T3-BSC-913

THE POLITICS OF SUBNATIONAL GOVERNANCE

Edited by

Deirdre A. Zimmerman
New York State Division of the Budget

Joseph F. Zimmerman
Graduate School of Public Affairs
State University of New York at Albany

UNIVERSITY
PRESS OF
AMERICA

LANHAM • NEW YORK • LONDON

Copyright © 1983 by

University Press of America,™ Inc.

4720 Boston Way
Lanham, MD 20706

3 Henrietta Street
London WC2E 8LU England

Printed in the United States of America

ISBN (Perfect): 0-8191-3438-4
ISBN   (Cloth): 0-8191-3437-6

All University Press of America books are produced on acid-free
paper which exceeds the minimum standards set by the National
Historical Publications and Records Commission.

Library of Congress Catalog Card Number: 83-14581

TO MARGARET

iii

TABLE OF CONTENTS

PREFACE

Several good quality state and local textbooks are on the market and as introductory volumes typically attempt to cover the entire spectrum of subnational governance. One consequence of the broad coverage is the author's inability to deal in depth with most of the current issues facing states and their political subdivisions. The principal objective of this volume is to make available to the introductory student materials not commonly found in standard textbooks. Hence, the readings supplement and do not supplant the textbooks.

Editors face difficult choices in selecting appropriate readings as an ample supply of quality readings on some subtopics is available and a shortage of such readings exists on other subtopics. Furthermore, space limitations necessitate that a number of first class articles be excluded from this volume. The editors have made a deliberate decision to exclude articles that might be labelled "high powered" research ones emphasizing quantitative methods because they would be above the level of the introductory student. Nevertheless, we have made an effort to include selections reflecting the great variety of research studies on subnational institutions, politics, and processes; their problems; and recommended solutions.

In contrast to a book of commissioned essays, the readings in this volume do not conform to a unifying theme or themes, and are not designed to represent a particular viewpoint. The intent is to present articles reflecting a diversity of approaches and opinions on subnational issues, hopefully stimulating discussion among the readers.

A debt of gratitude is owed to authors and publishers for granting reprint permission, and to Diane Cardone, Edith K. Connelly, Suzanne Hagen, Maxine Morman, and Addie Napolitano for preparing the typescript.

Rensselaer, New York   D.A.Z.
Delmar, New York   J.F.Z.
August 1983

x

PART I

INTERGOVERNMENTAL RELATIONS

The politics of subnational governance occurs within the framework of a federal system established by the United States Constitution in 1788. The arguments over the ratification of the United States Constitution revolved around the question of the proper amount of political power that should be confided in the Congress. Opponents of the proposed document feared tyranny might flow from the degree of power centralization inherent in the Constitution and proponents attempted to dissolve these fears by arguing the Congress was a government of limited delegated powers and posed no threat to the liberties of citizens. The Federalist Papers--authored by Alexander Hamilton, John Jay, and James Madison--appeared as letters from Publius to editors of New York State newspapers and remain as cogent explanations of the nature of the new governmental system to be established by the United States Constitution.

The Federalist Papers can be read today with great profit and it will become apparent to the reader the governance system described by Publius does not exist today as the powers of the national government have expanded enormously since 1788. The power expansion is attributable to changing conditions which produced constitutional amendments, judicial decisions, and statutory elaboration of delegated powers resulting in a governance system dominated to a large extent by the national government. Publius could not have visualized the growth of national powers to the extent that a state law relating to any aspect of the electoral system within the state may not become effective until approved by the United States Attorney General or the United States District Court for the District of Columbia if the state is covered by the Federal Voting Rights Act of 1965 as amended.

The growth of national powers has disturbed many government officials and citizens. President Richard M. Nixon and President Ronald Reagan have called for a reversal of the centralization of political power in Washington, D.C., and each has promoted a program labelled "New Federalism" which would weaken the political power of the national government.

1

Reading number 1 by Richard S. Williamson, Assistant to the President for Intergovernmental Affairs, contains a clear explanation of the general goals of President Reagan's New Federalism. In particular, the President is seeking to reduce the size of the national government and its intrusion into the affairs of state and local governments. Inherent in the President's plan is a swap of functional responsibilities between the national government and the states.

Mr. Williamson, in reading number 2, deals specifically with a key element in the President's program for revitalizing the federal system; replacement of narrow categorical federal grants-in-aid with block grants increasing the discretionary authority of state and local government officials. In his first year in office, the President was able to persuade the Congress to place fifty-seven categorical grant-in-aid programs in nine new or modified block grant programs. Critics of the "New Federalism" launched a strong attack upon the new block grant programs and Mr. Williamson answers their criticisms.

A different perspective on President Reagan's New Federalism is contained in reading number 3. Professor Roy W. Bahl, Director of the Metropolitan Studies Program at Syracuse University, presents a careful analysis of the strengths and weaknesses of the Reagan National Urban Policy Report. In particular, he faults the plan for its adverse impact on the urban poor and for failing to address clearly several important issues, including the state role in resolving urban problems and helping declining region adjust to major shifts in the economy.

In reading number 4, Professor Daniel J. Elazar, Director of the Center for the Study of Federalism at Temple University, views the governance system in the United States as a non-centralized system and argues that the nature of the system has been misunderstood by individuals viewing the system in hierarchical terms. Professor Elazar argues that partnership intrinsically is the principle underlying the federal system and the national government should view states as polities.

Dr. David B. Walker, Assistant Director of the United States Advisory Commission on Intergovernmental Relations, in reading number 5 describes the American governance system as "increasingly dysfunctional federalism..." and incomprehensible to the average citizen. Dr. Walker documents his diagnosis with signs and explains some of the underlying causes of the problem. Although he clearly outlines possible reform approaches, he concludes that "what the prescriptions will be is not clear."

STATE-LOCAL RELATIONS

While the term "Dual Federalism" has been employed to describe the nature of the relationship existing between the national government and the states, no one described the relationship between a state and its political subdivisions in terms of a dual political system until constitutions in a number of states were amended to provide for a system of local discretionary authority labeled Imperium in Imperio or an empire within an empire. Professor Zimmerman, in reading number 6, traces the development of local discretionary authority in the various states, and places particular emphasis upon the Imperium in Imperio approach and the devolution of powers approach. The reading concludes that the system of state-local legal relations is incredibly complex and concepts--such as Dillon's Rule, Imperium in Imperio, and devolution of powers--do not explain adequately the legal relationship of local governments to their states.

INTERSTATE RELATIONS

The drafters of the United States Constitution were fully cognizant of interstate problems and the need for a mechanism to solve such problems and promote multistate cooperation. Recognizing that an adjudicatory forum was needed to resolve authoritatively legal disputes between the states, the drafters of the national Constitution assigned the United States Supreme Court original or trial jurisdiction in suits brought by one state against another state. The Constitution implicitly promotes interstate cooperation by authorizing two or more states with the consent of the Congress to enter into compacts. The United States Supreme Court in 1893 (Virginia v. Tennessee, 148 U.S. 503) held that the consent of Congress is required for states to enter into agreements with each other only if the compacts are "political" in nature. Relative to a number of subjects, such as forest fire prevention, the Congress has granted consent in advance for states to enter into compacts.

3

In reading number 7, Professor Zimmerman traces the procedural steps involved in establishing an interstate compact and highlights the obstacles to the successful negotiation of a compact. Experience has demonstrated that it is difficult for states to agree upon the terms of an interstate compact. Furthermore, should the states reach agreement, their plans may be frustrated by the refusal of the Congress to grant consent to the compact or by long delays in the granting of consent.

1. The Self-Government Balancing Act: A View
   From the White House*

   Richard S. Williamson

President Ronald Reagan has a dream.

His dream is not to cut the bloated federal budget,
though he has been successful with the largest budget
cuts in history. Both the Republican Senate and the
Democratically controlled House passed a budget resolution last summer which is sweeping in its size and
scope.

His dream is not about tax cuts, though the
reductions in the marginal tax rates which the President proposed and were passed by Congress are the
largest in history.

His dream is not about regulatory relief, though
the Presidential Task Force on Regulatory Reform which
is chaired by Vice-President Bush has cut the volume of
regulations published by one-third and saved billions
of dollars for the consumer by eliminating needless
overregulation.

Rather, the President's dream is to change how
America is governed. He wishes to shrink the size of
government. He is trying to change the presumptions
which have been directing Americans and led them in
recent years to turn first to the federal government
for answers. He is seeking a "quiet revolution," a
new federalism which is a meaningful American partnership.

Ronald Reagan, throughout his public career, and
especially during his two presidential campaigns in
1976 and 1980, discussed the breakdowns of the federal
government. He echoed the points made by the Advisory
Commission on Intergovernmental Relations when they
identified the federal system as overloaded, congested
and inefficient. He told the American people that
there is accountability lacking in the federal system.

*Reprinted with permission from the National Civic
Review, January 1982, pp. 19-22.

Those in Washington are too distant from their constituents, too hard to reach, too unsympathetic to the real local concerns that face all Americans on a day-to-day basis.

Furthermore, the President has stated that he embraces a point made by one of the founders of the National Municipal League, Louis Brandeis, when Justice Brandeis said that the states were laboratories of experiment. The President feels that such diversity is good. When a mistake is made in Washington, it affects all 55 states and territories. When a decision is made in Springfield, Illinois, or Boston, Massachusetts, or Salem, Oregon, the other states and territories can learn from those decisions and adopt them according to their own needs and desires.

Finally, President Reagan does not believe that Washington, D.C., has any corner on wisdom. He recognizes that state and local governments have strong leadership of their own with a greater sensitivity to local problems, a great concern for their fellow citizens, and a wisdom about how best to address local problems with local solutions.

In the first 10 months of his administration, President Reagan has made substantial federalism initiatives. Throughout his economic package, federalism priorities are reflected.

The very budget cuts the President proposed reflect his desire to cut back the size of the federal government and thereby curb federal usurpation of state and local governments and other important institutions. Further, the budget cuts themselves reflect a reordering of budgetary priorities so that the national budget addresses truly national needs.

Also, within the President's budget proposals adopted through reconciliation, he proposed that 88 categorical programs be combined into seven block grants.

The growth of categorical programs, with all their mandates and controls, had a devastating impact on the strength and viability of state and local governments. In 1959, there were only 40 grant-in-aid programs. By

1970, the categorical grants had grown in number to
130. By 1978, there were 492 programs. Seen in the
light of this rapid growth, perhaps the President's
proposal of blocking just eight categorical programs is
modest. However, in light of others' experience, it was
sweeping.

The President was successful in getting 57 categorical programs combined into nine block grants. It was
not all that the President sought but, nonetheless, it
was a significant accomplishment. It is interesting
that the political partnership in support of these programs was the President in union with state and local
officials (Republican and Democrat) versus the power
structure in Congress. The block grant proposal
suffered as much from the Republicans as the Democrats
in Congress. Congressional leaders sought to protect
their power fiefdoms. Nonetheless, as noted above,
there was great success.

The vast majority of states has opted into the
block grants. All but three states have opted into at
least some of the block grants. Further, the block
grants have been a vehicle for significant regulatory
relief to state and local governments. For example,
regulations for those categorical grants under the
jurisdiction of Health and Human Services that were
blocked, moved from 318 pages in the Federal Register
to just six pages. The Office of Management and Budget
estimates that the reduction in paperwork for state and
local officials as a result of this regulatory relief
will be 5.4 million manhours per year, an 83 percent
reduction.

Furthermore, the tax cuts, while aimed at
increased investment and productivity, reduced the
oppressive levels of federal taxation which have
usurped revenue sources which otherwise might have been
available to state and local governments. The type of
economic growth that will result from the incentives
unleashed by this tax cut will significantly increase
the economic strength and viability in the local
communities. And, it is important to note that one of
the incentives addressed itself to encouraging
reinvestment in existing plants and equipment which
would substantially benefit mature cities.

7

In the area of regulatory relief, the President has made substantial progress. More than 200 state and local officials have submitted recommendations which identified over 500 questionable regulations which bind and limit local and state governments. Of the first 130 regulatory relief actions taken by that task force during its first six months, over 30 percent primarily benefitted state and local governments. For example, the 504 regulations which would require buses to have facilities for the handicapped have been amended so that alternative transportation services can be provided. Therefore, the national purpose is achieved but local governments are given the flexibility to derive the best possible standards for their own needs.

In addition to the economic package, each department and agency has taken major initiatives in returning authority and responsibility back to state and local governments. For example, HUD is moving to give greater local control of public housing. EPA is reconsidering its noise emission standard for garbage trucks. Noise pollution is a local matter and should be handled by local governments. HUD is drafting a policy statement which will enhance the abilities of neighborhoods to engage in service delivery or economic development activities. The Justice Department has ordered the United States Attorneys to set up coordinating committees with state and local law enforcement organizations and to begin a more cooperative approach to prosecution. HUD is developing a legislative proposal for streamlining the urban development action grant application and implementation process.

The President has also established various structures for addressing federalism issues. He has set up a Federalism Advisory Committee under the chairmanship of Paul Laxalt, who served as a county official before his election as lieutenant governor and then governor of Nevada, and presently serves in the United States Senate. The full advisory committee met on June 23. Subsequent subcommittee meetings have been held to consider revenue return, welfare, housing and other issues. This committee is providing valuable input into the Administration as decisions are being made, and will continue to do so.

The Administration has created greater activity by the Executive Department, and the advisory committee has created greater activity than its recent predecessors with respect to involvement in the Advisory Commission on Intergovernmental Relations.

The President has asked each of his Cabinet members to ensure that there is a high-level person with responsibility for intergovernmental affairs in their department or agency. The President has instructed Cabinet members to conduct "early and genuine consultations" with state and local officials concerning program and policy changes. This last request is evidenced by the consultations that are ongoing right now with state and local officials regarding entitlements, the fiscal year 1983 budget, and the meetings of the subcommittees of the Federalism Advisory Committee.

Furthermore, the President has devoted more time than any of his recent predecessors to meet with state and local officials. In the first 10 months of his Administration, Ronald Reagan met with more than 1,200 state and local officials in the White House, often in meetings either individually or in small groups of one to two dozen.

Just in the last few months there has been an important meeting of the U.S. Conference of Black Mayors with the Vice President for a candid exchange of concerns and views. The President also met with mayors and county officials on the issue of revenue sharing.

Ideally, the changes the President is proposing to realize his dream, the changes in how America is governed, will be made at a time of expanding resources. Unfortunately, that is not possible. The United States now faces a critical economic situation which requires rough budgetary decisions.

The Administration recognizes that the transition which is taking place in federal/state/local relations is not painless. We seek to minimize the dislocation caused by this realignment. Nonetheless, we think this realignment is inevitable and critical if we are to change the way America is governed, return to a proper balance between the citizen, local governments and the federal government.

We must address fundamental questions of structure. We all must seek to sort out what functions belong where. The issue of swap must be addressed. The revenue return issue must be developed so that long-term structural changes that are necessary can indeed occur.

It is Ronald Reagan's dream to revitalize our federal system. It is my responsibility to help realize this dream.

2. Block Grants--A Federalist Tool*

Richard S. Williamson

President Ronald Reagan is committed to a
revitalized federalism. Through his two terms as
governor of California, while a candidate for president, and since inauguration, Ronald Reagan has
remained committed to restoring the proper balance
between the federal government and state and local
governments. He is determined to make government work
again. To do this, he recognizes the need to provide
greater authority and responsibility to state and local
governments.

Over the years a system of allocating federal
funds to state and local areas developed that was
organized into a myriad of specific categorical grants
that serve narrowly defined groups. The system has
become a confusing tangle of small programs which overlap, conflict, and overregulate. These categorical
grants have systematically taken discretionary
authority away from state and local officials and
transformed them into administrators of federal programs. The growth trend and proliferation of these
categorical grants is dramatic.

On June 16, 1959, during hearings which resulted
in the creation of the Advisory Commission on Intergovernmental Relations, Senator Edmund Muskie made the
following observations:

> There is a feeling on the part of some people
> that states are always reaching out for federal
> dollars. There are upward of 40 grant-in-aid
> programs depending on how they are classified.
> I don't know how you keep track of them all.[1]

In 1959, the total federal spending for these
grant-in-aid programs was $6.7 billion, accounting for
1.4 percent of the gross national product (GNP). By
1970, there were 130 categorical grant programs, and by
1980 the number of categorical programs stood at 492;
total federal spending had skyrocketed to over $90

*Reprinted with permission from State Government,
Vol. LIV, No. 4, 1981, pp. 114-17.

billion, a 1343 percent increase since 1959, accounting for 3.5 percent of GNP.

Furthermore, the categorical grant programs described by Senator Muskie in 1959 dealt principally with transportation and income security programs. The present 492 programs cover virtually every facet of state and local government.

President Reagan made clear his desire to provide greater flexibility to state and local governments throughout his campaign. In his speech accepting the Republican Party nomination for president last year, he said:

> Everything that can be run more effectively by state and local governments we shall turn over to state and local governments along with the funding sources to pay for them. We are going to put an end to the money merry-go-round where our money becomes Washington's money to be spent by states and cities only if they spend it exactly the way the federal bureaucrats tell them to.[2]

Despite the president's campaign rhetoric and his reiteration upon taking office that he intended to provide greater flexibility to state and local govern-ments, few thought he could be successful. As Governors Richard Snelling of Vermont and James Hunt of North Carolina wrote in August, "Last year, knowledge-able observers predicted that legislation proposing new block grants would never be scheduled for a hearing in the Senate or the House of Representatives; enactment was viewed as an impossibility."[3]

Surprising the skeptics, defying the opposition, President Reagan formed an effective political partner-ship between his administration and the nation's governors, state legislators and many local officials. He made dramatic proposals to consolidate nearly 90 categorical grants into six block grants.

This year's Reagan block grant proposals were the most far-reaching effort that had ever been attempted in the consolidation of federal grant-in-aid programs. Only five block grants have been enacted out of approximately 20 which have been proposed over the last two decades: Title XX of the Social Security Act, Comprehensive Employment and Training Act, Law Enforcement Assistance Act, Community Development Block Grant, and Partnership for Health. But none of these initiatives has fully relieved state and local officials from the burden of federal strings.

The president's proposals did not pass Congress in their entirety; however, he did achieve substantial and unprecedented success. Fifty-seven former categorical programs have been combined into nine new or changed block grants with budget authority of over $7.5 billion. This success is characterized by the National Governors' Association as follows:

> Seven months after taking office, President Reagan has changed the direction of a federal aid system that was becoming increasingly rigid and fragmented . . . . (I)t represents some progress toward greater flexibility for state and local officials at a time when aid to state and local governments is shrinking.[4]

Despite these significant initial successes, the president intends to battle with renewed vigor for further flexibility for state and local governments and for new block grants. The following are some of the compelling reasons the administration will seek more block grants.

First, our governmental system, at present, is not working. The federal government is overloaded, having assumed more responsibilities than it can efficiently or effectively manage. This is a large part of what the election on November 4, 1980, was all about.

From the full spectrum of social services to housing to transportation to education and beyond, the federal government has become the decision-maker and manager of the public sector. It has crowded out state and local governments, treating them as if they were mere administrative provinces of the federal government.

The Reagan budget and further block grants will begin the process of making government work again by decentralizing government decision-making. As the president said on March 20, 1981:

> We are not cutting the budget simply for the sake of sounder financial management. This is only a first step toward returning power to states and communities, only a first step toward reordering the relationship between citizen and government.[5]

Second, the block grants will permit government decisions once again to be made by state and local officials who can be held accountable for those decisions. There has been a breakdown in our governmental system because there has been a breakdown in accountability between decision-maker and voter. President Reagan does not think that officials in Washington who are isolated from the voters should be making major decisions affecting the social fabric. He believes that the people have a right to participate in and determine those decisions complished by allowing government decisions to be made at the local level.

Third, significant administrative savings will result. The programs proposed for consolidation in just the health and social services areas alone encompass 437 pages of law and 1,200 pages of regulations. Once the awards for 6,800 separate grants are made, over 7 million man-hours of state and local government and community effort are required each year to fill out federally required reports.

A recent Washington Post article reported that Mohammad N. Akhter, the director of the Missouri Division of Health, said that 20 percent of his employees work to comply with federal regulation of the more than 40 health programs funded by Washington. He said that the Missouri Health Division could do a better job with 75 percent of the funds it now gets from Washington if the federal mandates were eliminated. Similarly, in a 1976 study by the Office of Management and Budget, it was found that the Community Development Block Grant resulted in a 25 percent reduction of total staffing in the Department of Housing and Urban Development for community development programs.[6]

14

Fourth, block grants will result in greater innovation and permit the states to serve as true "laboratories of democracy." The history of state government is replete with examples of such innovation. It was the Northern states that brought the question of slavery to the forefront of American politics. It was California that led the way in advancing the nation's environmental concerns long before it was fashionable to do so. It was states like Wisconsin and Illinois that developed the first welfare programs in the nation prior to federal pre-emption. And, unlike the federal government, when a state makes a mistake, it will not be required to be repeated in every other state of the union.

Finally, enactment of the block grants will reduce the impact of the budget cuts by permitting state and local officials to target diminishing resources to areas and individuals whose needs are the greatest. Such targeting will not occur if the decision-making authority is left with unelected, unaccountable federal bureaucrats in Washington, D.C.

RESPONSE TO THE CRITICS

During the debate on block grants, a number of arguments have been advanced against this new proposal. Some are meritorious; some specious. But, when you cut through the fog, there are three key arguments which are made by those who oppose block grants.

First, it is argued that the block grants will result in massive reductions in federal aid to cities, because funds which have traditionally gone to the cities will now be funneled through state capitals. This is simply not true. Consider the following facts:

• General local governments (cities, towns and counties) now receive only about 5 percent of non-education grants directly from the federal government.

• More than 80 percent of the funding in the non-education programs being folded into new block grants already goes to state governments.

• The brunt of the cuts in the block grants will thus fall on states, not local governments.

15

It is true that the administration has proposed changing the Community Development Block Grant so that the states would administer approximately $1.1 billion for cities of less than 50,000 population. But the administration has not proposed a change in the current administration of the Community Development Block Grant program for cities of greater than 50,000 in population.

What big city mayors are concerned about, as expressed in their meetings with the president in June, is whether the relationship between the federal government and the cities will be altered by future block grants. During the course of those meetings (attended by 21 Democrats and 35 Republicans in five separate sessions) the president assured the mayors that they will be fully consulted before any future block grants are proposed.

It should also be noted that recent studies by the National Governors' Association and the National Science Foundation showed that aid flowing to cities from state capitals is more responsive to need than aid coming directly from Washington, D.C.[7]

Second, it is argued that governors and state legislators are not competent to handle the block grant funds which they are being asked to administer. This argument ignores the extraordinary advancements which have been made in state government over the last two decades.

With respect to state legislatures, in 1962 only 19 legislatures met annually. By 1978, 43 legislatures held regular sessions in both years of the biennium. Compensation for state legislators has increased and staffs have become more professional. State legislatures have also been reapportioned along one-man, one-vote principles.

State executive branch work forces have also been professionalized, along with the modernization of state administrative and planning systems. Many states have also undertaken comprehensive reorganizations of their executive and administrative structures.

16

In addition, technical assistance will be available from the federal government to assist the states in making the adjustments to the new block grant system. For example, the Community Development Block Grant contains a special allocation of $15 million for such technical assistance.

Third, it is argued that even if state officials are competent, they are not sufficiently caring or compassionate to meet the needs of the people in their states. This argument goes to the heart of the debate over block grants and everything that President Reagan and his administration stand for.

Either you believe in democracy or you don't. President Reagan believes in people and their ability to govern themselves. And he believes that state and local officials across this country are every bit as compassionate and competent and caring as any official in Washington, D.C.

To those elitists who believe that somehow Washington, D.C. has a corner on wisdom and compassion in this country, there is nothing that President Reagan or those who serve him can write or say that will change their minds. But that is where the intellectual and political battle will be joined.

Just as we believe economic decisions should be made in the freedom of an unburdened economic market-place, so too should political and governmental decisions be made in the free and open political process. There will be winners and losers. But at least decisions can be made at a local level where decision-makers can be held accountable for their actions.

None of us in this administration has any mis-conception that block grants are a magic panacea. But we are convinced that they will help make government work again. The pressing needs of individuals and institutions in this nation will continue to be met. The only real losers from block grants will be the bureaucratic middlemen--the grantsmen--who siphon off funds from those greatest in need.

Following the recent budget reconciliation process for fiscal 1983, the president addressed the annual convention of the National Conference of State Legislatures and in his remarks he reaffirmed his pledge to work with the states for more block grants and greater flexibility. He said:

A major aspect of our federalism plan is the eventual consolidation of categorical grants into blocks. Today there are too many programs with too many strings offering too small a return . . . .
Block grants are designed to eliminate burdensome reporting requirements and regulations, unnecessary administrative cost and program duplication. Block grants are not a mere strategy in our budget plan, as some have suggested; they stand on their own as a federalist tool for transferring power back to the state and local level.
In normal times what we've managed to get through the Congress concerning block grants would be a victory. Yet we did not provide the states with the degree of freedom in dealing with the budget cuts we had ardently hoped for. We got some categorical grants incorporated into block grants but many of our block grant proposals are still on the Hill. That doesn't mean the end of the dream. Together you and I will be going back and back and back until we obtain the flexibility you need and deserve.[8]

The Reagan administration's efforts to return a proper balance between the federal government and state and local governments have just begun. And, the president intends to work with his partners in state and local government to gain congressional passage of further block grants, an important federalist tool to transfer power back where it belongs.

NOTES

1. Senator Edmund Muskie, Senate Committee on Government Operations, "To Establish an Advisory Commission on Intergovernmental Relations," June 16, 1959.

2. Ronald Reagan, Acceptance Speech, Republican National Convention, Detroit, Mich., July 17, 1980.

3. Governors' Guide to Block Grant Implementation, Council of State Planning Agencies and National Governors' Association, Aug. 1, 1981.

4. National Governors' Association, "President Reagan Has Changed the Direction of Federal Aid System," Governors' Bulletin, Aug. 7, 1981, p. 2.

5. Ronald Reagan, Remarks before the Conservative Political Action Committee, Wash., D.C., March 20, 1981.

6. Office of Management and Budget, "Assessment of the Administrative and Organizational Consequences of Grant Consolidation Reform," October 1976.

7. "Bypassing the States: Wrong Turn for Urban Aid," National Governors' Association, Center for Policy Research, 1979; G. Ross Stephens and Gerald W. Olson, Report to the National Science Foundation, "Pass-Through Federal Aid and Inter-Level Finance in the American Federal System, 1957-1977."

8. Ronald Reagan, Address to the National Conference of State Legislatures, Atlanta, Ga., July 30, 1981.

3.   A Reaction to the National
          Urban Policy Report*

Roy W. Bahl

An urban policy report should state the
general approach the administration will take toward urban problems and list the specific initiatives proposed. On the first count, the Reagan
administration is to be commended for clearly
stating its philosophy of how urban problems can
be resolved. These principles suggest marked
changes in federal involvement:

. less federal aid to cities;
. a dominant role for state governments;
. much more reliance on private-sector and
  voluntary organization initiatives;
. increased user charges, revenue bonds and
  special district financing;
. much less concern with direct governmental
  efforts to redistribute income through the
  financing of pro-poor services; and
. a general shifting of financing responsibility from federal to state and local
  governments.

Such a program is quite consistent with the
administration's general approach to economic
recovery. If the economy can be strengthened by
giving incentives to higher-income investors, the
benefits eventually will trickle down to the poor.
The urban policy is to reduce federal assistance
to cities, shift financing responsibility and

---

*   Roy W. Bahl, "A Reaction to the National Urban
     Policy Report," Governmental Finance (Chicago:
     Municipal Finance Officers Association of the
     United States and Canada, ©1982). Reproduced
     with permission from publisher.

service choices to those who are willing and able to pay and hope that the poor will eventually share in the fruits of cities' improved financial position and management. This thrust may not have universal appeal, but it is an approach. The Carter administration's urban policy, by contrast, tried to please so many different interests that no clear statement of policy emerged.

In terms of specific initiatives, the Reagan administration's report is less impressive. The report proposes the "newest federalism," with its swap and turnback components, but it does not provide estimates of the impact of these changes on cities, on the urban poor or on the detail of the amounts of funding involved. It is also silent on how to encourage increased private-sector involvement, how to make state governments behave more responsibly toward cities and how declining and distressed local governments can cope with short-run fiscal problems.

I do not think this is the right urban policy for the United States of the 1980s. The policy's impact on poor cities and poor people will result in social problems that the administration apparently has ignored or ruled out as unimportant. In some ways the policy goes in the right direction, but it goes too far.

Following is a discussion of what I think are the report's greatest strengths, its important weaknesses and some areas where the basic analysis seems flawed.

STRENGTHS OF THE ADMINISTRATION'S REPORT

I agree with three basic tenets of this report: 1) federal policy ought not to be built around reversing the Snow Belt-Sun Belt shifts in economic activity; 2) state governments' role is pivotal and ought to be clearly stated; and 3) local governments ought to be pushed to improve their financial management and planning practices and to better understand what they can afford.

Regional Shifts. One might take either of two
positions about proper federal policy toward the
shift of population and economic activity from
the Northeast and Midwest to the growing Southern
and Western regions. One policy would be to create
a set of competitive subsidies to attempt a
reversal of the current trend, i.e., to use government subsidies and penalties to offset the comparative disadvantages of the declining region. This
seems to be the approach taken by the Carter
administration's Urban Policy Statement of 1978,
which included a National Development Bank, the
targeted employment tax credit, neighborhood commercial reinvestment programs and expanded Urban
Development Action Grant funding. The problem with
this approach is that there is little evidence that
such revitalization programs work or have any
effect on the economic base of declining cities.
Certainly the European experience with such regional subsidies is not encouraging. At a time of slow
national economic growth, the United States can
scarcely afford to create such inefficiencies.

An alternative approach is a kind of compensation policy accepting the notion that market
forces are affecting a reallocation of population
and income within the country and attempting to
compensate the most financially pressed governments
and families during the adjustment period.

The Reagan administration proposes such a
policy, but comes up short in several respects.
First, the administration does not elaborate on
what kind of program could be worked out to ease
the pain of regional shifts during the transition
period. Moreover, other policies in this urban
report suggest that low-income families would not
be protected from the pain of economic decline and
that central city public services would not be
subsidized during the transition. For example,
the swap, turnback and federal aid reductions
would leave declining area governments in the
position of doing less for families most hurt by
economic decline.

22

The administration is correct in realizing that the issue is how to help governments through a painful adjustment period, not how to reverse the current pattern of regional shifts. On the other hand, the administration is unwilling to face the issue that federal assistance is an important element of an adjustment program.

State government role. The administration's policy gives state governments the key role in strengthening and financing urban governments. This reverses a longstanding ambiguity wherein the state government shares of total state and local government financing and spending have been increasing while federal assistance has increasingly bypassed the states. State governments' role and responsibility had become so unclear by the time of the New York City emergency aid that the question--how far New York State had to go before federal aid would flow--was never even raised.

Moreover, boundary problems lie at the heart of urban fiscal problems and city-suburban fiscal disparities in the declining regions. Whether these problems are to be dealt with an annexation, consolidation or regional financing schemes, it is clear that reform must begin at the state government level.

The Reagan program properly recognizes the need for state governments to play a key role in dealing with urban problems, but the program has not addressed the issue of what steps the federal government must take to insure that state governments will address metropolitan fiscal disparities. After all, state governments' track record in this respect has not been good.

Financial planning. The administration's program encourages local governments to improve financial management practices and will increase the incentives for improvement by reducing the flow of federal aid. The New York City crisis and its aftermath convinced many city administrators that financial planning and control is essential. Experience since that time has shown that significant

23

improvements can result from using control systems, fiscal forecasting techniques, debt and cash management models, etc. The administration's policy, by placing more responsibility in the hands of state and local governments, increases the premium for improved financial management.

WEAKNESSES OF THE ADMINISTRATION'S REPORT

The Reagan urban policy statement does not address three important issues essential to formulating a complete urban policy. The first is whether the federal government has any responsibility for the adverse effects of business cycles on state and local government finance. The second is the consequences of the administration's policy for the urban poor. The third is the position to be taken about the comparative tax advantage of resource-rich states in the West and Southwest and the distribution of future federal assistance.

Business cycles. The foundation for the administration's urban policy is the economic recovery program. The argument is that cities will benefit from whatever national growth occurs. The administration's economic recovery program, however, has so far produced a 9 percent unemployment rate, a "misery index" (unemployment rate plus inflation rate) not much different from the 20 percent of the Carter recession and left central cities in the declining region with high unemployment rates. The administration's report does not raise the possibility that it has some responsibility to compensate state and local governments for the compromising effects of inflation and recession. Surely if the cornerstone of the administration's urban policy is its economic recovery program, then it must also have a compensatory policy to bear some of the responsibility for the recovery program's failure.

The business cycle and inflation have dramatic effects on state and local government's financial health. The severity of the last recession was the catalyst that pushed New York City

over the edge and brought many other local governments and at least one state dangerously close to
fiscal insolvency. Because swings in economic
activity do induce substantial changes in relative
fiscal health, one might argue for an explicit
recognition of business cycle effects in federal
intergovernmental policy.

In a sense this was done with counter-cycli-
cal aid and acceleration of other components of
the economic stimulus package in the 1975-1978
recovery. The present administration does not
propose such a policy. State and local governments
are on their own in coping with the budgetary
effects of recession and inflation.

Income redistribution. The administration's
policy is not targeted on the needs of the urban
poor. One could argue that if this urban policy
succeeds, it could markedly worsen income distribution.

First, by proposing the swap and turnback
components of the New Federalism, the administration is proposing that the federal government view
income redistribution as much more of a state and
local government responsibility than before. Not
only would states have responsibility for Aid to
Families and Dependent Children and food stamps,
but the total amount of federal assistance would
be cut. Since state and local governments must
compete with one another with tax and expenditure
policy (and the administration's proposal encourages such competition), it seems clear that state
and local governments themselves can place much
less emphasis on providing redistributive service.
Even if state and local governments did move to
increase taxes to offset some of the federal grant
loss and to provide improved services, the net
effect would be a shift from a progressive
federal income tax to a proportional or regressive
set of state and local government taxes.

Second, there are other aspects of the Reagan
proposal which are not pro-poor. The increased
use of user or benefit charges to finance public

25

services can effectively exclude those who cannot afford to pay the charge. What are the social costs of pricing the poor out of the use of public facilities? Similar problems emerge in the administration's proposal to increase the involvement of the private sector. The privatization of services such as day care will certainly have impacts on low-income workers.

Another example is the administration's citation of private-sector involvement in urban renewal: it may be a good way to reconstruct parts of the city, but experience does not suggest that the poor are direct beneficiaries. This may not doom such programs, but these effects need to be recognized.

Resource-rich states. An important policy issue is what will be done about states that have gained a substantial comparative advantage in their fiscal position due to the location of natural resources within their boundaries. With deregulation, the various types of severance and extraction taxes in the energy-rich states have markedly improved their comparative fiscal positions. The courts have now ruled that under certain conditions, these states may continue to tap the energy base and thereby further increase their comparative fiscal advantage. What is the proper response of the federal government? In particular, will the distribution of federal assistance among the states take into account this increased taxable capacity? The administration's urban policy statement, which deals with many similar issues, is silent on this issue.

IMPORTANT ISSUES NOT CLEARLY ADDRESSED

Several issues raised in the urban policy report were either not fully addressed or not properly thought through. In some cases, the policy statement raised the problem, suggested the desired outcome and went no further. In others, the reasoning appeared flawed. These issues include:

. how to implement the new state role in
  dealing with urban problems;
. what to do about the infrastructure
  problem;
. how to help declining regions adjust
  to regional shifts;
. what methods to use in stimulating
  public-private cooperation; and
. the wisdom of promoting the idea of
  interprise zones and competitive
  subsidies among local governments.

Further discussion on these subjects is
necessary.

The state role. State governments have always
had the power to effectively deal with urban problems. States could liberalize annexation and
consolidation regulations, they could create
regional financing districts or they could adjust
state aid formulae to recognize the particular
needs of cities. In fact, however, states have
performed poorly in all these areas. So poorly,
in fact, that it has fallen to the courts to
correct city/suburb fiscal and service-level
disparities. Particularly in the Northeast and
Midwest, where most distressed cities are located,
states have not done what was necessary to address
the urban problem.

The administration's policy places the responsibility for urban policy at the state level by
giving the state governments more control over
federal assistance. But there is no safeguard,
other than a few passthrough regulations, that
will insure a change in state attitude toward
cities. There are reasons to believe that states
will be even less sympathetic to city problems.
The recession and federal aid reductions have cut
into state revenues, a factor likely to lead to
reductions in state aid. Moreover, state legislatures are increasingly dominated by a suburban
influence, which means they may be even less responsive than before to central city needs.

There is probably a great opportunity to

27

deal with urban problems by increasing the role of state governments, but more is needed by way of giving states incentives (and penalties) to properly address these problems.

Infrastructure issues. As noted in the urban policy report, the infrastructure problem is a major national issue. While much ado is made about public-private cooperation, elimination of cumbersome regulations and better financial and capital facility planning, it seems clear that the Reagan proposals will further reduce the amount spent by state and local governments on capital investment and maintenance. The fact is that with further reductions in federal aid and with tight fiscal positions, state and local governments will defer expenditures which are most easily deferred-capital spending and maintenance. Especially if governments are required to borrow the funds for major renovations or construction projects, high interest rates provide a further incentive to postpone.

This approach is strongly inconsistent with the administration's economic recovery plan, which emphasizes capital investment. But public and private investment adds to the economy's productivity. It is reasonable to believe that further deterioration of the capital infrastructure-e.g., roads, public utilities, ports-in urban areas can impede increases in productivity. A similar statement could be made about investments in human capital, i.e., education and health services.

The president's statement, while arguing that public infrastructure investment is important for the country, is silent on how to increase the rate of such investment. Indeed, the fiscal strains of the newest federalism and the fiscal 1982 budget deficit may combine to dry up state and local government capital project activity.

Structural adjustments. The administration is correct in arguing that regional shifts in economic activity probably cannot be reversed and that it

28

is not good public policy to offer subsidies as
incentives to maintain jobs and people in declining regions. The administration also correctly
recognizes that in the transition period, the
governments and low-income persons in declining
regions face severe adjustment problems. What the
administration does not offer is the method by
which the federal government could begin to ease
the pain of this adjustment period.

A comprehensive urban policy would begin by
addressing the needs--resulting from population
declines--of poor people and poor local governments. Perhaps it would be possible to give structural adjustment assistance to local governments as
part of a program whereby the localities would
bring their budgetary activities in line with the
realities of their new, lower level of population
and economic activity. The administration's
urban policy report does not offer any suggestions
about how one might deal with such adjustments.
In effect, the declining areas will be left to
their own devices, with less federal aid and more
servicing responsibility.

Public-private cooperation. The urban policy
report stresses the possibility of making use of
the market, and about relying more heavily on public-private cooperation. The report gives several
examples of private-sector initiatives which have
led to substantial physical renewal in the center
of metropolitan areas. Very little was reported
about the impact of these activities, however.
Were these activities successful in increasing
the net employment in the region? Did they have
any negative effects--such as displacing the poor
from certain areas of the city? Have they contributed substantially to a revitalized city economy,
and where they have not, has the city shared in
the losses? Have local governments gained back
more in increased tax revenue benefits than they
gave up in the form of fiscal subsidies?

The public-private cooperation in urban
renewal may be an important way to physically
revitalize cities, but it also has its costs.
There is much more that we need to know about the

29

impact of these activities than was reported here.

Enterprise zones and tax incentives. The administration's urban policy report is different from most other studies in this area in that it encourages local government use of tax incentives, etc., as a competitive device. The usual argument is that competitive subsidies are probably a windfall gain to the business concern, i.e., an unnecessary giveaway by the local government. When local governments compete by offering these subsidies, they shift part of the burden of financing local services from the owners of business to local residents. The administration's recommendation for more use of competitive subsidies is almost startling in light of the great amount of evidence that these subsidies do not work in attracting jobs. Certainly competitive subsidies are not in the national interest.

The administration also is proposing the establishment of enterprise zones. Presumably, the enterprise zone will attract jobs and economic activity to areas of the city where businesses would not ordinarily have located. In the urban policy report, the administration also claims that the activities attracted may not have been initiated without these subsidies. This should immediately cause one to ask whether such activities will continue to exist without the subsidy, and if not, is the establishment of these activities in the national or the local interest.

A great deal more homework on this issue is necessary. It is not at all clear that enterprise zones can accomplish the objectives set for them; the initial proposals to establish enterprise zones can be questioned on many grounds.

NATIONAL URBAN POLICY

Most observers agree that the Carter administration's national urban policy did not address many important issues. The following issues were basically ignored:

. whether the federal government ought to
  attempt revitalization of declining regions
  or offer compensation for these regions'
  losses during a financial adjustment
  period;
. what to do about declining city economies;
. whether inflation and recession ought to
  be viewed as a part of intergovernmental
  policy;
. what roles should state governments play
  in the intergovernmental system; and
. what will be the federal policy toward
  big city financial disasters?

The Reagan urban policy report addresses two
of these problems. It identifies the state governments as the key actors in the state and local
government sector, and it would not favor policies
to reverse regional shifts. On the other hand,
the administration does not go very far in spelling out the implementation problems in these areas.

Like its predecessor, this administration has
not dealt with the other issues. There are discussions of enterprise zones as methods of revitalizing central cities, but no consistent policy
has emerged regarding how to deal with regional
disparities. Surely the federal government has a
major role to play in this area, i.e., the regional
allocation of substantial increases in defense
spending, the allocation of federal grants, deregulation of energy and the method of taxing
energy resources.

Finally, the administration is making no
statement about intentions to compensate state and
local governments for the effects of inflation and
recession. Indeed, the administration has increased the hardships on state and local government budgets associated with increasing unemployment. Unemployment compensation benefits have
been altered to the detriment of local government areas with substantial amounts of unemployment;
state and local governments will be left to their
own devices to finance a larger share of welfare-
related costs; and countercyclical assistance and
public works programs have been eliminated.

4. States as Polities in the Federal System*
Daniel J. Elazar

In recent years there has been a tendency on the part of many, including decision makers, to view the states principally as the "middle level" in the federal system. Following the hierarchical principles of contemporary management doctrine, the states are seen as cogs in an administrative chain of command. "New federalists" seek to have Washington give them increased administrative tasks. "Urbanists" seek to minimize their role in favor of that of the central cities. "Decentralists" want to strengthen their management capabilities while "centralists" want to transform them into shells exercising only those functions which cannot be housed elsewhere. Even friends and leaders of the states have come to accept this definition of state roles uncritically, squaring as it does with the commonly accepted managerial view of contemporary government.

This view is a misperception of the states' true role in the federal system. As such, it has had and will continue to have important consequences in shaping their present and future role.

1. *The states as polities*. The true role of the states in the federal system is to function as polities, not as middle managers. The United States, in the words of *The Federalist*, is a compound Republic, partly national and partly federal. That is to say, the United States consists of a national polity with the whole country for its arena and served by the general government (the nineteenth century phrase carries much meaning) plus the several state polities each with its state for an arena and served by its own government. In the words of *Federalist* No. 39 (1787):

> Among a people consolidated into one nation, . . . supremacy is completely vested in the national legislature. Among communities

*Reprinted with permission from the National Civic Review, February 1981, pp. 77-82.

united for particular purposes, it is vested
partly in the general and partly in the
municipal legislatures. In the former case,
all local authorities are subordinate to the
supreme; and may be controlled, directed, or
abolished by it at pleasure. In the latter,
the local or municipal authorities form
distinct and independent portions of the
supremacy, no more subject, within their
respective spheres, to the general authority,
than the general authority is subject to them,
within its own sphere. In this relation,
then, the proposed government cannot be deemed
a *national* one; since its jurisdiction extends
to certain enumerated objects only, and leaves
to the several States a residuary and inviolable
sovereignty over all other objects.

The governments of both elements that together compound
the Republic are complete or essentially complete.

    2. *The states as polities are designed to play a
political role in the largest sense of the term.* This
means that the states' principal tasks are to govern--
to make and implement policies within their spheres of
competence, not simply to administer programs developed
outside of their jurisdiction, and to govern the
conduct of politics for the Republic as a whole. These
roles are constitutionally correct and historically
accurate. The states are recognized as polities in the
federal constitution. When they were at the height of
their power, they were actively governing even though
they may have done much less administering of programs
than they do today. Moreover, until recently, their
role in governing the conduct of politics was un-
challenged from any quarter.

    James Wilson, the Pennsylvanian who was the
strongest advocate of a strong national government at
the federal constitutional convention, put it this way:
"(There is a) kind of liberty which . . . I shall
distinguish by the appellation of *federal liberty* . .
. . When a confederate republic is instituted, the
communities, of which it is composed, surrender to it a
part of their *political* independence . . . . The states
should resign to the national government, that part,
and that part, only, of their *political liberty*, which,

placed in that government, would produce more good to
the whole, than if it had remained in the several
states. While they resign this part of their political
liberty, they retain the *free and generous exercise* of
all their other facilities, as states, so far as it is
compatible with the welfare of the general and super-
intending confederacy." (Emphasis added)

3. *The states' important administrative responsibilities should not suggest that their primary
function is managerial.* Quite properly, as the
velocity of government has grown, so, too, have the
administrative functions of the states increased. This
is especially visible in intergovernmental programs,
for obvious reasons. Given the current American
tendency to think in managerial terms, this has led to
a subtle reconceptualization of the states' role,
suggesting that it is one of "middle management,"
functioning within policy parameters set by the federal
government with some discretion in setting the policy
parameters for their local subdivisions. (One
consequence of this is to encourage federal bypassing
of the states wherever Congress or a federal agency
wants to set policy parameters for local governments
directly.) Thus, states are expected to administer,
not govern, and, indeed, are even chastized if they
attempt to act as governors.

4. *The American system is not a management
hierarchy but a matrix of arenas, each designed to be
politically responsive to its citizens.* In this
respect, federalism is like democracy, which, as
George F. Will quoted G. K. Chesterton, the British
essayist as saying: "Democracy which is not like
writing poetry or playing the church organ, because
these things we do not wish a man to do at all unless
he does them well. Democracy is, on the contrary, a
thing analogous to writing one's own love letter or
blowing one's own nose. These things we want a man to
do for himself, even if he does them badly."
(George F. Will, *Washington Post*, July 28, 1977)

The federal system is not a power pyramid organized on the basis of the federal government on top, the
states in the middle, and local governments on the
bottom (and, by implication, the people under them
all); rather, it is a matrix of arenas with the federal

34

government framing the whole, the states serving
smaller arenas within that whole, and local governments yet smaller ones. While there is a size
difference, there are no "higher" or "lower" arenas.
Each arena is as important for its purposes as any
other. The hierarchical model not only reinforces the
notion of the states as middle management but also
creates the illusion that policy making and coordination are best undertaken at the top where things all
come together. Under this model, at best, powers are
decentralized from higher to lower levels. The matrix
model, on the other hand, suggests the reality we all
know, namely the constitutionally mandated non-
centralized diffusion of powers among the various
arenas.

    5. *Historically, the states' position in the
matrix has been maintained through their political
role*. The states were powerful because their governments saw their function as one of governing, not
simply administering. Much of that governing was done
by legislative policy making in which the actual tasks
of program administration were placed in the hands of
the localities. Many of the tasks involved federal-
state relations but in a way that recognized the
states' proper role.

    The states were additionally powerful because the
conduct of electoral politics was their preserve. The
parties were organized within their boundaries and
barely had a national dimension, and the patronage
system gave the state and local party leaders control
over most federal officials within their jurisdictions.
As Morton Grodzins pointed out two decades ago, there
is an intimate relationship between the degree of
diffusion of power in the party system and federalism.

    6. *More recently, there has been a trend away
from non-centralization, to the view that the federal
government should mandate state administrative tasks*.
This takes two forms: congressional legislation
establishing programs which the states must implement
as if the states were creatures of the federal government and federal executive or judicial mandating of
conditions which the states and their localities must
meet in implementing their own programs. Both of these
are reflections of the new view of the federal system

35

as a decentralized pyramid rather than a non-centralized matrix. Two factors have made this possible: a change in constitutional understanding brought about by the courts and the universities, and a decline in traditional party politics with its reliance on state and local organization. It is a tribute to the strength of federalism in the United States and the states in the federal system that, in most cases, non-centralized modes of policy making and administration still prevail.

The most recent blatant examples of this can be found in: (1) the Carter administration's recommended countercyclical economic program which would bypass the states to target in on 27,000 local communities across the country identified by a computer in Washington; (2) a revised law enforcement block grant which would guarantee local high crime areas special funds on a mandated state passthrough basis and would also require state and local officials to submit to binding arbitration if they disagree on intrastate allocations; (3) a proposed metropolitan transportation program that would bypass the states; and (4) President Carter's urban proposals included a state incentives program which, while seeming to offer incentives to encourage greater state involvement in urban problems, would actually put the federal government in the business of coercing the states to undertake "modernization" along lines that would meet with Washington's approval.

7. *The present situation is a kind of stand-off; hierarchical assumptions prevail in theory while older forms of noncentralized government still dominate in practice.* The states have not done as badly in recent years as the foregoing comments might suggest. As a group, their governments are fiscally the healthiest of any in the federal system, they have increased the level and range of their activities many-fold, they have improved their governmental machinery, and they have become more responsive to their citizens than at any time since the Civil War. Moreover, they are in the best position to meet the needs of the American people across many fronts. At the same time, as polities, they are under greater assault than ever before.

8. *The future role of the states depends on the way in which the stand-off between the two conceptions*

of the states as polities or as middle managers is resolved.

> Obviously the preservation of local self-government is essential to the very idea of a federal union. Without the Town-Meeting, or its equivalent in some form or other, the Federal Union would become *ipso facto* converted into a centralizing imperial government. Should anything of this sort ever happen--should American towns ever come to be ruled by prefects appointed at Washington, and should American States ever become like the administrative departments of France, or even like the counties of England at the present day--then the time will have come when men may safely predict the break-up of the American political system by reason of its overgrown dimensions and the diversity of interests between its parts.[1]

This is an eminently practical question which requires resolution in the minds of opinion molders and decision makers first and foremost. Right now it could still go either way but time is running short.

9. *The central organizing concept for the proper understanding of the role of the states as polities in the federal system remains partnership.* Real partnership must be based on the reaffirmation of constitutional non-centralization. It requires the states to see themselves as polities that govern and lead where and when it is necessary to do so. It requires that the federal government be mindful of the states as polities and that Congress, in particular, be required to return to representing state interests rather than compete with them. It requires that the non-centralized party system be renewed. Perhaps most of all it requires that the federal courts restore (or refrain from interfering with) the constitutional basis for non-centralization.

John W. Burgess, the leading political scientist in the post-Civil War years, put it this way in his classic article on "The American Commonwealth" which appeared in the first issue of the *Political Science Quarterly* in 1886:

37

Blot out the national government, and you
still have the nation physically and ethnically,
which, by its own innate power, will restore
its political organization; but blot out the
government of the commonwealth (state), and
you have a territory measured by the chain of
the survey or, with a population governed
exclusively by the nation's organs, and restored
to local self-government only by the nation's
act.   (Page 15)

In the *Federalist* No. 1, Alexander Hamilton suggested
that the possibility of constitutional choice was one
of the greatest blessings conferred by Providence on
the American people:

It seems to have been reserved to the people
of this country, by their conduct and example,
to decide the important question, whether
societies of men are really capable or not, of
establishing good government from reflection
and choice, or whether they are forever destined
to depend, for their political constitutions,
on accident and force.

The federal system was one product of that power to
choose. Its future, which affects the future of the
entire American experiment, depends on the continuing
exercise of correct choices by the American people.

The twentieth century was a time in which
objective conditions caused state roles to diminish.
As many students of the subject have pointed out,
whether the states acted responsibly or not in meeting
the century's challenges, they found the federal
government stepping in as senior partner or more.
There are many signs that objective conditions in the
twenty-first century will require different responses.
Conditions of size and scale will reduce the utility of
the federal government as a problem solver and increase
that of the states. Changes in the patterns of urban
settlement will continue to reinforce that trend.
Finally, the closer integration of an international
community whose members increasingly will rely on
federal principles in their own organization will
increase the international role of the states,
including a closer relationship with their counterparts

in other federal systems. All told, the auguries for the future are good if the states and the American people as a whole have the will to respond to these conditions and do what has to be done.

Notes

1. John Fiske, *American Political Ideas Viewed from the Standpoint of Universal History* (New York: Harper and Brothers, 1885), p. 92.

5. Intergovernmental Relations and Dysfunctional Federalism*

David B. Walker

During the past two decades, drastic changes have occurred in the American federal system. These changes, when combined with some standpat political attitudes and practices, have produced neither a dual nor cooperative brand of federalism (and certainly no "New Partnership"), but an increasingly dysfunctional federalism. Contemporary intergovernmental relations, then, have become more pervasive, more intrusive, more unmanageable, more ineffective, more costly and, above all, more unaccountable, and chiefly because of the expansion of the federal role over the past 15 years.

The Signs: The prime symptom of this deepening dysfunctionalism is the continuing tendency to "intergovernmentalize" seemingly everything that becomes a public issue--and, increasingly, everything becomes a public issue. Its signs are everywhere, hence there is no need here to detail the degree to which:

--The old line between private and public concerns has been obliterated;
--The very real distinctions between federal and state-local matters of the early sixties have been lost;
--State and local budgets have become ever more fiscally dependent on grant revenues;
--State and local programs are involved in intergovernmental fiscal transfers, conditions and court orders;
--State and local regulatory processes are circumscribed by federal statutory and court sanctioned constraints;
--State and local policies and administrative processes have been affected by the Supreme Court's extraordinary expansion of what is "absorbed" within the orbit of the Fourteenth Amendment;

---

*Reprinted with permission from the National Civil Review, February 1981, pp. 68-76 and 82.

--Federal grants-in-aid have been "used" to serve
national regulatory--not promotional, supportive, or
additive--purposes;
　　　--State and local governments have been "used" to
implement wholly national policies; and
　　　--The federal government has been "used" to further
what not so long ago would have been a wholly local, or
at best, a state concern.

　　　Some Underlying Causes:　It has been the collapse
of certain basic constraints in the constitutional,
fiscal and political areas that has nurtured these
troublesome trends, along with the rise of relatively
unfettered individual policy entrepreneurs--usually in
Congress--each pushing his or her own favorite program
initiative from conception to enactment that has spurred
federal growth.　Yet, this has almost always been in a
regulatory or grant assistance role, not in a direct
servicing capacity.

　　　Judicially, the Supreme Court has ceased to be the
"umpire" of the federal system, and is more accurately
described as either spectator or player.　From an
intergovernmental perspective, this is reflected in (1)
the fairly steady adherence to the old New Deal court's
passivity regarding Congress' seemingly unbridled right
to regulate commerce, even for mandating purposes, and
its willingness to use it in areas undreamed of before
1960.　This absence of an umpiring role is even more
dramatically reflected in the federal judiciary's
unwillingness to check Congress' power to spend for
the general welfare, even when some of the conditions
attached to grants in the seventies have amounted to
coercion or arbitrary intrusion into the administrative procedures of state and local governments.　The
"passivity" in the last two areas has had the practical
effect of accelerating the activism of the federal
political branches, and its reflects a sustained
effort to ignore the very great changes in the grant
system since the early sixties.　The basic protection from the Tenth Amendment in the grant-in-aid area,
the judicial theory still holds, is the capacity of the
states and localities to say "no" to a grant.　The
third basic sign of a non-judicious approach to
federalism is found in the activist stance of the high
court in its extraordinary expansion of the Fourteenth
Amendment.　This includes not only broad interpretations of the "equal protection" and "due process"
clauses, but also the steady "absorption" within the

amendment of most of the federal Bill of Rights.

Fiscally, the federal government began the period
with a much stronger revenue system than that of the
states and the localities. Buttressing the federal
fiscal strength in the sixties were its broad-based
income tax, the responsiveness of this levy to
conditions of growth and inflation, the growing acceptance of deficit spending, the separate system for
financing social insurance, and the ability to shift
funds from defense to the domestic sector. These
combined to produce the notion in the sixties that "the
resources are there, if only we have the will to reach
out for them". And, thus, the myth of the federal
cornucopia was born.

Politically, the changes in attitudes, the mode
and extent of participation, and the process over the
past two decades probably have been the most dramatic.
American political history suggests that the major
parties either singly or in combination have provided
their own cluster of constraints on the expansion of
the federal role in the system. Political factors made
questions of federalism a major source of congressional
debate from Washington to Kennedy, and they combined to
keep the federal intergovernmental role a comparatively
modest one clear through to the mid-sixties. The
constitutional constraints had collapsed by the late
thirties, and the fiscal were linked largely to the
political. Yet, over the past decade and a half most
of these political curbs have disintegrated. Witness
the:

--Steady decline in the strength of local and
territorial interests in the governmental and political processes:
--Rapid rise of a host of newer types of interest
groups based on sociomoralistic (anti-abortion, etc.)
and demographic (black, Hispanic, Indian, women's,
youth and senior citizen) causes, alongside the traditional economic (business, labor, farmers and doctors)
and programmatic (highways, welfare, public health,
etc.) groups;
--Increased efforts on the part of state and local
government to lobby Washington, even as their own
traditional strength at the national level was growing
weaker--thanks to the growing array of programmatic,
sociomoralistic and demographic groups that usually are

aligned against them and to the growing insensiti-
vity of their national legislators to their jurisdictional worries;

--Steady deterioration of the capacity of the
political branches of the national government to
"pacify" this plethora of pressure groups, especially
in a period of ostensibility "democratic" and "open
access" congressional "reforms" and of a populist
Presidency;

--Steady decline in the voting differences between
Democrats and Republicans in the Congress on federal
role and grant-in-aid issues; and

--The slow, but clear change in the manner that
Congress handles grant and grant-related legislation,
from partisan and ideologically dominated, usually
executive-branch-initiated, yet geared to reaching a
rough consensus process in the sixties, to a
functionally-oriented, congressionally-dominated,
cooptive process in the seventies.

The Crucial "No Change" Area: Even with the
drastic changes in the constitutional, fiscal and
political areas, the dysfunctional traits of contemporary American federalism would not be as pervasive and
as potentially dangerous as they are if continuing
elements of "standpatism" also were not present. The
critical cluster of static attitudes and practices includes;

--No basic change in the size of the federal
bureaucracy and in the presidential and congressional
desires (regardless of party or ideological persuasion)
to keep it relatively small, despite an ever mounting
number of assignments given to it;

--No basic change in relying almost exclusively on
grants-in-aid as the primary instrumentality for
carrying out the national government's prime domestic
servicing responsibilities (except Medicare and the SSI
program);

--No basic change as the above would suggest, in
the national government's direct servicing role from
that of 1960 (or of 1940, for that matter);

--No basic change in the congressional and
presidential view that relying on state and local
governments and administrators even for the most
"national" of programs is "administratively

convenient," cheap, a curb on federal bureaucratic growth and politically clever;

--No basic change in the dominance of the old public administration approach to intergovernmental program management that with adequate conditions and sanctions state and local administrators can be rendered properly accountable, hence a part of a "chain of command" whose pyramidal peak is in Washington;

--No change in the belief of liberals that with the right formula or the right administrator (depending on the form of the grant) equity and "targeting" can be achieved; and

--No basic change on the part of most state and local officials and their representational groups in Washington that federal aid is a first rate way of alleviating their fiscal pressures, and that with a few more "push ups" and "jogs around the track," especially if a President or a key committee chairman is exercising with them, federal aid can be had without federal conditions.

What Impact on the System? In combination, these attitudes, along with the political and economic conditions noted earlier, have led to an overloading of the intergovernmental system, with precious little cooperation and a lot of inevitable conflict. Cooperation after all rests on shared goals and mutual trust, are rare commodities in this period of controversial and conflicting program goals, creeping conditionalism and chronic buckpassing.

A rather fanciful form of federalism, then, has emerged. Basic policies in most program areas appear to be made in Washington either by the court or Congress, or their implementation is achieved through decisions, orders, mandates, conditions, regulations and the lure of federal loot by 12 million state and local civil servants. All this is fanciful, of course, because the subnational governments, their elected officials and bureaucracies are capable of a highly differentiated response to all this in terms of compliance, cooperation, participation and conflict. Equally fanciful is any notion that the federal aid system as a whole protects the interests of the needy or equalizes levels of public service.

44

Matters of operational efficiency also are seldom brought into focus, either before or after the fact. Potential benefits are usually dramatized; potential costs are frequently ignored. Not only are many inter-governmental programs poorly designed to accomplish their stated objectives; most are not "designed" at all; and their objectives are seldom specified in operationally meaningful terms. Furthermore, few programs are evaluated once they are in place, and fewer still are modified or scrapped in consequence. Above all, perhaps, no real debate has occurred regard-ing the questionable administrative assumptions on which grants' management rests.

Where does this leave the electorate? Frustrated, fearful angry and alienated. The system has become largely incomprehensible even to those whose job it is to have an overview understanding of it. No wonder the average citizen, who is skeptical of politics and politicians but who still trusts our basic govern-mental institutions, is endlessly frustrated by the complexity, confusion and no-so-occasional corruption of the system.

Yet, the system as it has emerged since 1960 makes eminent sense in short-range, pressure group and poli-tical terms. From this perspective, it works. It helps elected officials to get reelected; it provides golden opportunities to congressional freshmen and sophomores (that is to say, the majority) to play "ombudsman" and to parlay this role into political asset; it keeps a range of interests somewhat "pacified." It conveys the impression of governmental response and of responsiveness. It has helped to keep the majority party together and provide valuable lessons on how the minority might become the majority. But does any of this make sense, in any other but personal incumbent and immediate political party terms? We think not.

Future Scenarios: Some Possible, Some Unreal: Other than the dreary, deadening prospect of more of the same--more aid programs, more formal conditions and constraints, more buckpassing and less real dollars--at least three basic alternative reformist strategies confront anyone concerned with the condition of the system.

On the two extremes stand the "system is already responding" and the "system requires drastic constitutional change" schools of thought. The former is based on a reading of recent events that suggests that the hyper-responsiveness of the system in the seventies to the immediate concerns of a plethora of pressure groups also applies to the long-range and basic concerns of the majority of the electorate. Advocates note the emergence of some elements of fiscal and political constraint. The early years of the decade witnessed the disappearance of the "fiscal dividend" that the prosperity of the sixties had generated and which fueled the expansion of the public sector. Growing pressures for budget balancing as a means of curbing inflation have arisen, and inflation is now deemed the number one public finance agenda item. In addition, defense outlays are slated to rise and the social security system appears to be in need of alternative sources of funding, both probably at some cost to domestic programs. The Carter budgets for fiscal 1981 and 1982, Congress' handling of its own reformed budget procedures this past year, and talk of revamping the congressional power structure are cited in evidence of a new behaviorial pattern. These incrementalists also warn that no drastic reform proposals are really necessary and that continuing political pressures will correct the imbalances, inefficiencies and ineffectiveness of the present system, thus rendering it more accountable and simpler to the electorate.

Opponents counter with the argument that fiscal retrenchment in domestic program areas need not involve basic intergovernmental program and regulatory reform, but merely a cutback in aid dollars. On the basis of current and projected experience, it only adds up to as many (if not more) aid programs, and more conditions attached thereto, but less money in constant dollar terms. From the state and local perspective, as well as that of the system as a whole, this would be the worst of nearly all possible worlds. To accept the "already responsive" thesis, they claim, is to ignore the dynamics of interest group lobbying, and Congress' perennial tendency when confronted with fiscal constraints to adopt the "parity of pain principle." This leads to no real assessment of intergovernmental programs and regulations, to avoiding the choice between those grants that make sense from those that are nonsense, of ignoring the differences between those that are fat and those that are lean, of separating out those that are genuinely intergovernmental from those that are patently parochial and political.

At the other extreme, the constitutional reformers contend that the political pressures are too great, that the system's responsiveness continues to be excessive, and that constitutional curbs are needed to foster an environment in which national decision makers can say "No"! The curbs range from the less dramatic like a presidential item veto, to the more drastic like constitutional limitations on taxing or spending and the changing of the terms of House members (and sometimes of the President) to the most drastic which involve the instituting of a quasi-parliamentary system, and the redrawing of state boundaries and clarification of state powers.

Opponents argue that none of these is feasible or even desirable, and that reforms short of the constitutional variety can do the job. Between the two extremes, and rejecting them, stands the "basic reform short of constitutional change" school of thought. Five approaches are found within this group.

One of these "middling" scenarios focuses on the collapse of internal governmental constraints. Hence, it calls for "sunset legislation," income tax indexation, grant consolidation, fiscal notes, a regulatory budget, statutory taxing and spending limits, congressional veto of administrative regulations, and committee reorganization on the Hill as ways of building greater discipline into the operations of the political branches of the national government.

Opponents of this approach contend that procedural changes without basic attitudinal and political ones will accomplish nothing but more charades, more complex and unfathomable national governmental operations, and more intergovernmental uncertainties.

A second mid-range scenario assumes that the problems are basically political and that if they are corrected the other difficulties will be resolved fairly easily. One group here focuses on party reform and advocates restriction on the political action committees of pressure groups, a reduction in the number of presidential primaries, closed primaries, enhancing the role of elected officeholders in all conventions, mid-term conventions, public financing of congressional candidates with funds donated to the parties and retention of the electoral college with a few changes.

A very different faction within this political process group centers its attention on the sovereign citizen. For it, a few of the above proposals are appropriate, but the direct election of the President, public financing of congressional and other campaigns, -a national initiative and referendum process, easier and simpler voter registration, the easy creation of new political parties, along with public financing of citizen witnesses appearing before regulatory agencies are central points in the reform agenda.

Opponents of the strengthened parties alternative argue that procedural props are no substitute for needed substantive functions and that the national parties perform no functions presently that other mechanisms and groups could not provide. To call for a responsible, accountable two-party system at this time, they claim, is to ignore the reality of contemporary American politics and the attitudes of the electorate toward the parties and the system they pretend to constitute.

Critics of any further focusing on the voter as sovereign policy maker in the system point to recent efforts to enhance direct participation in the system and their disappointing results. Periodic pushes for more populism and more participatory democracy, they point out, have done nothing but to enthrone a new breed of special interest group politics.

A third reform approach centers on the role of the federal judiciary and emphasizes that its authoritative role should be harnessed to render the system more accountable, more balanced and more effective. The present system, it is noted, is in large part a byproduct of court decisions relating to commerce and the conditional spending powers, and more balanced realistic future decisions in these twin constitutional areas could establish a new climate for and some enforceable means of curbing the seemingly uncontrollable assertion of national authority.

Critics of this strategy claim that it would lead to even greater judicial intrusion into essentially political matters than prevails now and that it rests on the fallacy that the Supreme Court is a neutral arbiter of intergovernmental conficts rather than a national body which, with only a few historical lapses, has favored national power and growth over its nearly 200-year history.

A final middle-range reform strategy concentrates on state and local governments, and their representatives and national associations in Washington. Its underlying thrust is to challenge the subnational governments to find ways and means of saying "no" (where appropriate) to federal programs, dollars and conditions. Decongestion should be as much, if not more, a part of the agenda of state and local governments as it should be uppermost with the national government. A somewhat changed role for the national associations is envisaged, one that is conscious of and vigilant about the long-term consequences of an ever accelerating federal role, of the need for trade-offs and bargaining, of the costs as well as the benefits of federal subventions. Moreover, a greater capacity and willingness to resort to the courts is sought when unjustified or excessively burdensome conditions are attached to grants and when Congress exercises its commerce power in a mandating fashion.

Critics of this approach claim that the real problem is with the array of interest groups that have no hesitancy in undercutting and undermining state and local governments if doing so will advance their own causes. The excessive responsiveness of federal policy makers to such pressures, they maintain, has pushed the states and localities to mount greater representational efforts over the past decade and a half. Moreover, some within this group argue forcibly that the rivalries between and among the

49

subnational governments and their national associations, and the differing needs and fiscal positions of some states and many localities assure a continuing focus on Washington.

A final middling perspective concentrates on surgical ways of decongesting today's overloaded inter-governmental network. What is needed, this group urges, is a sorting out of roles and of some of the functions that unwisely have become intergovernmentalized. This is no return to the old style dual federalism, they caution. Instead, this strategy seeks to place squarely on the federal government's shoulders the full fiscal and administrative responsbility for key national func-tions (like public welfare and health insurance) and to recognize the ineffectiveness, inequities, inefficiencies and unaccountability that the present patchwork approach to these two multi-billion programs has produced. There is no call for retreat for the federal government, but rather a facing, for the first time really, of its full responsibilities in these areas of clear national con-cern and obligation. The myths of managerial conven-ience, of bargain basement administration, of inter-governmental equity must be identified for what they are, so this group maintains, as myths--just myths.

At the same time, these surgicial reformers also call for a devolution of a range of activities the federal government now is aiding and pretending to "run." But the details at this point become somewhat blurred. Some of them argue for grant consolidation (and, in effect, the elimination of certain narrow categoricals). Others call for a trade-off: consolida-tions for a cut in their funding. Still others on the 440 grants that account for 10 percent of the federal aid total urge their elimination through mergers or devolution to state and local governments. Using the percentage of state-local outlays that specific federal aids provide is yet another approach, advocated by some. If it constitutes less than 10%, say, of the total of state and local expenditures in the affected program area, this group would say "scrap it". The subnational governments already are the dominant providers and all the federal aid provides is marginal fiscal help with major administrative headaches.

Advocates also point out that several functions by their very nature would remain intergovernmental--transportation, the environment, energy, natural resources and community development to mention only the more obvious. The goal of this partial sorting out strategy, they insist, is to decongest the system, to reduce the focus on Washington for a range of secondary public policies and programs, to enhance the discretion of subnational governments, and, above all, to inject greater accountability into the system.

Critics of this approach contend that it is totally infeasible, untraditional and undesirable. Once an issue gets to Washington or an aid program gets started there, it is nigh impossible to push it back into the state and local realm, they warn. Moreover, the number of programs and especially the large number of puny aid programs is a small price to pay for political accommodation, for pressure group pacification, for achieving a rough approximation of some consensus. The old theory that whatever passes muster in the chambers and corridors of Capitol Hill and is signed by a President is still a good test of what is in the national interest, they believe, and artificial efforts to reduce the pressures on the national legislative and administrative processes, especially as they are presently conditioned, will come to naught.

Conclusion. The basic question remains: how is the system to be rendered more functional, more accountable, and more comprehensible? Both the distant and the immediate past, as well as the present, provide fairly clear reasons as to why this now is the prime issue facing American federalism. We think we understand the dynamics of contemporary change, the prime actors and the consequences of our recent actions. Yet, we see the future no more clearly than anyone else. The foreign policy imponderables, the domestic political and economic uncertainties, the course of the court (and perhaps a possible switch in time to save far more than nine, to revise the old saying) are all problematic. But the present condition of American federalism is clear to us. Our diagnosis is that it is seriously ill. What the prescriptions will be is not clear.

51

6. State Dominance
or Local Autonomy?*

Joseph F. Zimmerman

The best system of substate governance has been
a subject of dispute for more than a century and a
half. At the heart of the controversy is a difference
of opinion on the degree to which states sould be involved in the local governance system. Here, two
theories have been in competition. One stresses the
integration of political authority and the other sup-
ports the fragmentation of such authority. To some
observers, the clash is between elitist theory and
democratic theory. To others, it is a clash between
functional and dysfunctional governmental approaches.
The key question is: On what level of government
should policy be made?

As the superior government, the state historically has been involved deeply in the local governance system. The nature of this involvement, however, has changed significantly in a number of states
during the past three decades.

Beginning in the 19th century, local government
officials sought constitutional protection against
interference by the state legislature in what were
perceived by the officials to be "local affairs,"
and later sought constitutional and statutory authorization for broader discretionary powers. Arguments
advanced by local government officials in support of
additional discretionary powers emphasized the importance of local self-government in a democratic
society and the ability of officals on the local
level -- in contrast to remote state officials -- to
determine the best course of action to solve problems.
In the 1950s, support for local self-government came
from a new group -- public choice theorists -- who
maintained that local governments possessing broad

---

* Reprinted from Measuring Local Discretionary
   Authority (Washington, D.C.: United States Advisory Commission on Intergovernmental Relations,
   1981), pp. 11-13 and 16-21.

discretionary powers afford citizens the opportunity
to "vote with their feet" by establishing residence
within the jursidiction of a political subdivision
offering the types and quality of services, as well as
the taxes, the citizens find most satisfactory in
terms of their needs and preferences.[1]

THE DIVISION OF STATE-
LOCAL POWERS

Governmental power at the subnational level may
be placed in three broad spheres -- a state controlling sphere, a local controlling sphere, and a shared
state-local sphere. The state possesses complete
responsibility for several governmental functions,
many local governments possess complete or nearly
complete responsibility for others, and the state
and certain local governments share responsibility
for the remainder.

These spheres of control have been shifting in
recent decades in response to economic, political,
and social changes. Some of these trends conflict,
however, since a number of states grant additional
local discretionary authority to some or all local
governments but at the same time preempt -- partially
or totally -- responsibility for functions that had
been the responsibility of local governments. Although the resulting kaleidoscopic nature of functional
authority assignment is generally apparent, relatively
little detailed information is available on the variations in discretionary authority currently possessed
by the several types of local government in each of
the 50 states. This lack of information and the
complexity of the relationships between the state
and the various units of local government make the
system of local government both relatively incomprehensible to most citizens and often confusing to
federal, state, and local officials.

The amount of discretionary authority granted by
the states to local units or their legal voters generally may be placed within four distinctive categories
-- structual, functional, personnel, and fiscal. Typically, the broadest discretionary powers apply to
governmental structure and functions and the narrow-
est to finance. The amount of discretionary authority

in personnel matters varies considerably from function to function.

DETERMINING FACTORS

The precise allocation of local discretionary authority within a particular state is influenced by five principal interdependent factors:

1. The political culture of the state is an important determining force.[2] Traditional beliefs regarding the proper repository of legal authority, if strongly held, make exceedingly difficult attempts to change the distribution of local authority within a state.

2. The length of the legislative session determines in large measure the opportunity for legislative control of local governments. The Kentucky General Assembly, for example, meets biennially for a 60-day regular session and, consequently, is unable to exercise the type of detailed control over substate governments that the Massachusetts General Court, which meets annually for nearly the entire year, can exercise. This factor was reflected in a national study of state mandates revealing mandates in only 28 of 76 specific program areas in Kentucky compared to mandates in 46 areas in Massachusetts.[3]

3. The number of units of local government also influences the degree of legislative control, since the legislature can devote only a limited amount of time to local issues. Southern states generally have the smallest number of political subdivisions on a per capita basis.

4. The complexity and length of the state constitution and ease of the amendment process influence the extent to which the state constitution or legislation is employed to grant or restrict powers of political subdivisions. In Vermont, heavy reliance is placed upon statutes because its 7,600-word constitution

54

stipulates that the senate, by a two-thirds vote every fourth year, may propose amendments if a majority of the members of the house of representatives concurs.[4] A proposed amendment approved by the legislature in this manner is referred to the subsequent biennial session of the general assembly, which, if it approves the proposed amendment, must submit the proposal to a statewide referendum. In other words, up to eight years may be required to amend the state constitution. It also should be noted that in 17 states voters may employ the constitutional initiative.

5. Finally, the political strength of associations of local officials and public service unions affects the amount of discretionary authority exercisable by local governments. Unions representing firemen and policemen have been successful in a number of states in persuading the legislature to mandate action by local governments favorable to their members.

CONSTITUTIONAL VARIATION

Although each state constitution contains provisions relative to local governments, not all constitutions grant authority to local governments or their legal voters: No powers are granted by the state constitution to any type of local government in Alabama, Arkansas, Delaware, Indiana, Kentucky, Mississippi, North Carolina, Vermont, and Virginia. Relatively broad discretionary powers, however, may be granted by statute as in New Jersey....

Georgia's constitutional grant is unique. Whereas all other states with a constitutional provision relative to local discretionary authority grant powers to municipalities only (or to their legal voters) or to municipalities and counties (which legally are municipal corporations in several states), the Georgia constitutional provision limits such powers to counties. Nationwide, the legal system of state-local relations is mixed with a constitutional grant of local discretionary authority restricted to certain types of local units (such as cities and towns in Colorado and Oklahoma) or by population size (such as cities in Texas with a population exceeding 5.000).

The constitutional grant of authority may or may
not be self-executing. The grant in Rhode Island is
triggered by the adoption of a locally drafted charter
by a city or town. Although the self-executing nature
of the Tennessee constitutional grant of local discretionary authority was not made explicit, the Tennessee
Supreme Court ruled that "an examination of the Journal
and Proceedings of the Constitutional Convention of 1953
shows that the authors of these home rule provisions
intended them to be self-executing."[5] In the 24 self-
executing states, powers not delegated by the Constitution are subject to Dillon's Rule -- rule of strict
construction -- which is explained in a subsequent
section. In other states, legislation is required
to implement the constitutional grant of authority.
The Nevada legislature has not implemented the constitutional provision.

COMPLICATED SYSTEMS

The variety of state-local relations in the 50
states and within certain states strains comprehension.
The number of local governments in 1977 varied from
four in Hawaii to 6,643 in Illinois. . .and in Hawaii
the state has preempted complete responsibility for
corrections, education, hospitals, and welfare -- with
the result that approximately 80% of all state-local
functions are performed by the state.

Understanding the system of local discretionary
authority within a state can be complicated if voters
employ special provisions, such as that in Illinois
authorizing local electors by referendum in cities
over 25,000 population to vote to exclude their city
from the constitutional grant of power. No Illinois
city, however, has exercised this option.

In Massachusetts, an "acceptance" or "permissive"
statute does not apply within a city or a town unless
the city council or the town meeting, respectively,
votes to accept the statute. In addition, a town
of a population under 15,000 may rescind its acceptance of a special law relating to town employees,
authorizing a capital expenditure, or involving
participation of the town in a regional district unless the statute specifies another method of revision.
Towns over 15,000 population lacked this power until
1979.

56

Further complicating the system of local governance is the fact that many local governments seek the enactment of special laws by the state legislature instead of exercising their own discretionary authority. Similarly, a city may decide to adopt an optional charter prepared by the state legislature (as in Massachusetts and Washington), instead of drafting and adopting its own charter.

Constitutional prohibition of special legislation has not been completely successful, as exhibited by the fact that Philadelphia, Pittsburgh, Allegheny County, and Scranton each is placed, by statute, in a separate class in spite of the Pennsylvania constitutional prohibition of special legislation.

In California, "general law" cities today possess approximately the same powers as so-called "home rule" cities, thereby in effect making the constitutional grant of local discretionary authority of relatively little significance.

Cities and counties in New Mexico, although granted certain discretionary powers by the state constitution, must submit their budgets to the state local government division for approval. A most interesting perspective was provided by a North Carolina respondent, who wrote:

> In some states, the local government commission's responsibilities and regulations would be looked upon as highly restrictive, as would state responsibility and funding for schools, highways, and prisons. It is looked on here as providing freedom from responsibilities, rather than restrictive.

In 1979, the West Virginia Supreme Court invalidated most of the statutory grant of local discretionary authority and in effect limited cities to selecting one of four statutory forms of government and determining the dates of local elections.[6] In Vermont, the so-called statutory "home rule" provision is inoperative, because bond counsels advise cities and towns that the provision is unconstitutional.

Public understanding of the amount and type of
local discretionary authority has been inhibited by
the failure of state constitutions to define terms,
such as "local concerns" and "municipal affairs," resulting in a case-by-case examination of state-local
conflicts by the courts. Poorly drafted provisions --
such as the use of "not inconsistent" or "denied" in
the Massachusetts constitution -- cause problems because a local action not denied by the constitution
or laws is inconsistent if the action does not follow
existing statutes.

Regardless of the amount of discretionary authority
granted by the state constitution or statutes -- structural, functional, fiscal, or personnel -- the key determinant of the ability of a local government to exercise fully the grant of powers is adequate finance.
Typically, the state reserves a large measure of control over finances, thus critically limiting the ability
of most local governments to exercise fully the grant
of discretionary authority.

DILLON'S RULE

In interpreting the formal powers granted to local
governments, state courts traditionally adhered to a
rule of strict construction that became known as
"Dillon's Rule," or the rule of state omnipotence
relative to local governments. In 1868, Judge John
F. Dillon held:

> The true view is this: Municipal corpora-
> tions owe their origin to, and derive their
> powers and rights wholly from the legisla-
> ture. It breathes into them the breath of
> life, without which they cannot exist. As
> it creates, so may it destroy. If it may
> destroy, it may abridge and control. Unless
> there is some constitutional limitation on
> the right, the legislature might, by a single
> act, if we can suppose it capable of so
> great a folly and so great a wrong, sweep
> from existence all municipal corporations
> of the state, and the corporations could not
> prevent it. We know of no limitation on
> this right as the corporations themselves
> are concerned. They are, so to phrase it,
> the mere tenants at will of the legislature.[7]

Later in 1868, an another opinion, Judge Dillon held:

> In determining the question now made, it
> must be taken for settled law, that a mu-
> nicipal corporation possesses and can exer-
> cise the following powers and no others:
> First, those granted in express words;
> second, those necessarily implied or
> necessarily incident to the powers ex-
> pressly granted; third, those absolutely
> essential to the declared objects and
> purposes of the corporation -- not simply
> convenient, but indispensable; and forth,
> any fair doubt as to the existence of a
> power is resolved by the courts against
> the corporation.[8]

In 1871, Judge Thomas M. Cooley of the Michigan
Supreme Court challenged Judge Dillon's opinion by
ruling that some rights of local self-government are
inherent in municipalities.[9] Judge Cooley also held
that legislation affecting local governments should
be general in nature. Although his ruling was followed
by courts in Indiana, Iowa, Kentucky, and Texas, for a
time, it is no longer followed in any state.

In 1903, the U.S. Supreme Court upheld the constitutionality of Dillon's Rule:

> Such corporations are the creatures, mere
> political subdivisions of the state for the
> purpose of exercising a part of its powers.
> They may exert only such powers as are ex-
> pressly granted to them, or such as may be
> necessarily implied from those granted.
> What they lawfully do of a public char-
> acter is done under the sanction of the
> state. They may be created, or, having
> been created, their powers may be re-
> stricted or enlarged, or altogether with-
> drawn at the will of the legislature; the
> authority of the legislature, when restrict-
> ing or withdrawing such powers, being sub-
> ject only to the fundamental condition
> that the collective and individual rights
> of the people of the municipality shall
> not be destroyed.[10]

In 1923, the U.S. Supreme Court again refused to recognize an inherent right of local self-government.[11]

Acting upon the basis of Dillon's Rule, in the 19th century state legislatures enacted numberous special laws affecting individual local governments. Some of these special laws correctly recognized that local communities were different in many respects -- including their climate, industry, population, topography, and transporation systems. Other special laws representing an abuse of legislative power were used as a means of arbitrarily controlling local governments. The state legislature was an incubus in the view of cities objecting to what were considered unjust special laws.

Despite the thrust of Dillon's Rule, it is a mistake to assume that all local governments have limited powers in a state where the rule applies. In Alabama, local legislation provides a broad array of powers to municipalities but not to counties. An expert correspondent in Kentucky wrote that "there is considerable home rule in practice. Dillon's Rule applies, but it is impossible for the legislature to enact any law affecting local government when there is considerable local opposition on a wide scale." In addition, it must be recognized that a number of state procedural controls -- a uniform system of accounting, post-audits, competitive bidding requirement, merit system for personnel selection -- do not affect local discretionary authority in a significant manner unless the controls prevent the adoption of a different system preferred by the local government. Furthermore, in 41 states the constitution offers political subdivisions some protection prohibiting special legislation from what often is viewed as excessive state intrusion into purely local matters.

Still, the basic impact of Dillon's Rule was to constrain local discretionary authority; and growing dissatisfaction with this trend in the 19th century led to a countermovement to expand that authority.

THE MOVEMENT FOR
LOCAL DISCRETIONARY
AUTHORITY

Constitutionally established as the creator and
controller of local governments, the state legislature
has had a deep involvement in the local governance
system since the end of the Revolutionary War in 1781.
Whereas some states have been concerned with the economy and efficiency of local governments and the prevention of corruption, other states have exhibited
little concern for these matters.

Abuses of the legislature's plenary power to enact
special laws led voters in several states in the 19th
century to approve proposed constitutional amendments
prohibiting the legislature from enacting special laws
elating to specific topics. The 1850 Michigan Constitution was the first to prohibit a specific law, when
it forbade the legislature from passing such a law
"vacating or altering" any road laid out by highway
commissioners.[12] Since 1874, the New York Constitution has forbidden the state legislature from passing
local bills laying out or discontinuing roads, drain-
ing swamps, locating or changing county seats, or incorporating villages.[13]

A second method of limiting the power of the legislature to control local governments involves constitutional provisions prescribing specific procedures
for the enactment of a local law. The Massachusetts
Constitution stipulates that the general court (legislature) may enact a local law only upon (1) the approval of a petition by the voters of the concerned
city or town, or mayor and council, or town meeting,
or (2) receipt of a recommendation for passage of a
bill from the Governor and its subsequent approval
by a two-thirds vote of each house of the legislature.[14] To protect against the enactment of "Ripper
laws," the pre-1970 Illinois Constitution granted
to Chicago a suspensory veto over special acts
applying to the city.[15]

A third method of restricting the power of the
legislature over political subdivisions is to limit
constitutionally the number of classes of local government that may be established, by the legislature, or

the minimum number of units in a class. The Massachusetts Constitution requires at least two local
governments in a class.[16]

A fourth approach is illustrated by the Wisconsin
constitutional provision that the legislature may approve only statewide bills uniformly affecting "every
city or every village."[17]

AFFIRMATIVE GRANTS OF POWER

The prohibition of special legislation may be
viewed as a negative constitutional right of local
governments. The first positive grant of power was
contained in optional charter laws allowing cities partial discretion relative to the structure of government.
Currently, New Jersey, New York, Utah, and Virginia
have optional charter laws for counties, and Massachusetts and Washington have such laws for cities.
New York counties have made no use of the optional
charter laws, but 19 of its counties have drafted
and adopted charters under special legislation or
the 1958 constitutional grant of power.

The first broad affirmative constitutional grant
of discretionary authority allowed cities in certain
states to draft, adopt, and amend charters -- a power
later extended to other local units in some states.
This movement for greater local discretionary authority
has been labeled "home rule" -- an emotionally loaded
term and a political symbol often employed without
definition.

According to proponents, advantages of a broad
grant of local discretionary authority include the
following:

1. Local experimentation to solve problems and
    provide services more expeditiously is en-
    couraged.

2. Citizen interest in local affairs is stimu-
    lated as the citizens possess the authority
    to initiate discretionary activities.

62

3. Education of residents in civic affairs is
    promoted because major decisions are made on
    the local level.

4. The most expeditious solution of public
    problems is promoted since local citizens
    know the problems best because of intimate
    knowledge of conditions.

5. A major legislative burden is removed, thereby
    providing additional time for the legislature
    to consider statewide issues and problems.
    In other words, local discretionary authority
    is a substitute for special legislation and
    also may be viewed as local initiative re-
    placing dependence upon the legislature for
    permission to initiate action.

6. Citizen alienation from government, that may
    result from decisions being made by state
    bureaucrats who are insensitive to the views
    of local residents, may be reduced.

In granting discretionary authority by constitutional provision to local governments, states followed
one or both of two avenues: Imperium in Imperio and
devolution of powers.

IMPERIUM IN IMPERIO

The early constitutional grants did not enumerate
local government powers, but such powers were implicit
in the grant of authority to draft, adopt, and amend
a charter.

In 1921, the National Municipal League proposed
a model constitutional provision based upon a type
of federalism within the state, with governmental
powers divided between the state and local governments.
This model provision would establish an Imperium in
Imperio, or a state within a state, by enumerating
local government powers and placing them beyond the
competence of the state legislature to affect. It
should be noted that the sixth edition of the Model
State Constitution (1963) lists the Imperium in
Imperio approach as an alternative and features the
devolution of powers approach.

In cases involving a conflict between the state
and a local government under this division of powers
or federated approach, courts apply the rule of exclusion (i.e., a constitutional grant enumerating
certain local powers automatically excludes all other
powers). The courts also interpret a specific word in
concert with other words on the same subject.

In theory, this approach to local discretionary
authority is inflexible, since a constitutional amendment is needed to change the distribution of authority.
In practice, the effectiveness of the Imperium in
Imperio approach has been limited by narrow judicial
interpretation of the scope of local affairs. In
other words, the traditional repository of control
has not been changed significantly since in most
cases the courts upheld the paramountcy of legislative power.

In 1955, Dean Jefferson B. Fordham criticized
the Imperium in Imperio approach by charging that the
"general-local distinction ranks with the governmental-
propriety test in tort and other matters as a major con-
tributor to the fuzziness of local government law doctrine and relatively high unpredictability in application."18

The Imperium in Imperio approach to providing a
constitutional grant of power to local governments was
a defensive movement to stop state interference in
what were perceived to be local affairs. This "layer
cake" division of powers and functional responsibilities
was more feasible when the approach was developed,
since society was less complex and not all local governmental functions had a clear state interest. The growing interdependence of levels of government led courts
to perceive a "state concern" in most functional areas
and to limit severely the scope of local discretionary
powers.

DEVOLUTION OF POWERS

Growing dissatisfaction with the Imperium in Imperio approach induced the American Municipal Association (now the National League of Cities) to employ
Dean Forhdam to study the problem of local discretionary

authority. In 1953, Dean Fordham drafted model constitutional provisions recognizing that local affairs cannot be divorced completely from state affairs,[19] and emphasizing that authority is granted to political subdivisions to enable them to discharge responsibilities.

His devolution of powers approach rejects the traditional division of governmental powers approach and removes from the judiciary the function of determining the dividing line between state and local powers. Under the proposal, the state constitution delegates to a municipal government, with two exceptions, all powers capable of delegation subject to preemption by general law. The exceptions are the power to enact "civil law governing civil relations" and the power to define and provide for "the punishment of a felony." This approach reflects a legislative supremacy approach, as did Dillon's Rule, but differs in that local governments under the former are free to act within the broad constitutional grant of power in the absence of general preemption statutes. Under Dillon's Rule, of course, no action can be initiated by a local government in the absence of legislative permission. Since the devolution of powers approach is self-executing, an Imperium in Imperio in effect is established automatically if the legislature fails to exercise its powers of preemption. The local charter, as well as general state laws and reserved constitutional powers, is more like a document placing restrictions upon the exercise of local discretionary powers than one granting such powers and, consequently, the charter is shorter than a Dillon's Rule charter. In Oregon, for example, most city charters are short because they provide for a general grant of powers under the Imperium in Imperio approach.

Under the devolution of powers -- and assuming the legislature through general laws reassesses continuously the powers devolved upon local governments -- the courts no longer have to determine the extent of the grant of local discretionary powers as they do under an Imperium in Imperio approach. The legislature, rather than the courts, is the arbiter of local powers and is omnipotent in its relationship to local governments if it decides to exercise fully its powers. As the late Professor Arthur W. Bromage of the University of Michigan wrote in 1955, "there is, with certain exceptions, no home rule power which is beyond legislative control" under the devolution of powers approach.[20]

Yet, the devolution of powers approach does not eliminate all state-local conflicts, since the legislature, in exercising its police power, may clash with a local government which maintains that the legislature is invading the sphere of local responsibility. Here, as under the Imperium in Imperio model, the courts are called upon to adjudicate the dispute on grounds of public policy rather than on law.

Recognizing that classified legislation may be a euphemism for special legislation, the model provisions drafted by Dean Fordham limit the number of classes of local governments to four, and stipulate that each class must contain at least two local governments.[21]

Only Alaska, Montana, and Pennsylvania have adopted the devolution of powers proposal en toto. With the exception of the 1958 Oregon county provision establishing an Imperium in Imperio, all states amending their constitutions since 1953 have followed the "devolution of powers" approach in general but reserved specific powers to the legislature. The Massachusetts constitutional provision, for example, contains the following limitations on local powers:

> Nothing in this article shall be deemed to grant to any city or town the power (1) to regulate elections other than those prescribed by sections three and four; (2) to levy, assess, and collect taxes; (3) to borrow money or pledge the credit of the city or town; (4) to dispose of park land; (5) to enact private or civil law governing civil relationships except as an incident to an exercise of an independent municipal power; or (6) to define and provide for the punishment of a felony or to impose imprisonment as a punishment for any violation of law.[22]

Discretionary authority is granted to political subdivisions by specific sections of some state constitutions in addition to the general grant of authority. To cite two examples, section 4 of article XVIII of the Ohio Constitution authorizes cities to acquire and operate public utilities, and section 5 of article

66

XIII of the Arizona Constitution authorizes cities to engage in private business. In addition, discretionary authority is granted to local governments by numerous general, classified, and special statutes in certain states.

CONCLUSION

Local government are nowhere mentioned in the U.S. Constitution. As Judge John F. Dillon stated in his classic decision, they are creatures of their states. The history of state-local relations since the mid-19th century is largely the story of local government's effort to modify this subordinate relationship.

At first, these efforts focused on preventing legislative abuses through various types of limits on special legislation. Then, they took a different tack -- an affirmative grant of authority from the state, through its constitution or legislation, to draft, adopt, and amend a charter and to supersede special laws and certain general laws. This affirmative approach, in turn, has taken two different paths. First came a constitutional provision establishing an Imperium in Imperio, or a state within a state, wherein local government affairs were enumerated and placed beyond the legislature's power to affect. Narrow judicial interepretation of the scope of local affairs, however, severely eroded the effectiveness of this approach. As a consequence, a second approach -- the "devolution of powers" -- was developed. This concept was designed to remove from the courts the function of differentiating between state and local powers, and instead to delegate to municipal government, through the constitution, all powers that the legislature can delegate but subject to the legislature's taking them back when it pleases. The "devolution of powers" generally offers localities the greatest amount of discretionary authority. With the exception of the Oregon county provision, all states seeking to alter the local government provisions of their constitutions have followed this approach in general since 1953.

A reasonable question is: How is each of the 50 states classified according to the threefold typology of Dillon's Rule, Imperium in Imperio, and the devolution of powers? Unfortunately, while these are three useful concepts in explaining the legal nature of state local relations, it is not possible to use them to classify the 50 states, because no one type applies to all general-purpose local governments in any state, and many states have a legal system that blends two or three of the types. A futher complication is the conflicting decisions issued by the highest court in many states with respect to the extent of local discretionary authority.

Two examples may suffice: The first type of problem is illustrated by a Massachusetts case. The Massachusetts General Laws specifically allow a town with a population of under 15,000 to rescind its previous acceptance of special statutes -- with the exception of statutes that (1) stipulate a different method of rescission, or (2) relate to the tenure and pension statuts of town employees, or authorize a capital expenditure, or involve participation of a town in a district.[23] However, a 1970 decision of the Supreme Judicial Court held that a special statute accepted by a town meeting in towns over 15,000 cannot be repealed subsequently by a vote of the town meeting.[24] Thus, the state has blended more than one approach in its relations with a single type of local unit.

Two Rhode Island Supreme Court decisions illustrate the second type of complication. In 1976, the court upheld the right of cities and towns to impose residence requirements on their employees.[25] While this decision broadened the power of cities and towns, the court subsequently ruled in another case that a local officeholder, Wilfrid L. Godin, could retain his state senate seat despite a City of Woonsocket charter ban on all dual office holdings.[26] Thus, the court gave both broad and narrow interpretations to the constitutional grant of local discretionary authority.

NOTES

1. See Charles M. Tiebout,"A Pure Theory of Local Expenditures," Journal of Political Economy, October 1956, pp. 416-24; and Robert L. Bish and Vincent Ostrom, Understanding Urban Government:

1. *Metropolitan Reform Reconsidered* (Washington, D.C.:
    American Enterprise Institute for Public Policy
    Research, 1973).

2. Daniel J. Elazar, *American Federalism: A View
    from the States,* 2nd ed. (New York: Thomas Y.
    Crowell Company, 1972), pp. 86-126.

3. ACIR, *State Mandating of Local Expenditures* (A-67),
    Washington, D.C.: U.S. Government Printing Office,
    July 1978, pp. 44-45.

4. *Constitution of Vermont,* § 72.

5. *Washington City Electric vs. Johnson City,* 350
    S.W. 2d 60. at 604 (1961).

6. *Hogan vs. City of South Charleston,* 260 S.E. 2d
    283 (1979). See also David A. Bingham, "No Home
    Rule in Virginia," National Civic Review, April
    1980, pp. 213-14.

7. *City of Clinton vs. Cedar Rapids and Missouri Rail-
    road Company,* 24 Iowa 455 at 461 (1868).

8. *Merriam vs. Moody's Executors,* 25 Iowa 163 at 170
    (1868).

9. *People vs. Hurlburt,* 24 Michigan 44 (1871).

10. *Atkins vs. Kansas,* 191 U.S. 207 at 220-21 (1903).

11. *City of Trenton vs. New Jersey,* 262 U.S. 182 (1923).

12. *Constitution of the State of Michigan,* art. IV, § 30
    (1850).

13. *Constitution of the State of Michigan,* art. III, §
    17.

14. *Constitution of the Commonwealth of Massachusetts,*
    art. LXXXIX, § 8 of the articles of amendment.

15. *Constitution of the State of Illinois,* art. IV, §
    34 (1870). See also the New York Constitution,
    art. XII, § 2 (1894).

16. Constitution of the Commonwealth of Massachusetts, op. cit.

17. Constitution of the State of Wisconsin, art. XI, § 3.

18. Jefferson B. Fordham, "Local Government in the Larger Scheme of Things," Vanderbilt Law Review, June 1955, p. 675.

19. Jefferson B. Fordham, Model Constitutional Provisions for Municipal Home Rule (Chicago: American Municipal Association, 1953), The Association never endorsed the proposal. Dean Fordham currently is a professor of law at the University of Utah.

20. Arthur W. Bromage, "Home Rule-NML Model," National Municipal Review, March 1955, pp. 132-33.

21. Fordham, Model Constitutional Provisions for Municipal Home Rule, op. cit., p. 15.

22. Constitution of the Commonwealth of Massachusetts, art. LXXXIX of the articles of amendment, § 7. Texas, as the result of a state supreme court decision, has had the devolution of powers approach in operation since 1948. See Forwood vs. City of Taylor, 147 Tex. 161 at 165, 214 S.W. 2d 282 at 286 (1948).

23. Massachusetts General Laws Annotated, Chap. 4, § 4A.

24. Chief of Police of Dracut vs. Town of Dracut, 357 Mass. 492, 258 N.E. 2d 531 (1970).

25. Louiselle vs. City of East Providence, 116 R.I. 585, 351 Atl. 2d 345 (1976).

26. Cummings vs. Godin, 377 Atl. 2d 1071 (1977).

7. Obstacles to Establishment of Interstate Compacts
Joseph F. Zimmerman

Interstate compacts do not spring full-blown on the mere whim of social planners or even senior public officials. On the contrary, establishment of interstate compacts on even the simplest of matters is problematical and time consuming. A brief review of the prerequisites to and history of such compacts demonstrates both the problems posed by attempts to establish them and why they have come to be used less frequently in recent years.

Interstate compacts have generally been used to solve only very straightforward interstate problems. Indeed, until the 1920s, almost all compacts concerned boundary questions and, with few exceptions, involved only two states. In more recent years, compacts have been used for planning purposes and mutual aid undertakings. Mutual aid compacts are standby agreements for interstate cooperation in periods of emergency and do not establish permanent agencies to administer the compacts. The Port Authority of New York and New Jersey, established by a bilateral compact in 1921, was the first permanent agency created to administer a compact. Few compacts have created agencies to administer major programs. As one expert put it, "The interstate compact commission, with very few exceptions, has not been used to carry out large substantive programs requiring intensive day-to-day administration," and "shares with other multiheaded bodies characteristics which tend to promote representiveness at the expense of effective administrative organization, . . ."[1]

Establishment of an interstate compact typically entails three basic steps. First, representatives of the states must negotiate and reach tentative agreement on the terms of the compact. Until the 1930s, these negotiations were generally handled by joint compact commissions established for a specific purpose pursuant to state statute and whose members were appointed by the governors of the participating states. In more

71

recent years, some compacts have been negotiated in the first instance by other types of groups. For example, the Interstate Compact for the Supervision of Parolees and Probationers was framed in the mid-1930s by the Interstate Commission on Crime, a group of attorneys-general and other state officials. Several compacts established since the 1930s have been negotiated by various pre-existing or ad hoc groups, such as the former New York State Joint Legislative Committee on Interstate Cooperation and the regional governors' conferences.

After negotiators reach agreement, the compact does not become effective until formally ratified by the legislatures of the participating states and approved by Congress if the compact is "political" in nature. A compact can not become effective until all the states have enacted virtually identical enabling legislation which, of course, is subject to a veto by the governor except in North Carolina. In addition, several compacts involving eastern states have provided that they will not become effective until executed by the governor after legislative approval.

Formal approval of the United States Congress is required before many compacts can become effective. Although Article I, Section 10 of the United States Constitution forbids states to enter into compacts without the consent of Congress, the Supreme Court has held that this requirement does not apply to all compacts.[2] But compacts that are of a "political" nature require Congressional approval.

After completion of these steps, the compact is established, and the compact's program may be implemented. Of course, if the compact is to be administered by a new compact agency instead of some pre-existing governmental body, the agency must be established and its members appointed before operations can begin.

These steps have proven not to be empty formalisms. On the contrary, for even the relatively simple compacts that have been established or proposed in the past, each of these steps has proved to be a significant, sometimes insurmountable obstacle.

The most fundamental obstacle has been the inability of the negotiators quickly to reach agreement on the terms of the compact. State negotiators must resolve the technical, financial, and substantive issues posed by the problem to which the compact is to be addressed; in this respect, they face all of the difficulties that would confront private entities in entering into contractual arrangements with others. In addition, however, state negotiators are constrained by a variety of factors unique to their status as public officials that impair their ability to reach agreement and make prompt agreement all but impossible. These constraints include their responsibility to the public, limitations on the states' abilities to commit funds for future years, and procedural requirements calling for voter and/or legislative approvals. As a result, negotiations concerning interstate compacts generally are prolonged and often unsuccessful.

Agreement has often been difficult to reach. For example, negotiations between California and Nevada concerning a bilateral compact for the allocation of certain water rights took twelve years, even though only two states were involved in those negotiations and there was only one real issue to be resolved.

Where a compact entails a risk or, especially, a commitment of long-term financial obligations for the participating states, special problems arise. In such cases, both customary inhibitions relative to assuming such long-term obligations and political pressures to avoid even an appearance of being "ripped off" for the benefit of private interests or other public bodies encourage extra caution and even more lengthy, difficult negotiations. One common result in such circumstances is increased state legislative oversight of the compact activities and on restricting the authority of the compact agency officials. For example, Article X of the Port Authority of New York and New Jersey Compact required the Authority to submit a comprehensive plan for its activities to the New York and New Jersey State Legislatures for approval prior to its implementation; Article XI requires that development plans "supplementary to or amendatory of any plan theretofore adopted" must be submitted to the two state legislatures for approval prior to implementation; and

Article XVI grants to both the Governor of New York and the Governor of New Jersey a veto power over any action taken by the Port Authority Commissioners.[3] Other compacts that entail a commitment of long-term financial obligations, such as that of the Washington Metropolitan Area Transportation Authority, attempt to protect the interests of the members by giving each of their representatives a veto over at least certain actions of the compact agencies.

While provisions of this sort may allay some state concerns about a proposed compact, they beget others because the provisions subject the interstate compact agencies to the political interests of the compacting states. Thus, for instance, Governor Brendan Byrne of New Jersey, exercising his right under the Port Authority of New York and New Jersey Compact, vetoed a number of actions taken by the Port Authority Commissioners in order to pressure them to develop a public transit aid plan acceptable to him and to roll back the May 1975 increase in bridge and tunnel tolls from one dollar and fifty cents to one dollar. Fears such political checks on the activities of the compact agency could be used to impair its functioning or injure other member states provide additional impetus to complex and prolonged negotiations, and negotiators may be charged with special instructions to safeguard their states' political interests.

Political concerns can delay and complicate establishment of a compact in other ways, as well. Obtaining approval by the state legislatures can be a lengthy process, and even the need for gubernatorial approval can prolong the period prior to establishment of a compact. For example, although the New York State Legislature approved the Interstate Compact for the Supervision of Parolees in 1936, the State did not become a member of the Compact until 1944 because of the refusal of Governor Herbert H. Lehman to execute the compact with the other states.[4]

Thus, for various reasons, history is replete with examples of long delays prior to establishment of an interstate compact. The Atlantic States Marine Fisheries Compact, effective in 1942, required five years to secure the necessary approvals. The Great Lakes Basin Compact was ratified in 1955 by Illinois, Indiana, Michigan, Minnesota, and Wisconsin and in 1956 by Pennsylvania; but it was not ratified by New York until 1960 or by Ohio until 1963. As noted, the California-Nevada Interstate Compact for water apportionment required twelve years of negotiation to gain the approval of just two state legislatures. Indeed, after examining sixty-five compacts, Wallace R. Vawter found that the average time required for negotiating, ratifying, and securing consent was four and three-quarter years, measured from the date of the first ratification to the date of Congressional consent.[5] He also found that thirty compacts relating to natural resources and nineteen compacts relating to river management and control required an average of six and three-quarters years and eight an three-quarters years respectively from the date of the first ratification to the date of congressional consent.[6]

The expenditure of large amounts of time does not always pay off for states repeatedly have set out to establish a compact only to fail after years of effort. A number of proposed interstate compacts--including the Interstate Tobacco Compact, the New England Development Authority Compact, the Interstate Crime Compact, and the Potomac River Basin Compact--have failed to be enacted by the requisite number of states. The proposed Potomac River Compact between Maryland, Virginia, and the District of Columbia was laid to rest in August 1976 when the states were unable to reach agreement after ten years of active promotion.[7] Although the Delaware River Basin Compact was approved in 1961, two proposed Delaware River Basin Compacts failed to gain approval in the 1920s, and a similar proposed compact in the 1950s died in a Pennsylvania Senate Committee after being approved by the other states and the Pennsylvania House of Representatives. The New England Pollution Compact, although approved by the Vermont State Legislature, did not become effective because the Governor of Vermont vetoed it on account of the failure of the Legislature to include in its act the compact's pledge to abate existing pollution.

Other compacts have failed because of an inability to obtain needed approval of the United States Congress. These include the Main-New Hampshire School District Compact, the Midwest Nuclear Compact, the

National Guard Mutual Assistance Compact, the North-
eastern Water and Related Rsources Compact, the Mid-
Atlantic States Air Pollution Control Compact, the
Interstate Environment Compact, and the California-
Nevada Interstate Compact.[8]

Even when Congress does give its approval, its
actions can be slow. The Susquehanna River Basin
Compact was approved by Maryland and New York in 1967
and by Pennsylvania in 1968, yet Congress did not
approve the Compact until 1970. The Washington Metropolitan Area Transit Regulation Compact was approved
by Maryland, Virginia, and the District of Columbia in
1958, but did not receive the consent of Congress
until 1960.

For all these reasons, it is difficult to disagree
with the conclusion of an authoritative study that
"there are weaknesses and difficulties in the use of
the interstate compact. The most obvious difficulty is
the necessity for securing agreement among several
jurisdictions."[9] And it is clear that "the ratification of a compact change by two or more state
legislatures is likely to be a lengthy process at best;
at worst it may constitute an impossible obstacle."[10]
As the National Resources Committee put it, "(w)hen the
problem is a continuing and complex one, the compact
method is not only ill-adapted to the planning function
but it leaves much to be desired from the standpoint of
effective administration."[11]

It is, no doubt, at least in part because of the
increasing recognition of these problems that interstate compacts have been used less frequently in recent
years than in decades past. Their heyday as a solution
to multi-state problems came in the 1950s and 1960s.
But a sharp drop in their use occurred commencing in
the 1970s.

NOTES

1. Wallace R. Vawter, "Interstate Compacts--The
Federal Interest" in Task Force on Water Resources and
Power, Report on Water Resources and Power (Washington,
D.C.: United States Commission on Organization of the
Executive Branch of the Government, June 1955),
vol. III, p. 1702.

2. Virginia v. Tennessee, 148 U.S. 503 (1893).
3. Similar provisions are found in the interstate compact between New Jersey and Pennsylvania creating the Delaware River Port Authority. Article III provides that the governor of each state can veto any action taken by the commissioners from his state, and Article XII requires that proposals for virtually all types of new projects be submitted to the legislatures for their approval.
4. Not only substantive problems, but also mechanical and procedural problems, can impede and delay the establishment of interstate compacts. After ratifying the Forest Fire Compact, for instance, Rhode Island recalled and repassed the ratification act to correct what appeared to be a typographical error. A similar problem delayed implementation of the New York State-Rhode Island Boundary Compact.
5. Vawter, "Interstate Compacts," p. 1693.
6. Ibid.
7. "After the Compact," Potomac Basin Reporter, September 1976, p. 1.
8. On at least one occasion, a compact was not established when the President vetoed a Congressional Resolution approving it. In 1942, President Franklin D. Roosevelt vetoed the act consenting to the Republican River Compact. Document No. 690, House of Representatives, 77th Congress, 2nd Session, April 2, 1942.
9. Frederick L. Zimmermann and Mitchell Wendell, The Law and Use of Interstate Compacts (Lexington, Kentucky: The Council of State Governments, 1976), p. 54.
10. Roscoe C. Martin, Guthrie S. Birkhead, Jesse V. Burkhead, and Frank J. Munger, River Basin Administration and the Delaware (Syracuse: Syracuse University Press, 1960), p. 131.
11. National Resources Committee, Regional Factors in National Planning and Development (Washington, D.C. United States Government Printing Office, December 1935), p. 41.

PART II

STATE CONSTITUTIONS

Whereas the United States Constitution has proven to be a lithe document capable of adjusting to changed conditions without frequent formal amendment, the typical state constitution is a rigid document replete with detailed material of a statutory rather than an organic nature. The average age of state constitutions in 1983 was about eighty-three years. Although the Massachusetts constitution (1780) is the oldest one, the document differs considerably today from the original document because of amendments.

Many state constitutions are long documents because of restrictions placed upon the powers of state and local governments in the nineteenth century, and the relative ease of amendment which facilitated efforts by interest groups to insert special provisions. Counting local government amendments, the Georgia constitution contains over one-half million words and is followed in length by the Alabama constitution which is approximately 129,000 words in length. As of January 1, 1982, the California constitution had been amended 438 times and was followed in terms of number of amendments by the Alabama Constitution (393). The New York Constitution contains 191 amendments. The constitution of Alaska and Hawaii, the two youngest states, are exceptions to the above comments. Both documents are relatively short and confined to fundamentals.

An examination of state constitutions reveals there is no agreement relative to matters considered to be worthy of constitutional status. Included in a number of constitutions are a hodgepodge of antiquated phrases and defective provisions which do not accomplish their purposes. The New York constitution even contains provisions relative to reapportionment of the legislature which have been invalidated by the United States Supreme Court as violating the equal protection of the laws clause of the fourteenth amendment to the United States Constitution.

Constitutional experts have praised the original
Hawaiian state constitution and one might surmise constitutional amendments seldom would be adopted. However,
the Hawaiian constitution requires that the question of
calling a constitutional convention appear on the referendum ballot once every ten years. Professor Norman
Meller and Richard H. Kosaki of the University of Hawaii,
in reading number 8, note that the thirty-four amendments
proposed by the 1978 constitutional convention were ratified by the electorate.

The authors of reading number 8 point out there was
no citizen demand for fundamental changes in the constitution, analyze the election of delegates and the composition of the convention, outline the organization and
operations of the convention, examine the role of interest
groups, and describe the product of the convention.

In recent years, conventions have debated whether
to submit their proposals, including an entire new constitution, to the voters as one package for ratification.
The 1967 New York convention decided to place a proposed
new constitution as a single proposal on the ballot and
the voters rejected it. Fearing a similar fate for its
proposed amendments, the Hawaiian convention submitted
its proposals as thirty-four separate amendments. All
were ratified. Meller and Kosaki point out that a controversy, leading to a legal challenge, revolved around
the form of the referendum ballot. Voters had the option
of voting for or against all amendments, or voting "no"
on one or more amendments with unmarked amendments being
recorded as "yes" votes. The result was that each proposed amendment was adopted by votes against other proposals and did not receive a direct vote of approval.

Deirdre A. Zimmerman, a management analyst in the
New York State Division of the Budget, in reading number
9 explains the organizational and fiscal principles included in the constitutions of Alaska and Hawaii to
facilitate sound management of the state governments.

Each constitution provides for a strong governor
by confiding control of the executive branch in the
governor by providing for a short ballot; incorporating
the principles of administrative integration, span of
control, and functional organization; and gubernatorially
initiated plans for reorganizing the executive branch.

Of equal importance are provisions in the two constitutions containing sound fiscal principles--executive
budgeting, budgetary comprehensiveness, capital budgeting, the item veto, and prohibition of borrowing for
operating expenses.

8. HAWAII'S CONSTITUTIONAL CONVENTION
1978

Norman Meller and Richard H. Kosaki*

The constitutional convention which met in
Hawaii in the summer of 1978 had its origins in
a legal squabble; and its immediate aftermath was
a judicial challenge which went to the heart of
citizen participation in constitution making.
Sandwiched in between was the adoption of a
sizeable number of substantive constitutional
changes ranging widely over such concerns as
environmental protection, benefits for a single
ethnic group, and imposing state spending limits
with mandatory refunds of governmental surplus.

At least once every decade in Hawaii the
question of whether a constitutional convention
shall be held must appear on the general election ballot. The popular vote in 1966 required
the legislature to set up the machinery for the
convention which assembled in 1968 (see the
League's study With an Understanding Heart--
Constitution Making in Hawaii). In 1976, the
general election was to take place six days
before the end of the 10 years, so the legislature
disputed over deferring the question until 1978.
Despite an attorney general's opinion permitting
delay, the question did appear on the 1976 ballot.
To help stimulate the interest of voters, the
Legislative Reference Bureau widely distributed
a small pamphlet discussing 20 possible subjects
which a convention might consider.

Almost 75 percent of the voters favored the
holding of a convention. A material factor may
have been the amorphous public dissatisfaction

---

* Reprinted with permission from the National Civic
Review, May 1980, pp. 248-57 and 271.

with the government following Watergate. It was
conceded that there were no overriding or pressing
issues which necessitated a convention.

The 1977 legislature fixed the number of convention delegates at 102, double that of the state
House of Representatives, and the largest constitutional convention to date in the state. Delegates were apportioned among the 27 representative
districts, with each entitled to at least two delegates, and with four or six allotted to the bigger
legislative districts. Precincts in the latter
were grouped so that in all cases two delegates
were elected from each delegate district. While
the larger body may be attributed to the popular
sentiment for a "grass roots" convention, it also
permitted accommodation of all incumbent legislators who might desire to become delegates.

The legislature directed that the special
election be held on May 21, 1978, and that the
delegates convene on July 5, less than two months
later. Monthly remuneration was set at $1,000,
with a maximum of $4,000, plus per diem expenses.
As the salary was to begin the day after the election and be paid semi-monthly, it practically
assured a short convention which would conclude
its work before the primary election scheduled
for early October. Anticipating this, the convention legislation also called for submission of
proposals to the voters at the general election
in November, unless the delegates decided to the
contrary. Approximately $500,000 was appropriated
to pay the costs of the special delegate election,
and over $2.5 million for all phases of the conven-
tion.

"Tooling Up" the Community. Once the legislature acted, the state swung into action in anticipation of electing delegates. The office of the
lieutenant governor issued factual releases on
choosing delegates and the mechanics of holding a
convention. The media encouraged broad public involvement and solicited reactions to probable
constitutional issues. Workshops were held on how

to campaign for a convention seat. Public forums
were scheduled throughout the state to examine a
range of matters which might be considered in the
convention. Polls taken under various auspices
sought to probe the public's formulation of
issues. These surveys initially provided the
grist for the candidates' campaigns and had as
their potential the instruction of the delegates
when they convened. Lacking any public outcry demanding fundamental reform, all of these efforts
collectively served to channel a myriad of concerns for changing one or more aspects of government into a single interest identified with the
election of delegates and the holding of the
convention.

The Candidates and Election Results. In the
decade since the previous convention, Hawaii's
population had increased by about 20 percent.
Even more startling was the dramatic jump in the
number of registered voters, from 242,827 in 1968
to 344,952 in 1978, more than twice the rate of
population growth. Despite these developments,
fewer people voted for delegates in 1978 than in
1968.

A record number of candidates--697--filed
for election for the 102 seats. One district had
30 candidates; more than 20 candidates filed in
each of seven districts; and the smallest number
of candidates was six (four districts), three
times the number to be elected.

The turnout was only 35 percent of the
registered voters, less than half the number that
voted on holding the convention and the smallest
recorded for any statewide election in Hawaii.
Votes were predictably fewer at special elections,
but this was extraordinarily low, and most observers were surprised. Either the voters were not
attracted by the field of delegates or there were
few matters at issue which stimulated public attention or, most likely, both.

While each district averaged more than 3,000
registered voters, the highest vote getter garnered

only 1,982 votes (77 percent of those voting
in his district), and one delegate was elected
with the low tally of 363 (20 percent of voters).
Given the large number of candidates in each
district, it is not surprising that 89 of the 102
delegates won their posts on plurality votes.
Coupled with the low voter participation, this
cast more than the usual doubt on the "represen-
tativeness" of the delegates. A runoff election
would have helped provide a greater legitimacy
to the convention.

Delegate Composition. Whatever the cause, in
composition the 1978 convention was noticeably
different from its predecessors. For one thing,
it was singularly lacking in familiar political
figures and persons with well-established community status. While incumbents and former legislators constituted 51 percent of the 1968 convention, they were only four delegates in 1978.
In 1968, 45 incumbent legislators filed as candidates and 37 were elected; in 1978, only two incumbents chose to run, and one of them had already declared his intention not to seek reelection to the legislature. Both were elected, and,
significantly, the active incumbent later lost
in his bid for another legislative term. The
difference in legislator participation can be
attributed principally to wide advocacy of a
"grass roots" convention. Public interest groups
and the mass media, particularly the newspapers,
extolled the virtues of other than lawmakers
running for convention seats. For their part, the
legislators appeared ready to forego the certain
risks and doubtful benefit to be obtained from
convention membership.

The 1978 Hawaii convention was a considerably
younger group than its predecessors. The median
age was mid-30s, compared to mid-40s in 1968, and
almost a third of the 1978 delegates was below the
age of 30 (contrasted with only 9 percent in 1968).
The convention's female component was tripled: 30
(29 percent) of the delegates, compared to 10
percent in 1968 and 8 percent in 1950. Both

factors were to tell in the shaping of the convention product.

In 1968 Island-born delegates comprised 84 percent of the convention. Among the 1978 delegates was a larger number of more recent residents, so that locally-born delegates made up only 70 percent of the convention. The last three conventions have registered the dominance of the Japanese and Caucasians in the population. Caucasian delegates constituted 43 percent of the 1950 convention, and the Japanese 30 percent; in 1968 they reversed numerical precedence, but maintained about the same ratios. The Japanese delegates' numerical dominance was whittled away a little in 1978, to about 38 percent. As the third largest ethnic group, delegates of native Hawaiian ancestry constituted 14 percent of the 1978 convention, an increase of 10 percent over 1968 but less than the 1950 proportion of 19 percent. The Hawaiian component utilized its minority position skillfully, and realized material benefits for the Island's indigenous peoples.

In terms of occupations, in 1978 there was a marked drop in lawyers and other professions, and an increase in governmental employees, educators, students and retirees. Business and law-related, in that order, still comprised the largest occupational groupings, accounting for approximately one-quarter and one-fifth of the delegates. Their predominance aided the consideration of changes in governmental finance.

In 1978 there was no organized and overt political party involvement in the delegate election, compared to heavy activity in 1950. To a degree this paralleled today's generally low level of party visibility in the state, but it was also the result of pressures to secure a grass roots convention. Some of the delegates were holding or had held partisanly-cleared governmental employment, so that they were not political neophytes. In general, however, the parties kept a low profile and did not attempt to

86

exert direction over the day-to-day operations of the convention.

The selection of delegates was by nonpartisan ballot, but the party affiliations of most candidates could be discerned should they be considered material. Hawaii's shift from a heavily Republican territory in 1950 to a dominantly Democratic state by 1978 was reflected in the conventions: Republicans controlled the 1950 convention, while the Democrats outnumbered the Republicans in 1968 (68 percent to 28 percent) and 1978 when the convention was 86 percent Democratic with the remainder mostly Republican.

As has been noted elsewhere, the basic cleavage within most conventions is not between political parties but between preservers and reformers. This division seemed evident in the 1978 pre-convention organizational efforts, which found the delegates split into two camps--a loosely joined majority group whose members for various reasons were more status quo oriented, and a minority, often referred to as independents, many of whom were reform minded. While the delegates' backgrounds in terms of political experience, occupation, age, sex and ethnicity sometimes helped to explain stands on particular issues, generally the convention did not divide clearly along any of these lines. The convention had its share of "stand-ins" (those who represented vested political interests) as well as a full quota of "aspirants" (those who were using the convention as a launching pad for careers in elective politics). A few of the delegates could be labeled "idealists" or "statesmen," but they were in a minority.

Convention Organization and Operations. With the election of 102 disparate and mainly inexperienced delegates, convention structure became an especially challenging and crucial issue. Not surprisingly, one of the two legislator-delegates assumed a leading role in organizing the convention. He met with key labor and corporation

87

lobbists and rounded up a core of approximately
40 delegates. Next he fashioned a coalition with
a group of young lawyers who loosely shared an
ideological position, labeled "palaki* power,"
aimed at resisting the introduction of change by
newcomers to Hawaii, and whose leader was to play
a main role as unofficial floor leader in the
convention. The resulting slim minority permitted a shaky control over convention actions, but
the weak allegiance of its members never assured
an easy margin on issues. Repeating the experience of 1968, despite the convention's overwhelmingly Democratic composition, a Republican
was elected as President.

The minority did not function as a unit.
Mostly, the "independents" coalesced around their
objection to the organizational tactics of the
majority. While they leaned toward the side of
"reform" on such issues as the initiative and
unicameralism, on others they seldom voted unanimously.

The majority-minority feuding was especially
obvious in the initial days of the convention.
In plenary sessions and in committee meetings,
considerable time was consumed in arguing points
of parliamentary procedure. The long hours spent
on parliamentary rules and their interpretation
were prompted to some degree by a desire for
"fair play" on issues over which there was sure
to be a division of views, but were also a symptom of inexperience and bruised personal feelings.

To expedite its work, the convention established 16 committees. In number and jurisdiction
they were fairly similar to those of the 1968
convention. It should be noted that Hawaiian
Affairs and Ethics were designated as the responsibilities of separate committees, and Environment preceded Agriculture, Conservation and Land

---

*The name of the humble cotton cloth once worn
by Hawaii's plantation workers.

in the title of the committee assigned to
consider those matters. The new committee titles
portended the attention that these subjects would
receive during the course of the convention.
Each delegate was assigned to five or six committees, and only members of the majority faction
were appointed as chairmen.

Special interest groups were active in the
convention. Among the most prominent was the
state's largest public employee union, whose
volatile leader was accused of controlling the
convention. Other union and corporate lobbyists,
and representatives of public interest groups were
also present. The state executive and legislative
branches publicly proclaimed a hands-off policy,
but it was evident that they did not favor the
adoption of major substantive changes. The judiciary, led by the chief justice of the supreme
court, actively sought and succeeded in convincing
the delegates to approve the amendment creating an
intermediate court of appeals.

The convention received broad coverage, including full discussion of its negative aspects.
Although convention committees scheduled numerous
public hearings, few attended or otherwise availed
themselves of the opportunity to participate in
the deliberations. The results of opinion polls,
which tended to show the public in favor of
specific "reform" measures, appeared to have little
influence on the delegates' decisions.

The Convention Product. By the time the delegates concluded their work, they surprised the
state and probably themselves by the number and
range of changes proposed. Part of the explanation
lies in the organization of the convention. The
majority had not been fashioned to implement a
program, but rather to oppose amendments which
threatened to disturb the status quo: attempts to
eliminate or modify public sector collective bargaining, converting the legislature to a unicameral
body, and the introduction of the initiative,
referendum and recall. The cost of maintaining

such a coalition was the inability to prevent individual members, frequently allied with special interests, from successfully championing their pet ideas.

The weakness of organized party control is attested to by the amendment reinstituting the Hawaii-style open primary election. Similarly illustrative was the lengthening by at least 50 percent of the minimum period between primary and general elections. The establishment of a state-supported fund to help finance campaigns, and the imposition of limitations on candidate spending and campaign contributions could be explained as safeguards to keep access to politics open, and not as aimed at any entrenched faction of presaging the emergence of a different balance of power. However, the provision that incumbents in elected office must resign when their terms do not coincide with those of new posts they seek was aimed specifically at Honolulu's mayor and his gubernatorial aspirations. A two consecutive term limit was also added to the offices of governor and lieutenant governor.

The article dealing with the legislature received its customary spate of amendments. State senators were returned to staggered, four-year terms, and the reapportionment commission will now also include congressional districts in its decennial review. A requirement for a split session was added, and procedures for the introduction and passage of bills were altered. Open committee meetings were mandated. Legislative salaries will be set automatically by a commission appointed for eight years, unless the governor or the legislature disapproves of its work.

Some executive branch amendments were designed to remove minor constraints. The apportionment of the nonpartisan board of education was changed to provide for election of both at-large and district candidates. Since the convention did not provide that board or the board of regents with any revenue raising powers, however,

90

it remains doubtful whether a prohibition against
legislative and executive interest in the internal organization and management of the public
school and university systems, other than by
general laws, will assure the independence desired by the educational agencies.

Of the three major branches of government,
most attention was given to the structure and
staffing of the courts and the judicial process.
An intermediate appellate court was created to
assume part of the work load of the state supreme
court, and constitutional status was given to the
district courts. As a compromise on the principle
of merit selection of judges, a judicial commission will screen the performance of incumbents
before renewal of their terms and the qualifications of persons to be considered for judicial
posts. Once the commission establishes a panel
of at least six nominees, gubernatorial appointment and senatorial confirmation are retained. A
commission will propose judicial salaries, instead of their being fixed in the constitution. A
judicial discipline commission will aid the supreme court in the exercise of enlarged disciplin-
ary powers. Limitations were placed on the time
within which cases may be decided. Jury trials
were guaranteed only in common law cases involving $1,000 (instead of $100) or more. A 12-mem-
ber jury was mandated in criminal cases, but
provision for smaller juries in civil cases was
retained. Independent counsel will advise the
grand jury, so that it will not have to depend on
advice received from the public prosecutor.

A number of amendments dealt with fiscal
issues and with matters sensitive to preserving
Hawaii's uniqueness. An underlying theme of
conservatism distinguished both.

The amendments with a fiscal base are easily
identified. The maximum state debt established
by the constitution was redefined so as to halt
borrowing when the cost of debt service payments
exceeds 20 percent (18.5 percent starting in
1982) of average general fund revenues. Probably

as a trade-off, the legislative vote necessary
for bond authorization was reduced (to a majority
from two-thirds). Revenue bonds were authorized
to enable the obtaining of lower interest rates
on money borrowed for designated non-governmental
activities, and they will not be counted within
the state debt limit. Capital improvement authorizations that are not implemented will lapse
automatically after three years, forcing continuing review of long-range planning. General
fund expenditures cannot increase faster than the
state economic growth rate, unless the legislature
by extraordinary majority, justifies the necessity.
Deficit spending will be prohibited except where
the public health, safety or welfare is threatened. Should the state have a general fund surplus
in excess of 5 percent for two years, a tax refund
or credit was mandated. To help monitor these
provisions, and to end legislative-executive dis-
agreements, the estimates of a separate council
on revenues will control in the preparation of the
executive budget and its legislative appropriation.
To prevent undermining of the intent of the state
spending restrictions, the counties may not be
required to undertake additional functions without
the state also making provision for their financing. A tax review commission was established;
meanwhile, full discretion was granted to conform
the state income tax to the federal law. The
state seemingly adopted the policy of gradually
transferring the administration of the property
tax to the counties, albeit reluctantly as reflected by the length of time it will take and the
means adopted to assure statewide uniformity.

The islands-oriented amendments were comprised in part of an "Hawaiian-affairs package."
The Department of Hawaiian Homes Lands, a state
agency whose charter is under congressional protection, must now receive greater funding for the
rehabilitation of Hawaiians. A portion of the
public lands returned to Hawaii on statehood
will be held in trust for the benefit of Hawaiians, the proceeds to be administered by a board
composed of and elected by Hawaiians. Constitutional support is extended to rights

"customarily and traditionally exercised for subsistence, cultural and religious purposes." Supplementing these three major components are several other modifications, such as mandating that public educational institutions include a program promoting Hawaiian culture, the recognition of Hawaiian as an official language, the addition of a state motto, and the prohibition, with exceptions, against acquiring real property by adverse possession.

The other interests of the Islands-oriented group dealt with the maintenance of a life style not necessarily limited to Hawaiians, incorporating a concern for safeguarding the environment. The state is directed to protect and promote use of agricultural lands, and conserve ocean waters and adjacent lands, and is authorized to license mariculture and engage in public land banking. A new state agency will regulate the use of water resources. Provision is made for population growth management by both state and counties, and they are directed to protect and promote the natural beauty of Hawaii. One of the results of this bundle of changes may be to increase the state government's role in resource management, to the disadvantage of the counties. Somewhat as a crowning point, a "clean and healthful" environment is declared to be the right of every person, with legal standing to sue should degradation of the environment occur.

The generalized dissatisfaction of youth found embodiment in the convention in a wide-brush quest for reform. It overlapped the "palaka power" ideology among the delegates, and found partial expression in the amendments directed to "righting the wrongs" suffered by Hawaiians, and the prevention of development which would adversely affect the Island environment. It also accounts for a number of constitutional changes which otherwise appear as wholly disparate. Here fits the incorporation into Hawaii's bill of rights of the express recognition of each individual's right to privacy. Equally applicable is the

93

prohibition of discrimination in public educational institutions on the basis of sex, and the replacement of all single-sex words. Here, too, lies part of the explanation for requiring a two-thirds approval of the legislature before construction of any nuclear plant and the disposition of radioactive materials in the state. Finally, it helped fuel the extension of codes of ethics for officers and employees to include financial disclosure, to incorporate candidates for office, and to require the registration and restriction of lobbyists.

When the 1978 convention completed its work, it had agreed on 116 proposed changes. In reality, the convention had revised much of the constitution, but it did not want to place its handiwork before the voters on an all-or-nothing basis, and run the risk of objection to particular amendments causing rejection of the whole. Instead, the precedent set by the 1968 convention was adopted, and the changes were grouped into 34 separate proposals, with the contents of some only tenuously related.

"Grand Slam" at the Polls. With the amendments scheduled to come before the voters at the general election in November, the convention went to great effort to publicize their content. Summaries were mailed to the residence of every registered voter. An advertising supplement which purported to carry the full text of the amendments was distributed through the newspapers in all counties. A voter information booklet provided by the convention was circulated as part of the official ballot. News stories, editorial comment, and pro-and-con analyses prepared and publicized under non-convention auspices also supplied the voters with pertinent data and opinion.

The form of the ballot followed the three-part precedent adopted by the 1968 constitutional convention, with a single "yes" or "no" on all amendments, or a "yes-but" option that permitted voting against one or more proposals but

94

automatically registering a "yes" on the remaining unmarked proposals.

The Honolulu morning newspaper opposed three amendments and the evening five, with the "right to privacy" the only common target of opposition. On the eve of the election, both papers expressed concern about the possibility that all 34 proposals might be defeated.

Despite the wide range of controversial subjects, all of the proposals were adopted. Fewer than 60 percent of the voters who went to the polls cast marked constitution ballots; of those who did, 20 percent were in favor of the entire slate of proposals and almost as large a fraction cast a single "no" vote. This meant that each proposal was adopted because of votes against one or more other proposals, rather than because of expression of affirmative approval. The proposals which received the largest negative tallies included the "Hawaiian-affairs package," the right to privacy, resignation of incumbents on running for another office, campaign financing, and the transfer of the administration of the property tax to the counties.

To some commentators, the 1968 convention had invented a ballot form which had started out as an ingenious means to overcome voter inertia but which now threatened periodically to become a cynical manipulation of Hawaii's citizens. Protestors lodges several court challenges, but succeeded only in nullifying mostly minor parts of the proposed changes. In response to the major objection that the form of the ballot was biased in favor of an affirmative vote, the state supreme court refused to invalidate the results, holding that it was legally sufficient as long as the voters were fully and adequately instructed. Similarly rejected by the court was the fact that unrelated amendments were included with a single proposal; and the complaint that the electorate was presented with too complex an array of amendments to permit an intelligent decision was not

95

considered sufficient to warrant judicial interference with the electoral process. The court
did find, however, that information which the
convention released was incomplete on several
minor proposals, and thereby misleading to the
voters. Except for abrogating the limiting
definition of "native Hawaiian," none of the
amendments so invalidated were included in the
proposals which had drawn the most expression
of voter disapproval at the polls. Allowed to
stand was the vast bulk of the changes, a number
of which further emphasize the uniqueness of the
Island state.

9. ORGANIZATIONAL AND FISCAL PRINCIPLES IN THE CONSTITUTIONS OF ALASKA AND HAWAII

Deirdre A. Zimmerman

The typical state constitution contains antiquated and restrictive provisions and excessive details hampering effective and efficient administration of the state government. Two state constitutions are exceptions. The constitutions of Alaska and Hawaii contain a number of sound organizational and fiscal principles which could be adopted with profit by other states when amending their constitutions or adopting new ones.

ORGANIZATIONAL PRINCIPLES

Both constitutions ensure the Governor has strong administrative powers. Only the Governor and the Lieutenant Governor in Hawaii are popularly elected; there are no independently elected officials who share executive power with the Governor. Consequently, unity of command exists and the ballot is short. The Governor can be held responsible for administrative failures on election day: There can be no shifting of responsibility by the Governor to other administrative officials.

The organizational principle of integration is found in the two constitutions; the entire state administration is placed under the control and responsibility of the Governor. Coordination of administration is made difficult in many states by the division of administrative authority between the Governor and popularly elected administrative officials; uncoordinated administration has let to duplication and waste in many states. Clear lines of authority should run from the Governor at the apex to the bottom of the hierarchical pyramid.

Section 24 of Article IV of the Alaska constitution stipulates "each principal department shall be under the supervision of the Governor." There is no confusion regarding who is in overall charge of administration. Section 25 of the same article provides that all department heads are to be appointed by the Governor "subject to confirmation by a majority of the Legislature in joint session, and shall serve at the pleasure of the Governor." Section 26 provides that members of boards and commissions are to be appointed by the Governor

97

"subject to confirmation by a majority of the members of the Legislature in joint session and may be removed as provided by law...Each board or commission may appoint a principal executive officer when authorized by law, but the appointment shall be subject to the approval of the Governor." This latter provision ensures that executive officers will cooperate with the Governor.

Section 6 of Article IV of the Hawaii constitution authorizes the Governor to appoint department heads "with the advice and consent of the Senate" who "hold office for a term to expire at the end of the term for which the Governor was elected." The Governor also is authorized to appoint with the advice and consent of the Senate the members of boards and commissions which are the heads of principal departments. "The term of office and removal of such members shall be prescribed by law. Such board, commission or other body may appoint a principal executive officer....who may be removed by a majority vote of the members appointed by the Governor." This section also authorizes the Governor to "nominate and, by and with the advice and consent of the Senate, appoint all officers for whose election or appointment provision is not otherwise made by this constitution or by law."

One may question why the Alaska constitution requires the approval of gubernatorial appointments by the entire Legislature rather than by the Senate as is customary in most states. This type of doubt can be carried further by inquiring whether any type of legislative approval of gubernatorial appointments should be required? Should the Governor's power of appointment be encumbered by the requirement of legislative or senatorial approval? A strong case can be made for granting the Governor an absolute (unqualified) power of appointment and removal. Alaska has gone halfway towards this goal by granting the Governor the absolute power of removal. If it is good administration to give the strong mayor and the city manager an absolute power of appointment and removal, should not the Governor be given a similar power? Is the tradition established by the federal constitution requiring senatorial approval of appointments to be followed in the states without question? In Alaska there appears to be little reason for requiring legislative approval of gubernatorial appointments as a safeguard against a too powrful executive because the Governor is limited to two full consecutive terms.

The provision of the Hawaii constitution that the term of department heads expires with the expiration of the Governor's term is a good one since it facilitates gubernatorial control of the executive branch of the state government. The Governor's program in a number of states is hampered, if not frustrated, by department heads who were appointed by a previous Governor and refuse to cooperate with the present Governor.

An important principle of state administrative organization is the provision of staff agencies to assist the Governor. The complexity of modern state government makes it impossible for any Governor to properly administer the state without expert staff assistance. Section 5 of Article III of the Hawaii constitution contains an important provision requiring the Governor to appoint an administrative director to serve at his pleasure. This provision is similar to the chief administrative officer plan used in some cities and counties.

Reorganization of a state government should be continuous because new programs are created in response to new needs and old programs are eliminated or reduced in scope as the need for them dimishes. The question may be raised whether administrative reorganization is a prerogative of the Governor or of the Legislature?

The granting of broad reorganization power to the Governor by the Alaska constitution should prevent outmoded administrative organization: section 23 of Article III provides that "the governor may make changes in the organization of the executive branch or in the assignment of functions among its units which he considers necessary for efficient administration. Where these changes require the force of law, they shall be set forth in executive orders. The Legislature shall have sixty days of a regular session, or a full session if of shorter duration, to disapprove the executive orders. Unless disapproved by resolution concurred in by a majority of the members in joint session, these orders become effective at a date thereafter to be designated by the governor." This power is very similar to the reorganization power possessed by the President. The Governor's reorganization power is especially strong when one considers that the reorganization plans of the Governor must be rejected by a majority of the entire Legislature rather than by a majority of those present assuming a quorum.

Section 25 of Article III of the Alaska constitution provides that "the head of each department shall be a single executive unless otherwise provided by law" and section 6 of Article IV of the Hawaii constitution provides "each principal department..., unless otherwise provided in this constitution or by law, shall be headed by a single executive."

Boards and commissions usually do not function well for administrative work. The single-head department generally is preferred by administrative experts to the plural-headed department because the single-headed department is less expensive, permits the fixing of responsibility, and reduces delays in decision making. If a department performs a quasi-legislative and quasi-judicial functions such as the issuance of regulations and the hearing of tax appeals respectively, a board may function effectively.

The organizational principles of span of control and functional organization are found in section 22 of Article III of the Alaskan constitution limiting the number of major departments to twenty and provides that all offices and agencies are to be organized according to major purpose. However, the Legislature may create regulatory, quasi-judicial, and temporary agencies which are not required to be located within the principal departments. Section 6 of Article IV of the Hawaii constitution limits the number of principal departments to twenty and requires organization "according to major purposes as far as practicable." Experience in other states leads one to question whether a constitutional provision limiting the number of departments is effective. All agencies may be grouped within twenty departments, but many agencies may be operated independently of the department within which they are located. Coordination of administration and the introduction of performance budgeting should be facilitated by provisions in both constitutions requiring functional organization.

FISCAL PRINCIPLES

These two constitutions also contain an unusually large number of good fiscal principles which should help to ensure sound financial practices and a high credit rating for Alaska and Hawaii.

Budgeting is a topic of paramount importance which
is at the heart of every financial system. Fiscal experts generally agree that the chief executive of governmental unit should be repsonsible for the preparation of
the budget. Since budget preparation by the executive
facilitates advance planning and coordination in the
executive branch of the government. Budgeting and executive management are closely related since the budget
is one of the executive's principal control devices.

Section 12 of Article IX of the Alaska constitution
requires the Governor to submit to the Legislature a comprehensive budget setting forth "all proposed expenditures
and anticipated income of all departments, offices, and
agenices of the State. The Governor, at the same time,
shall submit a general appropriateion bill to authorize
the proposed expenditures, and a bill or bills covering
recommendations in the budget for new or additional
revenues."

Section 4 of the Hawaii constitution contains the
requirement that the "Governor shall submit to the legislature a budget setting forth a complete plan of proposed
general fund expenditures and anticipated receipt of
the State for the ensuing fiscal period...The Governor
shall also, upon the opening of the session, submit bills
to provide for such proposed expenditures and for any
other recommended additional revenues or borrowings by
which the proposed expenditures are to be met." It is
imperative that all expenditures of all departments and
agencies of the state government be included in the budget if it is to be a meaningful tool of management control
and responsibility.

One of the most widely accepted principles of budgeting is budgetary comprehensiveness; i.e., a budget document should set forth all proposed expenditures, anticipated revenues, and information on the debt position and
debt structure of the governmental unit. Unfortunately,
many budgets are expenditure documents only and fail to
consider revenues and debts. Legislators and the general
public should view proposed expenditures in relation to
anticipated revenues and the existing governmental debt.
The former might change their votes if presented with a
comprehensive budget document and might curtail deficit
spending if they knew that the incurring of additional
debt would cause the state to lose its top credit rating
with a consequent rise in the interest rate on new borrowing.

The provisions of the constitutions of Alaska and Hawaii relative to a consolidated budget are especially good. All proposed expenditures of the state come under review in one document at the same time and a decision can be made by weighing one proposed expenditure against other proposed expenditures, the available revenue, and the debt position and structure of the state government.

The Governor of Hawaii is required by section 4 of Article VI of the state constitution to compile the budget "in two parts, one setting forth all proposed operating expenditures for the ensuing fiscal period and the other, all capital improvement expenditures proposed to be undertakine during such period." The constitution of Alaska lacks a capital budget provision. The Hawaii constitution does not define what is meant by a capital improvement expenditure; this lack of a constitutional definition permits greated flexibility in the determination of what constitutes a capital item as conditions change. Capital items generally are defined in terms of the average life expectancy of an item and a minimum cost figure. To attempt to define capital items in these terms in the constitution would be a mistake.

A good capital budgeting program will permit the construction of capital facilities at the lowest possible cost and ensure that there is adequate advance planning and funds to provide new facilities when needed. Capital budgeting has the additional advantage of improving the credit rating of a state since capital budgeting assures the money market that the finances of the state are well managed. A capital budget needs to be revised annually and the priority schedule changed to meet new conditions.

Both constitutions fail to provide for a performance or program budget which stresses programs and how well they are being performed, yet this omission is not serious since both constitutions require functional organization of the executive branch of government which facilitates the introduction of performance budgeting. The Governor can readily install a performance budgeting system

Section II of Article III of the Hawaii constitution provides for a budget session of the legislature in even-numbered years. "At the budget session the legislature shall be limited to the consideration and enactment of the general appropriation bill for the succeeding fiscal year and bills to authorize proposed capital expenditures,

102

revenue bills necessary therefore, urgency measures deemed necessary in the public interest, bills calling elections, proposed constitutional amendments and bills to provide for the expenses of such session and the special session to be convened thereafter in accordance with the provision of Section 17 of this article."

An important provision to be found in each constitution is the one prohibiting legislative riders; i.e., acts which would be vetoed by the Governor if they were submitted to him independently of the appropriation bill. A Governor who lacks the item veto would hesitate to veto an appropriation bill even if undersirable riders are attached to it for fear of bringing the state government to a near stand-still if funds are not available to operate the government. Since the Governors of both states are armed with the item veto, the need for the prohibition of riders is not as great as it would otherwise be.

Section 7 of Article IX of the constitution of Alaska follows good budgetary practice by forbidding the dedication to any purpose of the proceeds of any state tax or license "except when required by the federal government for state participation in federal 1programs." The earmarking of the proceeds of the motor vehicle gasoline tax for highway construction and maintenance is an all too common example of the dedication to a special purpose of the proceeds of a state tax. Many state budgets omit assigned revenues and expenditures and, consequently, violate the rule of budgetary comprehensiveness. Revenue from dedicated taxes does not go into the general fund, but into separate accounts with the result there are several rather than a single state account. The Legislature, therefore, is not afforded the opportunity to examine annually all state revenus and to determine the priority of needs for the existing revenue.

The governors of Alaska and Hawaii are armed with the item veto. Section 15 of Article II of the Alaska constitution provides that the Governor "may, by veto, strike or reduce items in appropriation bills." The item veto may be overriden by a three-fourths vote of the Legislature; this povision arms the Governor with an extra-powerful weapon since it would be difficult for the Governor's opponents to muster a three-fourths vote in the Legislature. Section 17 of Article III of the Hawaii constitution provides that the Governor "may veto any specific item or items in any bill which

appropriates money for specific purposes by striking out
or reducing the same." The item veto may be overriden by
a two-thirds vote of all members of each house of the
legislature. The item veto provisions of these two constitutions are particularly interesting since they allow
the Governor to reduce as well as to strike out items.
If the Governor believes that an item represents a worthwhile purpose but the amount appropriated is too large,
he can reduce rather than eliminate the item.

To exercise tighter control over expenditures and
to eliminate requests for supplementary appropriations,
the Governor of many states uses an allotment system
based on a time period and sometimes on a category basis
(materials, personnel, and capital expenditures). Flexibility is introduced into the allotment system by permitting funds to be transferred from one category to
another and departments to exceed their quarterly allotments with the approval of the chief executive.

Section 7 of Article VI of the Hawaii constitution
stipulates that "provisions for the control of the rate
of expenditure of appropriated state moneys, and for the
reduction of such expenditures under prescribed conditions, shall be made by law." The constitutional pro-
vison authorizing the Legislature to control the rate
of expenditures can be questioned on the ground that
since the Governor is reponsible for administration, he
should be empowered to use his own discretion in controlling the rate of expenditures. A law relating to
allotments unless it is a general one or one delegating
authority to the Governor will introduce inflexibility
into the expenditure control system. Financial experts
agree that the chief executive should be responsible for
both the preparation and execution of the budget. The
latter function is a task of importance equal to that
of the preparation of the budget and the Legislature
should not encroach upon the execution by the Governor.

The Alaska and Hawaii constitutions reject rigid
debt and tax limits. Alaska with five specified exceptions and its political subdivisions can borrow funds
only for capital improvements and only if the proposed
borrowing is approved by the electorate. Section 8 of
Article IX stipulates that "the State, may, as provided
by law and without ratification, contract debt for the
purpose of repelling invasion, suppressing insurrection,
defending the state in war, meeting natural disasters,

or redeeming indebtedness outstanding at the time this constitution becomes effective." Alaska and its political subdivisions may borrow in anticipation of taxes, but such debt must be paid before the end of the next fiscal year. Section II of the same article provides that "the restrictions on contracting debt do not apply to debt incurred through the issuance of revenue bonds by a public enterprise or corporation. The restrictions do not apply to indebtedness to be paid from special assessments on the benefited property, nor do they apply to refunding indebtedness of the state or its political subdivisions."

The provision of the Alaska constitution allowing the state and its political subdivisions to borrow only for capital improvements is a good one since sound financial practice calls for meeting current expenditures out of current income. However, a capital budget should also be required. Borrowing should be sorted to only to finance capital or unusual expenditures such as the construction of public facilities or the provision of funds to meet disasters. Many governmental units have experienced financial difficulties because they have borrowed funds to meet current expenditures. The life of bond issued to finance capital improvement should not exceed the life expectancy of the capital improvements.

Section 3 or Article IV of the Hawaii constitution provides that "all bonds and other instruments of indebtedness issued by and on behalf of the State of a political subdivision thereof must be authorized by the Legislature, and bonds and other instruments of indebtedness of a political subdivision must also be authorized by its governing body." Tight state control of the indebtedness of its political subdivisions may improve the financial condition of the subdivisions, but opens the door to possible abuses since such control violates the concept of "home rule" which holds that local governments should be granted broad discretionary powers.

Section 3 also establishes a state debt limit of sixty million dollars, but allows the limit to be exceeded by a two-thirds vote of the entire membership of the Legislature "provided such excess debt, at the time of authoriziation, would not cause the total of state indebtedness toe exceed a sum equal to fifteen percent of the total of assessed values for tax rate purposes of real property in the State, as determined by the last tax assessment rolls pursuant to law." The state may borrow in anticipation of taxes, "to suppress insurrection, to repel invasion, to defend the State in war or to meet emergencies caused by disaster or act of God" without regard to the debt limit.

The debt of a political subdivision is limited to ten percent of the assessed value of real property and a political subdivision may not contract debt during a fiscal year exceeding two percent of the assessed value of real property. A political subdivision, however, may borrow in anticipation of taxes for one year. A statutory provision for the periodic payment of taxes such as quarterly payments would obviate to a great extent the need for borrowing in anticipation of taxes.

Section 3 of Article VI also provides that "the provisions of this section shall not be applicable to indebtedness incurred under revenue bond statutes by a public enterprise of the state or political subdivision, or by a public corporation, when the only security for such indebtedness is the revenues of such enterprise or public corporation, or to indebtedness incurred under special improvement statutes when the only security for such indebtedness is the properties benefited or the assessments thereon."

The provisions of the two constitutions exempting public corporations from the debt limit can be dangerous since the exemption is likely to encourage the formation of such corporations to evade the debt limit as it is approached with the result that the administrative structure of the government will be complicated and control and responsibility for administration diffused. The constitutions of the two states establish a sound governmental structure, but this structure can be complicated by public corporations.

The desirability of debt limitations is questionable since they provide a false sense of security for bondholders and taxpapers; relatively extensive debt limitations did not prevent governmental units from defaulting on their obligations during the 1930s. Furthermore, debt limitations introduce an element of rigidity which hampers financial planning. On the other hand, debt limits do slow down or reduce reckless deficit spending.

Section 3 of Article VI of the Hawaii constitution requries all bonds with a maturity date in excess of one year to "be in serial form maturing in substantially equal annual installments, the first installment to mature not later than five years from the date of issue of such series, and the last installment not later than thirty-five years from the date of such issue." Serial bonds lower the cost of borrowing since interest is paid only on the unpaid principal. In addition, serial bonds in contrast to sinking fund bonds are not subject to tampering. Some governments failed to build up adequate sinking funds by failing to make periodic payments and parts of sinking funds were lost by poor investments. Consequently, the sinking fund was inadequate when the outstanding bonds matured.

The constitutuion of Hawaii does not specify whether the straight serial bond plan providing for a specified percentage of the bonds to become due each year or the serial annuity plan providing for an equal payment each year to retire the bond issue is to be followed. Under the straight serial plan a specified percentage of the bonds and the interest on the unpaid balance are paid each year. Under the serial annuity plan payments on the principal are the smallest during the first year of the issue because interest payments are largest this year. During each succeding year principal payments are increased as interest payments on the unpaid balance decrease so that the annual payments are equal in amount.

The requirement of the Alaska constitution that all proposed borrowing must be approved by the electorate is questionable. The average voter lacks the time or the opportunity to become thoroughly acquainted with a proposed bond issue so that he can intelligently pass upon the merits of the proposed issue. Besides, experience has demonstrated that the voters have little interest in bond elections: The turnout in bond elections is small with the result the decision whether to borrow is made by a minority of the voters who may represent primarily a pressure group with a selfish interest in the proposed issue.

Section 14 of Article IX of the Alaska constitution requires the Legislature to appoint a certified public accountant as an auditor to "conduct post-audits as prescribed by law and" to report to the legislature and the Governor. Section 8 of Article of the Hawaii

constitution authorizes the Legislature to appoint an
auditor for a term of eight years. "It shall be the
duty of the auditor to conduct post-audits of all trans-
actions and of all accounts kept by or for all departments, offices and agencies of the state and its political subdivisions, to certify to the accuracy of all
financial statements issued by the respective accounting
officers."

Alaska is to be commended for its constitutional
requirement that the auditor be a certified public accountant; this provision should ensure competent post-
auditing. The post-auditor who is either popularly
elected or appointed by the Governor, may be politically
popular rather than an expert auditor.

Section 3 of Article IX of the Alaska constitution
stipulates that assessment standards are to be prescribed
by law, thereby helping to ensure relatively uniform
assessment policies throughout the state. The absence
of a provision requiring assessment at fair market
value or some similar standard is commendable since
these standards seldom are observed in the other states.

The lack of a provision in either constitution
relative to the accounting system may be considered a
serous sin of omission by some financial experts since
the efficacy of financial control depends to a large
extent upon the type of accounting system used. Either
the accrual system or the cash system of accounting is
used by governmental units. The accrual system provides
for the recording of financial obligations as they are
incurred and accurately records the current financial
position of the government. Under the cash system of
accounting expenditures are recorded when payments are
made by the government. Many governmental units have
experienced financial difficulties as the result of using
the cash system of accounting because they did not know
the current status of their obligations.

CONCLUSIONS

Older state constitutions typically have been amended
on numerous occasions as detailed restrictions have been
placed upon the powers of the Legislature. While the
reason for the adoption of many such restrictions in the
nineteenth century is clear, there is relatively little
evidence that such restrictions are necessary today.

Furthermore, ingenious legislators frequently find ways to skirt the restrictions.

A more serious problem with older state constitutions is the lack of provisions incorporating sound organizational and fiscal principles designed to help ensure that the state government is operated in the most efficient and economical manner possible. Models to remedy this problem are readily available in the form of the organizational and fiscal provisions incorporated in the constitutions of Alaska and Hawaii.

PART III

POLITICS OF STATE GOVERNMENT

The readings included in this part were selected
to provide the student with exposure to a number of the
important issues involving state government ranging from
election campaigns to legislative-gubernatorial relations
and from small claims courts to labor relations in the
public sector. Based upon academic research or practical
experience, each reading provides insight into the actual
workings of aspects of the state governmental system.

The first reading deals with the partisan primary,
a preliminary election designed to reduce the number of
candidates seeking public office. A primary may be open
to any registered voter, or it may be closed to voters
who are not registered in the party, or it may be a
modified open primary in which a party member may vote
only in his party's primary but an independent voter
may vote in the party primary of his choice.

In reading number 10, Richard C. Kelley and Sara
Jane Weir of the University of Washington examine the
unique Washington State primary system which allows
voters to split their votes for candidates among candidates of the various political parties. The intent of
the blanket primary, a product of the progressive movement in the early days of the twentieth century, was to
weaken political parties.

Kelley and Weir conclude the blanket primary has
weakened party machines and is similar to a non-partisan
primary. Their analysis reveals that party raiding is
not increased significantly by the blanket primary, but
candidates spend extra money in the primary in an attempt
to appeal to a larger number of voters.

In reading number 11, Owen E. Newcomer of Rio Hondo
College briefly reviews the literature on nonpartisan
local elecitions and analyzes data from eight partisan
ballot type cities and eight nonpartisan ballot cities.
He found that ballot type had little influence on voter
turnout or people's faith in local government. Political
activity and feelings of efficacy, however, were higher
in cities with nonpartisan ballots.

111

The United States Supreme Court's one-person, one-vote dictum has ended gross overrepresentation of rural areas in one or both houses of the legislature in a number of states, but has made deliberate gerrymandering easier to accomplish. David I. Wells of the International Ladies' Garment Workers' Union in reading number 12 strongly recommends that redistricting be based upon four criteria--contiguity, compactness, reasonable equality of population, and avoidance of excessive division of governmental jurisdictions. Wells contends that employment of these criteria will promote fair districting that does not deliberately favor one party or group.

In reading number 13, James R. Oxendale, Jr. of West Virginia Institute of Technology analyzes the relationship between compensation and voluntary turnover in the lower house of forty-one state legislatures to determine whether higher levels of compensation reduce turnover rates. Oxendale concludes that there is little relationship between legislative salaries and turnover, and suggests that many factors influence turnover.

THE STATE LEGISLATURE

Reading number 14 contains an evaluation of the non-partisan, unicameral Nebraska legislature. Professor John C. Comer of the University of Nebraska points out that unicameralism is not an issue today, but that non-partisan elections remain controversial. He evaluates the performance of the Nebraska legislature in terms of the criteria of responsibility, responsiveness, accountability, and leadership structure, and concludes that the legislature rates relatively high with respect to the first two criteria but does not measure up as well with respect to the latter criteria. He cautions, however, that a change to partisan elections might improve accountability at the expense of responsiveness.

Should the state legislature be involved in decision-making relative to the use of federal funds received by the state? Since most federal funds received by states until the advent of block grants in 1966 and general revenue sharing in 1972 were in the form of relatively narrow categorical grants-in-aid, the legislature could exercise little discretion in the spending of such funds since the purposes for which the funds could be spent were targeted by federal conditions. In <u>reading number 15</u>, Carol Weissert of the National Governors' Association describes the three forms of legislative oversight of federal funds and judicial decisions with respect to whether the legislature possesses the authority to appropriate federal funds. She concludes the article by articulating the reasons why it is difficult to determine whether legislative oversight of federal funds makes a difference in terms of ensuring executive adherence to legislative priorities, reducing additional state financial commitments to support federal programs without legislative approval, and ensuring improved delivery of federally funded services.

Deirdre A. Zimmerman, a management analyst in the New York State Division of the Budget, in <u>reading number 16</u> continues the theme of legislative action to ensure that its intent is followed by the executive branch by examining the Congressional Budget and Impoundment Control Act of 1974 and a controversy over executive impoundment of appropriated funds in the State of New York. Ms. Zimmerman points out that it was several New York State local governments, and not the legislature, which challenged the authority of the governor and his budget director to impound appropriated funds. The Court of Appeals, the State's highest   court, ruled in favor of the plantiffs. The article concludes with the suggestion that a modified federal impoundment system might work well in the Empire State.

THE GOVERNORSHIP

Dr. Herbert E. Alexander, Director of the Citizens Research Foundation and Professor of Political Science at the University of Southern California, in <u>reading number 17</u> analyzes the changes in the financing of campaigns for the office of governor duing the 1970s. A major development has been the growth of partial public funding of election campaigns in a number of states. Nevertheless, private funding remains the dominant form of financing election campaigns. Professor Alexander provides a case study involving election expenditures in California and notes that the cost of gubernatorial campaigns remained approximately the same when expressed in constant dollars over the period 1958-78.

S. Nagel and Bradley C. Canon on the party affiliation
of members of state supreme courts. Whereas Nagel reported the supreme court in twenty-five states lacked
minority party representation, Lee discovered the number
of such states had fallen to eleven with eight located
in the south.

A long standing complaint against the judicial system has been the plaintiff's cost of securing justice in
civil disputes. In cases involving relatively small sums,
one approach to lowering the cost of justice has been the
small-claims court. Reading number 23, prepared by Consumers Union of the United States, Incorporated, explains
the procedures of such courts, how to handle your case,
and how to collect a judgment. The reading also contains
advice for defendants and recommendations for improving
such courts, and concludes with a description of a night
in Manhattan's Small-Claims Court.

Relative to criminal cases, the historic grand jury
has declined in importance and its use for felony indictments is mandatory in only twenty states. Associate Executive Director Donald M. McIntyre of the American Bar
Foundation in reading number 24 examines the functions
of the grand jury and its criticisms. McIntyre finds
the grand jury to be an important form of citizen participation and a desirable instituion provided certain
limitations on its role are recognized.

PUBLIC EMPLOYEE BARGAINING

One of the most striking developments of recent
years has been the sharp growth of membership in public
employee unions. In reading number 25, Seymour Z. Mann
of the American Federation of State, County, and Municipal Employees notes that the public unions have achieved
their greatest success in organizing employees in service
occupations, an area where unions in the private sector
have had limited success in organizing employees. Dr.
Mann attributes the growth in public employee union
membership to worker dissatisfaction with conditions
of employment.

The great political strength of public employee
unions in a number of state and local governments has
raised concern about the impact of unions upon the
governance system. Dr. Mann is convinced that such

114

Reading number 18 contains an interview by Joseph
F. Sullivan of The New York Times with Governor Thomas
H. Kean who reflects upon his first year in office. The
Governor describes surprises--such as the amount of paper
work--pressing budgetary and prison problems, and his
relations with the legislature controlled by the oppo-
sition party. The interview concludes with Governor
Kean stressing his role as a promoter of the state.

Reading number 19 examines the process by which a
Governor selects individuals for appointment to public
office. Editor Robert de la Vega of the Twin Cities
Citizens League provides a summary of the remarks of
officials who served under two former Minnesota governors and an individual working on the governor-elect's
transition team relative to the factors considered by
a governor in making appointments in his administration.
Comments in particular were addressed to the desirability of an open selection process.

Whereas the previous reading focuses upon the procedures employed by governors in making appointments,
reading number 20 describes and analyses innovations
in state cabinet systems. In addition to the traditional cabinet found in forty states, subcabinets concerned with broad issues have been established in
twenty-five states, and many states have created temporary task forces to deal with specific problems.
Lydia Bodman and Daniel B. Garry of the National Governors' Association explore the variety of cabinet innovations and their relative strengths and weaknesses.

Professor Zimmerman, in reading number 21, presents
a case study of the resurrection of the item veto in
New York State. The governor of this state has possessed the authority to disallow items in appropriation
bills since 1874, yet the authority seldom had been
exercised subsequent to 1943 until 1981. The reasons
for the decline in the exercise of the item veto are
explained as is the sudden disallowance of 158 items
by Governor Hugh L. Carey in the 1981 executive budget
appropriation bills.

THE JUDICIAL SYSTEM

Professor Francis G. Lee of Saint Joseph's College
in reading number 22 updates earlier studies by Stuart

unions play an important role in defining issues and providing representation for their members in the halls of government.

10. UNWRAPPING THE BLANKET PRIMARY*

Richard C. Kelley and Sara Jane Weir

Since the 1935 enactment of Washington's blanket primary, the political parties have complained that the system intrudes upon their right to choose the candidates who will represent them. Independent voters and non-party political actors have just as consistently supported the blanket primary system for the greater choice of candidates and greater leverage over nominations which it gives them. Recent Supreme Court decisions have been more sympathetic to parties' claims of a right of association.

The blanket primary is a unique form of direct primary election that does not require the voter to declare a preference for one party or another. It allows the citizen the freedom to choose, for each office, among the candidates of all parties, thus making ticket splitting in the primary election a possibility.

The blanket primary controversy relates to the ability of political parties to perform their traditional role of mediating issues between voters and the government. This note will examine the effect of the blanket primary on that role, along with other aspects of the blanket primary more directly related to its operation, including the effects of ticket splitting, the "raiding" of one party's primary by voters of the other party, and the effects on campaign expenditures.

For purposes of comparison, we will contrast the effects of the blanket primary with the traditional closed primary. In the closed system of nomination, the voter must choose from among the candidates of the party in which he is registered. It should be noted that most states' systems fall somewhere in between the two, having elements of both the closed and blanket primary systems: most of these are called "open" primaries.

---

*Reprinted with permission from Washington Public Policy Notes (Institute for Public Policy and Management, University of Washington), Vol. IX, No. 3, Summer 1981, pp. 1-6.

BACKGROUND

The blanket primary was enacted in Washington State, through an initiative sponsored by the Grange. Replacing a closed primary electoral system, it represented the ultimate expression of the "non-partisan" Progressive reform movement. By allowing voters unrestricted choice among all the candidates for a particular office, the blanket primary statute gave the voter the same sort of options available in the general election.

Washington State law allows a candidate to seek the nomination of only one political party, and for only one partisan office. Within each party, the nomination goes to the candidate receiving the most votes, provided that he or she polls 10 percent of all votes cast for that party's highest vote getter.

The blanket primary has met with much criticism from partisan politicians and party advocates on the ground that it denies political parties the right of free association. They claim that in allowing independents and members of the other political parties to participate in the candidate selection process, the blanket primary denies the party the right to decide who will participate in the selection of the party's nominee for the general election. They further believe that as the descendant of the party slating meetings and nominating conventions, the primary should be restricted to members of the party. In 1945, there was an unsuccessful attempt to convert the Washington blanket primary to a more traditional open primary, which would have allowed voters to cast their votes in either party but not to split their ballots between parties in a given primary.

Independents and other non-partisan supporters of the blanket primary, on the other hand, believe that the input of all eligible voters in the candidate selection process must take priority over the right of political parties to make exclusive decisions as to who the nominees will be in the general election. These supporters of the blanket primary argue that it allows the expression of many points of view rather than only those of the members of the party. They argue further, that some crossover voting is possible in any open primary election: the blanket primary

differs only in that it allows the voter to cross over
to vote for a candidate of particular interest, without being forced to cast meaningless votes for the
candidates for all other offices, as is the case in
the typical open primary election.

Survey results have shown that fewer partisan
voters than independent voters split their tickets in
the primary. The evidence indicates that crossover
votes from the other party have not determined the
outcome of most elections; in most cases, they have
simply resulted in an even greater margin of victory
for an already popular candidate. There has been
little evidence in the state of Washington of "raiding" by regulars of the opposition party in order to
secure the nomination of a candidate felt to be a
weaker opponent.

The surveys show that ideologically, independent
voters tend to fall between the two parties, being
more liberal than Republicans and more conservative
than Democrats. The blanket primary allows the
independent voter to vote for candidates selectively
and without regard for party label, thus altering the
ideological mix of voters in each party's primary for
each office. Moreover, the blanket primary does not,
on the whole, appear to be unpopular with citizens of
the state; rather it appears to be the accepted method
of candidate selection. Yet there remains the
question of the right of a party to choose who will
represent it in the general election, and it is to
this question that we now turn. The article will
first look at recent relevant court decisions, then
examine actual voting patterns and thereafter campaign expenditures. Finally the implications of these
findings will be considered.

FREEDOM OF ASSOCIATION

The blanket primary poses a difficult constitutional issue. The First and Fourteenth Amendments to
the U.S. Constitution guarantee citizens the right to
freedom of association in political activity. The
blanket primary allows independents and members of
other parties to participate in a party's central
decision as to who will represent it in the election,
thus diluting the influence of party members over

their nominations. The legal issue is whether this involvement of non-party members in party nomination decisions infringes on the party's right of association.

The freedom of association doctrine, which crystallized in Supreme Court opinions in the 1950s, almost immediately acquired an unsavory air because of its use in attempting to defend discriminatory activity as, for example, in Southern "white-only" primaries. After the Second World War, in a series of cases involving such primaries, the Court found that the right of blacks to equal protection of the law outweighed party rights of association. When freedom of association is not achieved at the expense of such a fundamental right, it has been taken very seriously by the Court, particularly in the political arena.

In Marchioro v. Chaney (1979), a case concerning the Washington State Democratic Party, the Supreme Court was asked to rule upon a state statute regulating the power of political parties to organize and operate; the decision, while stopping short of overturning the statute altogether, greatly increased the parties' control over their own business. Again, in The Democratic Party v. LaFollette (1981), a Wisconsin case in which the Democratic Party challenged Wisconsin's open presidential primary, the Court ruled that the state's allowing non-Democrats to vote in the primary burdened Democrats' right of association. The Court further ruled that the burdening was not justified by the state's interest in the electoral process.

The Wisconsin case comes very close to the issue in Washington's blanket primary; the only significant difference is that Washington's law deals not with presidential but with state, local, and congressional nominations. The language of the Court at several points is relevant: (the freedom to associate) " . . .necessarily presupposes the freedom to identify the people who comprise the association, and to limit the association to those people only." The Court also states in the Wisconsin decision:

> On several occasions this Court has recognized that the inclusion of persons unaffiliated with a political party may seriously distort its collective decisions--thus impairing the

party's essential functions--and that political
parties may accordingly protect themselves
'from intrusion by those with adverse political
principles' . . .it is for the National Party--
and not the Wisconsin legislature or any
Court--to determine the appropriate standards
for participation in the Party's candidate
selection process . . .

Thus the Court seems to be moving in the direction
of expanding the control of political parties over
their own governance, membership, and nominating processes. In the face of such movement, it would appear
that Washington's blanket system could have a difficult
time surviving a legal challenge on constitutional
grounds.

SPLIT-TICKET VOTING

We have analyzed the votes for statewide races
held in Presidential election years from 1936 through
1980. Analysis of eight partisan statewide races for
their deviation from the year's average party vote
reveals a steadily increasing rate of ticket splitting
by Washington voters over the 44-year period. The
percentage of deviation for all the races in each year
was averaged and compared with each of the other
general elections since the enactment of the blanket
primary in Washington. In 1976 the average deviation
for all races was 10.5 percent; this compared with an
average deviation of 5 percent in 1936, the first year
of the blanket primary.

Ticket splitting has increased most noticeably
during the last twenty-five years in the highly visible
races other than Governor, particularly for the positions of Secretary of State and Attorney General. The
increasing deviation from party voting is the combined
effect of an increase in the ranks of persons who
regard themselves as "independents" and a growing
incidence of crossover voting. The first trend can be
documented by survey results; the second, by voting
patterns.

National surveys indicate a significant increase
in the number of voters who do not affiliate with a
political party. These "independent," voters presumably make their choices according to some factor other

than party label. The greatest growth in the independent block has come among younger voters, new to their participatory role in the political system. Instead of choosing the party of their parents, as young people have traditionally done, or choosing one party philosophy over the other, many of these voters look to such factors as the candidates' stands on the issues or the candidates' images to guide their choice for each position.

Independent voters can be divided into two rather distinct groups. The first group, the smaller, is issue oriented and educated. Although these individuals may well be ideologically compatible with one party or the other, they do not affiliate with a particular party. The second group of non-partisan voters are those individuals who are on the fringe of the political system. They vote according to image or select candidates in a near-random fashion. They are independent because they have neither the knowledge nor the interest to vote according to issues or identify rationally with a political party.

The second trend contributing to deviation from party voting totals is partisan crossover voting. An example of this phenomenon is the 1936 Gubernatorial race in which a massive Republican crossover defeated a liberal for the Democratic nomination. That race is discussed further in the next section.

RAIDING AND THE INDEPENDENT VOTER

A persistent objection to the blanket primary is the opportunity it creates for raiding. A party's primary is said to have been raided when independents and voters of the other party cross over and nominate a weak candidate, for whom they do not intend to vote in the general election. This could be done with the intent of either picking an opponent who will be weak in the general election, or defeating an effective or outspoken incumbent in the primary with a candidate whose views are less threatening to those crossing over.

The model often presented for the raiding scenario is the 1936 Democratic primary for Governor. Incumbent Clarence Martin, a conservative Democrat, seemed destined for defeat by John Stevenson, a populist liberal. On primary day, Stevenson did carry most of the Democratic areas by wide margins, yet Martin was renominated thanks to the crossover votes of tens of thousands of Republicans, particularly in conservative areas of Eastern Washington.

This historical example is worth examining in some detail. Indisputably, Republicans decided who would be the Democratic nominee: this in itself seems an abuse. Yet the next chapter also needs telling: Martin went on to victory in the general election. Many or most of the Republicans who crossed over in the primary also voted for Martin in the general election. Thus, by our definition above, they were not raiding the Democratic primary to beat the Democrats; rather, their votes indicated an intention to have two candidates in the general election representing their own philosophy, and none representing the opposing point of view. Thus, in 1936, the action of Republicans in the primary for Governor effectively disenfranchised mainstream Democrats in the general election.

The recent career of Dixy Lee Ray offers another illustration. In the 1976 primary for Governor, Ray was widely perceived as a middle-of-the-road Democrat running against two liberals; she won the primary. By 1980, her image had shifted, in many voters' minds, from the middle-of-the-road to the right wing, because of her stands in favor of business and nuclear power, and against poverty programs and environmental protection. This time she lost the primary. Both primaries showed large apparent crossover votes, but Ray's vote in each apparently showed the extent of her real support, not raiding.

Senator James McDermott, who defeated Ray in the 1980 primary, was himself defeated in the general election. But the size of the Republican sweep in that election, and the poor showings of Democratic candidates for many offices, suggest the McDermott primary victory was a straightforward expression of preference but that he succumbed to the Republican tide in the general election.

The effect of the blanket primary's operation is thus to reduce the range of choices available to the voters in the general election. Polls in Washington State, and elsewhere, have consistently shown that there are significant ideological differences between the parties, with Democrats clustering around the more liberal positions, Republicans around the more conservative, and independents somewhere in between. The blanket primary makes it easier for those candidates to win nomination who do not represent the views of the party whose name they use. Typically, conservative Democrats like Clarence Martin, Henry Jackson, and John Cherberg, and liberal Republicans like Dan Evans have prospered under the system. By effectively creating one pool of primary votes, the blanket primary tends to reward middle-of-the-road candidates in the same manner as does the nonpartisan municipal election.

An element in the rationale of the creators of the blanket primary was the belief that party voters voted on party label alone, while independents and other groups (like the Grange) who were committed to issues and not to a party, were more discerning and informed. This perception was important both as a strategy for political power and as justification for the change in the primary system. As a strategy, the prospect was of a mobile block of votes responsive to the Grange or to any issue or set of issues, outflanking the stand-patting voters in both parties. As an ethical rationale, the more informed and public-spirited independents were presented as offering enlightened alternatives to the boss-controlled candidates endorsed by mindless partisan voters.

The use of punchcard voting systems in some counties has made it possible legally to obtain anonymous individual voting records to examine the crossover phenomenon with greater precision; opinion survey data have also provided insights. (It should be emphasized that there is no way for the researcher to connect a ballot with the individual who cast it; thus, the confidentiality of the ballot is entirely preserved.)

The strategic equation for the control of party primaries by independents seems to hold up. Even though the individual-level data show more voters crossing over than the aggregate totals reveal, one-quarter to one-third of the voters still appear to cast all their primary votes within one party or the other. Party supporters, it seems, are not in fact as willing to use the option to vote in more than one party's primary; consequently, independents are able to make their preferences felt out of proportion to their

numbers. As a strategy for increasing the clout of
independents and voters loyal to special-interest
groups rather than to a party, the blanket primary
would seem to be a success.

What of the second argument, namely, that independents choose better candidates because they are more
educated and informed than party voters? Whether a
candidate is better is, of course, a question of judgment, not fact, so it is impossible to address which
have voted for "better" candidates. However, we do
have considerable knowledge of the characteristics of
the independent voter, both from national surveys and
Washington State individual-level data. National
surveys show that, while some independents are every
bit as educated, informed and involved as are party
voters, independents on the average are less informed
about politics, less involved in their community, and
less likely to vote than are party members. Analysis
of individual-level ballot data in Washington State
also shows that independents are much more likely to
"fall off," that is, to fail to vote on some offices
and ballot measures.

On balance, then, the blanket primary does seem to
increase the political power of independents. The
characteristics of independent voters, however, open up
to serious question any claim that their political
ascendancy is in the public interest.

CAMPAIGN SPENDING

An issue rarely addressed in discussions of the
blanket primary is its effect on campaign spending.

In a closed primary system, the rational candidate
will direct his pre-primary campaign spending and
effort to those voters who are eligible to vote in that
primary, namely, the members of the candidate's party.
Thus, typically, the candidate will be spending money
to reach one-third to one-half of the persons customarily voting in primaries. Only after the primary will
his advertising focus broaden to encompass all the
voters and his campaign expenditures rise accordingly.

Under Washington's blanket primary system, however, the candidate's task before the primary is not
nearly so manageable. Instead of advertising his

125

candidacy only to his own party at that stage, he must
protect himself from an adverse crossover vote by working on independents and members of the other party as
well. The problem is further complicated by the lack
of party registration. Even knowing how many voters in
the district consistently vote in the Democratic or the
Republican primary does not help much in reducing campaign costs: after all, the candidate has no way of
knowing which voters are Democrats and which Republicans.

The inevitable consequence of this increased uncertainty is to force candidates to spend more money
before the primary. A typical campaign in Washington
State will make between 40 and 50 percent of its total
expenditures before the primary. Moreover, that this
high primary spending is associated with the blanket
primary receives further confirmation from the fact
that even candidates unopposed in their primary races
typically spend large sums in the primary; presumably
this high level of expenditure is intended to guarantee
their share of the crossover vote, although it would
also serve to increase visibility for the general election. In a time when massive campaign expenditures are
seen by many thoughtful observers as a danger to democracy, this unintended effect of the blanket primary
should concern us.

PARTIES, SPECIAL INTERESTS AND CANDIDATES

Related to the effect of the blanket primary on
campaign expenditures is its effect on the political
parties. Whereas the blanket primary was intended by
its originators to weaken the control of the political
parties over the nominating process, it may at the same
time have undermined the party role in mediating political demands between citizen and government. The
likelihood of unmediated participatory democracy in an
Athenian sense arising in a state of four million
people is nil; the danger in the parties' loss of their
mediating powers is that the role will be assumed by
special interests which are heavily involved in financing both primary and general election campaigns. The
difference between mediation by parties and mediation
by interest groups is that the party machinery is
controlled by precinct committee people, elected by the
voters; in contrast, special interests, by their very
nature, are subject to no democratic controls.

126

As Karen Marchioro, State Democratic Chairperson said on May 8, 1981:

> We make our platform decisions democratically, in conventions of elected delegates. The problem is, with this blanket primary scheme, we can't affect how our elected officials act in office. If they do the opposite of what the platform promises, we have no power to say they no longer represent our party, and make it stick. If we take someone on in the primary, what usually happens is the special interests bury us in money, and the crossover vote kills us.

Thus, one effect of the blanket primary is to reduce the parties' ability to set their own agendas and resist special interest pressures. This, in turn, reduces the value of citizen participation in caucuses, conventions, and other party activities.

Related to the decline of political parties as mediating structures, and the increased number of voters who choose on the basis of candidate alone, is the growth of the individual candidate as a means of consensus building and interest aggregation. Candidate image and, to some extent, stand on issues has increasingly led to the popular support of individuals like John Anderson and others who go beyond party to gain citizen support. Individual candidates look to Political Action Committees (PACs) and the support of special interests to finance their campaigns.

It is unclear at this time whether the shift from party to individual candidates signals a change in the system of mediating structures or whether it is indicative of a coming realignment of political party membership. Such realignments occur traditionally every 30 to 40 years in the United States as new political coalitions are put together, often under the old party labels. In most cases these new coalitions bring a new majority party, as was the case with the last major political realignment which brought various interests together in Franklin Roosevelt's "New Deal" coalition, establishing the Democratic Party as the majority party. By increasing the ability of candidates to assemble coalitions which differ from those of their parties, the blanket primary hastens the

weakening of parties' ideological positions, thus
reducing their ability to perform a mediating function
in the political system.

THE VOTERS' CHOICE

Looking at the issue in terms of the relative
influence of different groups of voters, there is a
sharp contrast between the blanket primary and the
closed primary. Three separate choices are to be made
in both systems. First, which candidates will represent the parties in the general elections? Second,
which party's candidate will win the office? And
third, what will be the governing philosophy of the
state?

On the choice of candidates in the primary, the
closed primary gives the party voter strong, undiluted
influence over his own party's choice, and none over
the choices of the other party and the independents; it
gives the independent full influence over the choice of
independent candidates, and none over the parties'
choices. The blanket primary, on the other hand, gives
party voters a much diluted influence over their own
party's choices, while allowing independents and members of the other party the same.

On the decision as to which party's candidates
will win the office, the two systems are alike, except
in the case where crossover voting might defeat a
strong candidate in the blanket primary.

Finally, on the decision as to which philosophy
will govern the state, there is likely to be a difference in the range of choice offered. The closed
primary makes separate decisions within the (albeit
blurred and overlapping) separate philosophical realms
of the two parties, and the independent group then
presents alternatives to the voter in the general
election. The blanket primary, by contrast, typically
allows the parties to nominate candidates whose philosophies are acceptable to independents and marginal
party adherents, thus giving the general-election
voters a narrower range of philosophical positions to
choose among.

These differences in the structuring of the
voters' choices assume greater significance when we

remember the difference in turnout between the primary
and general elections. Our primaries typically draw a
turnout of between 20 and 45 percent; general elections
usually draw between 70 and 80 percent participation.

Thus the closed primary system can be viewed as
allowing more significant choices of philosophies to
the state, and giving party members who vote in
primaries more influence over their own party's
direction; the blanket primary gives predominant choice
of governing philosophy to primary voters, and
increases the influence of independents who vote in
primaries.

CONCLUSION

Without a doubt, Washington State's blanket primary does fulfill the intent of its initiators to
weaken the political parties and give more power to the
independent voter. This effect may not be entirely in
the public interest now.

Data derived from both individual and aggregate
voting records do not support the long-standing
criticism that the blanket primary lends itself to
raiding to nominate weak candidates. There is, however, some indication that the system increases
primary campaign expenditures by making it necessary
for the candidate to appeal to a larger and more
diverse group of voters in the primary.

The heavy incidence of ticket splitting makes the
blanket primary tend to resemble a non-partisan primary. Because it tends to produce middle-of-the-road
primary winners, parties are less able to offer clear
alternatives. Moreover, the recent rise of political
action committees and single-issue groups points to the
need for further study of the extent to which weakened
parties facilitate the domination of the political
system by special interests.

The blanket primary and other Progressive reforms
were aimed at breaking the strength of party machines
in the early part of the century. Recent Supreme Court
decisions, however, indicate a greater willingness to
recognize parties' right of association under the
United States Constitution. The greater sympathy shown
now by the Court and others toward the parties' need to

129

control their own decisions and nominations may reflect
a sense that there is a need to strengthen the parties
to restore some balance to their role in the electoral
process.

11. NONPARTISAN ELECTIONS: A LOOK AT THEIR EFFECT*

Owen E. Newcomer

The field of partisan/nonpartisan election comparisons is relatively unexplored. Of the researchers who have done such studies, Eugene Lee, Charles Adrian and Robert Alford stand out as the foremost authorities.

From the research of these political scientists has grown a strongly held view that nonpartisan ballots discourage voter turnout because they eliminate valuable clues as to the candidate's position on issues. Adrian has argued this viewpoint by comparing turnout in nonpartisan elections to that in "responsible party" systems. The problem with this is that the United States does not have a "responsible party" system and such a comparison fails to explain what difference, if any, the presence of party labels on electoral ballots makes.

Alford and Lee have also endorsed this belief. In "Voting Turnout in American Cities" (American Political Science Review, September 1968), they grouped cities with populations of 25,000 or more into one category and compared turnout for partisan elections. The methodological problems with this are demonstrated by their own findings in another section of the article. Among the factors that affected voter turnout were: (1) the type of governmental structure (with systems in which the mayor was elected by the people having a higher turnout than systems in which the office was rotated among council representatives), and (2)

---

* Reprinted with permission from the National Civic Review, October 1977, pp. 453-55 and 468.

the degree of explicit ethnic cleavages (the more distinct the cleavages the higher the turnout of voters). These factors as well as size may be more important than the type of ballot used.

Perhaps more useful is a comparison of the effects of nonpartisan and partisan ballots on citizens' (1) voting turnout, (2) faith in government, (3) political activities other than voting and (4) feelings of efficacy.

To make these comparisons, an analysis was made of a national survey conducted by the National Opinion Research Center for Sidney Verba and Norman Nie (Political Participation in America: Codebook, Ann Arbor, Inter-University Consortium for Political and Social Research, 1976). From /⁻these_/ data eight partisan ballot cities and eight nonpartisan ballot cities were selected. The cities selected were the largest in the sample. Only the absence of party labels was used as a determinant, not the level of party activity in a community.

The partisan ballot cities are New York, Philadelphia, Pittsburgh, Jacksonville, St. Louis, Waterbury (Connecticut), South Bend, and Baltimore. The nonpartisan ballot cities are Los Angeles/Long Beach, Detroit, Chicago, Newark, Atlanta, Amarillo, Salt Lake City, and Seattle. The total number of respondents was 722.

In addition to presence or absence of party labels, income and education were used in the analysis as significant predictors of political behavior and attitudes. The method was to cross tabulate voter turnout, faith in government, political activity and efficacy with ballot type. Contingency subtables were also run using the above variables and holding income and education constant.

It was assumed that voter turnout in local elections in partisan ballot cities would be lower than in nonpartisan ballot cities. It was found

that the form of ballot had little predictive
value. The percentage of citizens who always
vote in local elections was 45.5 in partisan
ballot cities and 50.4 in nonpartisan ballot
cities. Although the results at first seem to
support the hypothesis, the range of scores and
their statistical significance need to be considered. Partisan ballot cities ranged from a
low in Jacksonville, where only 23.7 percent of
the citizens always voted in local elections, to
a high in Pittsburgh, with 65.9 percent. Likewise, in nonpartisan ballot cities the range
was from 32.4 percent in Amarillo to 60.0 percent
in Seattle. The Chi Square significance was
0.488, which means one has approximately a 50
percent chance of being right when using a city's
type of ballot as a guide to predict voter turnout.

When contingency tables were set up much the
same results were found. However, there was one
statistically significant subtable and it strongly supported the hypothesis: Among voters with
less than a high school education only 35.2 percent always voted in local elections in partisan
ballot cities compared to 55.1 percent in nonpartisan ballot cities.

The traditional hypothesis that partisan
elections promote higher voter turnout than nonpartisan elections was not supported by the findings. It may be that ballot form is inconsequen-
tial as an influence on voter turnout.

The second test was whether the belief that
local government understood the needs of the
respondent differed in partisan and nonpartisan
ballot cities, the assumption being that the percentage would be larger in the latter. Once again
the results showed that ballot type was little
help in predicting the degree of faith in government. In the partisan ballot cities surveyed,
49.3 percent believed that local governments
understood their needs well, and in the nonpartisan ballot cities, 49.4 percent believed so.
When contingency subtables were run, much the same

133

results were found.

To test the level of political activity three variables were used. First, the frequency with which respondents discussed local problems with their friends and acquaintances was cross-tabulated with ballot type. In the eight partisan ballot cities, 35.7 percent discussed local problems once a week or more. This compared to 43.8 percent in nonpartisan cities which is significantly higher, as was believed.

The second and third variables were whether the respondent has helped to form a group to solve local problems, and whether the respondent had personally contacted a local government official or an influential person about some need or problem. None of the tables for these two variables was statistically significant.

In the partisan ballot cities, 19.2 percent of the respondents believed that people like themselves could have significant influence over local governmental decisions, compared to 26.3 percent in the eight nonpartisan ballot cities, which is significantly higher, supporting our assumption. When these variables were controlled for family income, one subtable was statistically very significant. In partisan ballot cities, 25.2 percent of the upper income respondents believed that people like themselves could have significant influence over local governmental decisions, compared to 45.7 percent in the nonpartisan ballot cities. One statistically significant table was also found when education was used as the control variable. Among those respondents with some high school education, 9.3 percent in partisan ballot cities and 20.8 percent in nonpartisan ballot cities felt that they could be influential.

The second measure of efficacy yielded one statistically significant correlation. Among respondents who had some college education, in partisan ballot cities 24.2 percent believed that local government council members would give

their complaints a great deal of attention.
This compared to 40.4 percent among nonpartisan
ballot city respondents.

In short, the absence of party labels
from election ballots does correlate with enhanced citizen feelings of efficacy.

The findings in this paper contradict those
of Alford and Lee. The reason may be due to
their use of actual voting turnout figures whereas this study relied on survey data. A more
likely reason, however, is that this study surveyed only cities with large populations that
formed the center of an urban area. Alford and
Lee used data from cities with populations of
25,000 or more and did not distinguish between
major urban centers and suburban areas. The
influence that location and population exert
includes daily newspaper and television coverage
of local politics in major urban centers as
opposed to more limited coverage in many suburbs.

A second influence relates to population
size: the larger the city, the more likely it is
to have a mayor-council form of government with
the mayor elected directly by the voters. As
Alford and Lee mentioned in their study, the
direct election of the mayor is correlated with
higher voter turnout than the system, as in most
council-manager cities, of having the mayor chosen
by and from among the council members. Alford
and Lee did not control for this factor; this
study used only cities in which the mayor was
directly elected. In short, it may be that daily
television and newspaper coverage and direct
election of the mayor instead of the influence of
a partisan ballot have a positive influence on
voter turnout.

As an influence on voter turnout, it seems
from this study that the type of ballot used for
local elections has little effect. But, citizens
in nonpartisan ballot cities are somewhat more
likely to vote than those in partisan cities.

Ballot type failed to have any significant influence on the number of people that expressed faith in local government.

A significant difference was found to exist between partisan and nonpartisan ballot cities for the two variables of political activity and efficacy. More respondents in nonpartisan ballot cities discussed politics at least weekly than in partisan ballot cities. And, clearly, respondents in nonpartisan ballot cities felt more efficacious vis-a-vis government than those in partisan ballot cities.

The findings on political activity and efficacy contradict projections by Adrian in the 1950s that partisan elections were more desirable because they stimulated higher levels of political activity and led to "responsible parties" which in turn enhanced the political efficacy of the voters. Adrian's measure of partisan elections did not distinguish between ballot type and the level of organized political party activity present in a campaign. He treated party activity as a function of ballot type. Nonpartisan ballots would suppress party activity and partisan ballots would encourage it. However, ballot type and level of party activity really are separable factors. Nothing in this study disputes the value of organized political party activity. What is disputed is the value of placing party labels on the election ballot.

12. HOW TO INHIBIT GERRYMANDERING: THE PURPOSE OF DISTRICTING CRITERIA*

David I. Wells

The basic purpose underlying the establishment of criteria--or, as they are sometimes called, guidelines or ground rules--in the process of delineating legislative districting boundaries should be to inhibit gerrymandering to the greatest extent possible. In this context, gerrymandering may be defined as the drawing of district boundary lines in such a way as to secure special, unmerited advantage for one party, faction or group over another, or for some prospective candidates over others.

Districting criteria can serve this purpose because, if they are properly administered and strictly enforced, they diminish, to a greater or lesser degree, the discretionary powers of those who draw the lines, and it is precisely that power--the ability to determine the placement of district lines--which is the very essence of gerrymandering. Clear, precisely worded criteria can transform the districting process into a rational and logical procedure in which, unlike gerrymandering, the cards are not stacked in advance for or against any party, faction, group or potential candidate.

Whatever the specific guidelines are, if they are to serve their purpose, it is vital that they be applied in a very specific order of priority. Merely to set forth districting rules without specifying an order of priority would serve little purpose, for it would enable those who apply the provisions to pick and choose from among the

* Reprinted with permission from National Civic Review, April 1982, pp. 183-87.

137

various rules. Rules which are more favorable
to one party or group could be given preference
over others which are less favorable. A specified, logical order is essential if the guidelines are to reduce or eliminate gerrymandering.

There need be only four basic criteria:
two of them rather simple, the other two somewhat
more complex and requiring some amount of elaboration. The simple ones are <u>contiguity</u> and
<u>compactness</u>; the ones requiring some spelling out
are <u>reasonable equality of population</u> and the
<u>avoidance of excessive division of governmental
jurisdictions</u>. And I would apply these in the
following order: first, contiguity (as I will
proceed to define it); second, reasonable equality of population; third, minimal division of
governmental units; and fourth, compactness.

<u>Contiguity</u>. Contiguity is inherent in the
concept of the word "district." Yet over the
years, in many states, parcels of land not
effectively connected to one another have been
politically attached to form districts. It
should, therefore, be required that, to the extent
possible, districts must consist of contiguous
territory: that is, pieces of land physically
adjacent to one another.

In most parts of most states, this requirement can be met quite easily. In some situations,
however, depending on the geography of particular
areas, the construction of districts made up of
pieces of land separated by bodies of water is
sometimes unavoidable. In such cases, a requirement should be included that the separate parts of
such districts must wherever possible, be connected
to one another by some man-made means: by bridges
or tunnels where they exist or by regularly scheduled ferry service where they do not. In other words,
the general rule of thumb should be that districts
be established in such a way that it is not necessary to go outside of the district in order to
travel from any one part to any other part. The
only exception should be for islands which are not

138

connected to the mainland by bridges, tunnels or
ferries. In such cases, the island should be included in the same district as the nearest area
within the same governmental jurisdiction.

Reasonable Equality of Population. The one-
man, one-vote rulings of the 1960s require the
establishment of districts with reasonably equal
populations. Prior to those rulings, there were
very wide variations among district populations
and a resulting wide disparity in the political
power of the residents of different areas. To
require that districts be exactly equal in population, however, without allowing for small
deviations to accommodate other logical districting rules, actually facilitates gerrymandering,
for it permits those who draw the lines to
justify virtually any districting arrangement
they choose to establish as long as the resulting
districts have equal populations.

After some experimentation in the late '60s
with very tight equal-population requirements,
the U.S. Supreme Court expressly reaffirmed an
earlier holding in which it had rules that, except
at the congressional level, "deviations from the
equal population principle are constitutionally
permissible...so long as the divergences are
based on legitimate considerations incident to
the effectuation of a rational state policy
(emphasis added)."

In light of this, it seems to me that a state
is well within its rights in establishing a set,
specified and reasonable maximum population deviation for state legislative districts (and presumably for local legislative districts, as well).
For example, a 5 percent maximum deviation from
the state average would seem to be well within
what is both reasonable and legally acceptable.
But such a deviation should be permissible only
if it results from the application of the other
criteria not if it is arbitrarily applied in some
areas and not in others. (For example, a deviation of up to 5 percent should be acceptable if
it can be shown to be the result of a desire to

avoid splitting up a county or town or city.)
In effect, therefore, with regard to the population equality requirement at levels other
than the congressional, reasonable allowable
deviation would mean that:

A)   Where there is no justification for
a deviation, all districts must be equal.
B)   Where there is justification--based
on the other criteria--such deviations may go
up to the specified maximum deviation.
C)   No deviation may exceed the specified
maximum regardless of whether or not it can be
justified on the basis of the other criteria.

At the congressional level, by contrast,
any statutory or self-imposed maximum deviation must be far smaller than at the state or
local level, and must be applied with great
caution, for the Supreme Court has not made it
clear whether or not even a very small deviation would be acceptable. Certainly, at this
level, no deviation of more than, say, 1 percent at most from the state average should
even be contemplated. (The Court probably
would be unlikely to strike down a congressional
districting plan solely on the basis of population variations of less than such a small
figure, but this is speculation.)

Avoidance of Excessive Division of Governmental Jurisdictions. Any set of guidelines
should include one or more provisions designed
to minimize the division of counties, towns and
cities among legislative districts not primarily
because there is anything sacrosanct about the
existing boundaries of such units or because the
boundaries are geographically "logical," but for
two other reasons: first, because the political
machinery of most states is based on counties,
towns, cities and other units of government, and
therefore the smooth functioning of the political
system would be facilitated by avoiding the needless fragmentation of such units; second, and, in
my mind, more importantly, because keeping such

fragmentation to a minimum serves as an important deterrent to gerrymandering. This is because the borders of counties, cities and towns are reasonably permanent; they are not frequently or easily changed and they are unlikely to be altered in order to win political advantage in the process of delineating district lines. If the boundaries of governmental units were ignored, it would be quite difficult to prevent those who draw the lines from splicing or severing territory at will, but the existing borders of such political subdivisions provide convenient, logical starting and stopping places for legislative districts, and these units make convenient building blocks for the establishment of districts. This is particularly true in rural and suburban areas. (In cities, where there are generally no similar internal lines to inhibit potential gerrymandering, only a compactness requirement can serve this function.)

In addition to a provision designed to prevent excessive fragmentation of governmental units--beyond the degree required by the population-equality requirement--it is also desirable to include as a kind of corollary to this criterion, a provision or set of provisions spelling out precisely how governmental units are to be divided up on those occasions when their division is unavoidable. Such a guideline might read, for example, as follows: "If, in order to comply with the population-equality rule, it shall be necessary to divide the territory of any county or counties among more than one district, there shall be as few such divisions as possible; geographic location permitting, more populous counties shall be divided in preference to less populous ones; and such counties shall be divided among as few districts as possible."

This kind of guideline is necessary for the same reason that a specific priority-order is required among the various guidelines themselves: to prevent those who draw the lines from being able to pick and choose among a large number of

141

alternatives. To allow a choice among many alternatives would defeat the basic purpose of guidelines: the limitation of discretion.

Compactness. Although it has the lowest priority among the guidelines suggested here, an enforceable compactness provision is, nevertheless, essential as an anti-gerrymandering tool. This is because probably the most common form of gerrymandering is that which seeks to create political advantage by stringing together isolated pockets of territory--often widely separated and scattered geographically--where the party or faction in control of the process has significant voting strength. It is this type of gerrymandering which produces the classic bizarre shapes which most of us associate with gerrymandering--and which, indeed, gave that practice its name almost two centuries ago. This form of gerrymandering tends to be particularly prevalent in large cities where, as previously indicated, there are frequently no internal jurisdictional lines to inhibit gerrymandering and to prevent district lines from wandering in and out of streets at will, creating odd-looking indentations, protuberances and squiggly lines. And in large cities, as is well known, the inclusion or exclusion of just a few blocks can often mean the difference between victory and defeat for a candidate on election day.

Because of the irregular shapes of the many counties, towns and cities, as well as the uneven distribution of population, no districting plan can be expected to produce districts all of which have neat, compact shapes. Some departures from absolute geometric compactness are unavoidable. It is possible, however, to keep such departures to a minimum. To do so, it is necessary to deal not with single districts, but with the totality of a districting arrangement. No compactness rule will work properly if it merely sets up an arbitrary rule relating to how each district must

142

be delineated, for a standard which would be
logical for one district or for one area of a
state might be totally inapplicable to another.
Instead, the most effective way to achieve the
maximum degree of compactness possible, given the
irregular shapes of counties, towns and cities,
the absence of any semblance of uniformity among
them, and the need to equalize district populations, is to require that after all the other
districting guidelines have been followed, the
total length of the boundaries of all the districts created must be as short as possible.
Such a rule would prevent the arbitrary pushing
of a particular boundary line a few blocks in one
direction or another to achieve political advantage, but will permit minor departures from compactness to achieve a greater degree of population
equality among districts.

It will be noted that the criteria suggested here take no account of demographics. Only
geographic factors are used. This is because I
believe that the use of demographic factors is
justifiable only by those who, unlike myself,
believe that there is something inherently desirable about politically or ethnically or ideologically homogeneous districts as contrasted to heterogeneous ones. While under almost any districting arrangement most districts will turn out to be
homogeneous (and therefore "safe" in the political
sense), there is nothing inherently wrong or
undesirable about districts which include in them
a mix of ethnic groups or of Republicans and Democrats or of liberals and conservatives. But that,
of course, is the subject of another discussion
altogether.

There are some who contend that those of us
who advocate very precisely framed guidelines are
attempting to take the politics out of the districting process. I do not accept that character-
ization. Rather, those of us who wish to thwart
gerrymandering in reality have greater faith in
the political system than those who would like to

143

see everything "fixed" and prearranged in advance. We, in contrast, would merely like to see the so-called "great game of politics" played with ground rules which do not, in and of themselves, favor any of the participants in the game.

13. COMPENSATION AND TURNOVER
IN STATE LEGISLATIVE LOWER CHAMBERS*

James R. Oxendale, Jr.

High rates of turnover among legislators
have long troubled writers and reformers concerned with state government in the United States
/1, pp. 8-10; 3, p. 40; 5, pp. 21-31; 6; 7, pp.
13-24; 8; 11/. Average turnover per session in
state lower houses between 1963 and 1971 was
30.4 percent. From Charles Hyneman's writings in
the late 1930s to William Keefe and Morris Ogul's
speculations of the 1970s, a recurring suggestion
for reducing voluntary retirement from the state
legislature has been to increase legislative compensation. Keefe and Ogul put the thesis persua-
sively:

> The best short-run answer for breaking
> the turnover cycle lies, we believe,
> in what is by now a part of the "con-
> ventional wisdom" of political scien-
> tists. The tenet holds that a seat
> in the legislature may become a full-
> time career for members if they are
> given a salary that is more in line
> with those available in business and
> professions. /6, p. 130/.

Hyneman made essentially the same point in
1938. He wrote, "I am of the opinion that the
chief reason why legislators find one or more
terms enough is a financial one; their experience proves...that it is money out of the

---

* Reprinted from State and Local Government Review,
  Vol. XI, No. 2, May 1979, pp. 60-63 by permission of the Institute of Government, University
  of Georgia.

pocket to serve in the legislature" /5, p. 30/.
Hyneman, Keefe and Ogul, and numberous others
assume that a relationship exists between low
compensation and voluntary turnover. Voluntary
turnover means a decision to terminate one's
career in the legislature; involuntary turnover
means that caused by election loss or death.[1]
It is assumed that if compensation were to rise,
then turnover would decrease.

This paper looks at voluntary turnover and
compensation in forty-one state lower chambers
during the 1975-76 session and attempts to
discover whether a relationship exists between
these two variables. If indeed states with
higher levels of compensation have lower turnover rates than do states with lower compensation,
then one could conclude that compensation rates
appear to influence turnover. Data on this
issue is presented in Table 1 and summarized in
Table 2.

Tables 1 and 2 do not support an assertion
that higher compensation will result in lowered
turnover. Using Spearman's coefficient of rank
correlation, the correlation between turnover and
compensation is +0.24. Statistically there is
no correlation between compensation and turnover
for the states for which data are available in
1976.

California and New Hampshire have the same
rates of turnover, yet California pays over
$65,000 more biennially than does New Hampshire.
Indeed, five of the top ten states in compensation
are among the states listed in the lower half
of Table 1.

High levels of compensation may have helped
lower turnover in states like Hawaii which is
eighth in salary and lowest in turnover or
Michigan which is fifth in salary and fourth in
turnover. At the same time, low compensation may
have caused high levels of turnover in states
like Montana or Utah which have extremely low

146

TABLE 1

VOLUNTARY TURNOVER AND COMPENSATION FOR
LOWER HOUSE LEGISLATORS 1975-1976 SESSION

State	Percentage Voluntary Turnover	Biennial Compensation*
Hawaii	4	$30,000
Nevada	8	7,680
Arizona	9	19,170
Michigan	9.1	38,000
Ohio	10	35,000
Virginia**	10	10,950
Iowa	11	21,580
Kentucky**	11	12,350
Mississippi	11	25,400
New Mexico	11	3,600
Georgia	11	16,640
North Carolina	12	18,300
Delaware	12	19,500
Oklahoma	12	22,620
Wisconsin	12	38,181
North Dakota	12	5,700
Oregon	13	20,010
Minnesota	14	23,855
South Dakota	14	6,575
Nebraska	14	10,000
Colorado	15	15,200
Indiana	16	23,565
Missouri	16	16,800
New York	16	47,000
Rhode Island	16	600
Connecticut	17	13,000
Pennsylvania	17	31,200
Alabama	18	8,100
Kansas	18	14,400
Texas	18	18,600
Illinois	19	45,976
Maine	19	7,825

147

TABLE 1

VOLUNTARY TURNOVER AND COMPENSATION FOR
LOWER HOUSE LEGISLATORS 1975-1976 SESSION

State	Percentage Voluntary Turnover	Biennial Compensation*
California	20	$66,300
Florida	20	24,000
New Hampshire	20	200
Tennessee	20	19,400
Idaho	21	7,800
Utah	23	3,200
West Virginia	23	12,900
Louisiana	24	16,500
Montana	27	6,954

*Compensation is computed as it generally is in the Book of the States, that is, compensation scales are taken from those offered during the 1975-76 session. In those states which pay per diem, the current rates are multiplied by the number of days in the 1973-74 session, since the total days of the session are not yet available. Compensation figures are derived from salary, per diem, and unvouchered compensation paid during or between sessions. Compensation for special sessions or vouchered expenses is not included.

**Turnover rates are taken from 1975.

levels of compensation and very high rates of turnover.

The above data could be criticized on the grounds that turnover patterns from a single year might vary from traditional norms. In order to adequately understand the impact of a compensation policy on lowering turnover, it is necessary to compare a given state's current turnover at a higher compensation with past turnover at a lower compensation.

TABLE 2

ANNUAL COMPENSATION AND VOLUNTARY TURNOVER
FOR LOWER HOUSE LEGISLATORS, 1975-1976

		Less than $15,000	$15,000 or more
Percentage Voluntary Turnover	Less than 15%	16	4
	15% or more	17	4

Unfortunately, few studies are available which distinguish between voluntary and involuntary turnover on a longitudinal basis. The present research is based on voluntary turnover data from the twenty-two states for which the 1976 data were available. The year 1968 was chosen because it provides an essentially tranquil election after the uncertainty created by Reynolds v. Sims, 377 U.S. 533, 12 L. ed. 2d. 506, 84 S.Ct. 1362. Forty states[2] reapportioned their legislatures between 1964 and 1966. Obviously such major shifts in legislative districts could have artificially created high numbers of voluntary turnover because of fear of running in new districts. Therefore, the 1968 election was chosen because it, like the 1976 election, had legislators seeking reelection from the same district in which they were elected. If the traditional hypothesis concerning the impact of compensation on turnover were to be supported, then those states which had the greatest increases in compensation between 1968 and 1976 should have had the greatest decreases in turnover.

Table 3 compares compensation and turnover between 1968 and 1976. The results are mixed. · Using percentage changes in compensation and turnover, the rank correlation, r = +0.42, indicates a slightly positive relationship between the two variables. However, using absolute changes in compensation and turnover percent, the rank correlation, r = 0.43, indicates a slightly negative relationship. All twenty-two states had changes in compensation. Increases varied from about $2,000 to about $30,000 per biennium; however, not all states had corresponding turnover reductions. Indeed, some of the results appear to be rather confusing if it is assumed that the major cause for turnover is insufficient compensation. For example, between 1968 and 1976 New Mexico increased legislative compensation from $1,800 to $3,600 biennially. This was accompanied by a turnover drop of 43 percent. It seems unlikely that an $1,800 compensation increase over an eight-year period is sufficient inducement to result in a 43 percent decline in turnover. In these situations, non-monetary factors must be examined in attempting to understand the causes for legislative retirement.

While compensation may not have affected turnover in all states, in Hawaii, Tennessee, and particularly Iowa, salary increases may be the major causes for reduced turnover because major reductions in turnover occurred concomitantly with major increases in compensation. However, there are no clear patterns for the entire group. California and Illinois had major increments in compensation with simultaneous

TABLE 3

RELATIONSHIP BETWEEN VOLUNTARY TURNOVER AND
COMPENSATION FOR LEGISLATORS WHO RETIRED IN
1968 and 1976

State	Percentage Voluntary Turnover	1967-68 Biennial Compensation	Percentage Voluntary Turnover	1975-76 Biennial Compensation
California	3.0	$37,922	20.0	$66.300
Connecticut	16.4	4,750	17.0	13,000
Florida	23.5	6,100	20.0	24,000
Georgia	18.0	10,525	11.1	17,640
Hawaii	15.7	8,220 or 9,185	4.0	30,000
Idaho	18.5	4,341	21.4	7,800
Illinois	12.0	18,000	19.2	45,976
Iowa	38.0	3,560	11.0	21,580
Kansas	19.2	7,150	18.4	14,400
Maine	39.0	2,224	19.1	7,825
Minnesota	9.0	11,042 or 11,763	14.0	23.855
Missouri	6.0	11,500	16.0	16,800
Nevada	12.5	3,900	8.0	7,680
New Mexico	54.3	1,800	11.0	3,600
New York	9.3	36,000	16.0	47,000
Oklahoma	11.0	10,220	12.0	22,620

TABLE 3

RELATIONSHIP BETWEEN VOLUNTARY TURNOVER AND COMPENSATION FOR LEGISLATORS WHO RETIRED IN 1968 and 1976

State	Percentage Voluntary Turnover	1967-68 Biennial Compensation	Percentage Voluntary Turnover	1975-76 Biennial Compensation
Oregon	23.3	$11,760	13.3	$20,010
Pennsylvania	12.4	14,800	17.2	31,200
Tennessee	34.0	6,300	20.8	19,400
Virginia	16.0	3,300	10.0	10,950
West Virginia	29.0	3,000	23.0	12,900
Wisconsin	14.0	18,600 or 20,490	12.0	38,181

increases in voluntary turnover. Indeed, the five
states which had the greatest increases in compensation also had increased turnover. The data from
the above states offer no support to a general hypothesis that if compensation rises, even at quite
impressive rates, turnover will decline. Turnover
may very well lessen, but there is no clear evidence to indicate that it will, or that, if it does,
it does so because of a compensation policy.

A SPECULATIVE OVERVIEW OF TURNOVER
AND SALARY QUESTIONS

When considering the problem of legislative
turnover at the state level, several factors should
to taken into account. Some of these have been
detailed elsewhere $/3$, 4, 6, $8/$ and will not be
considered in this brief summary.

Two important variables which influence turnover have not been given the attention they deserve:

1. For most new members of the state
legislature, especially the lower chamber, this is their entry into politics
$/13/$. Invariably there is the problem
of adjustment. For some the psychol-
ogical adaptation is difficult, and
this frequently results in voluntary
retirement. According to Barber, some
legislators are too rigid to adapt;
others cannot accept a beginner's place
in the system; and still others cannot adjust to the hectic schedule or
the instrumental rather than consum-
matory social relations in the legislature $/1$, pp. 151-154; $8/$. For
these legislators salary is of little
or no importance and rarely inhibits
their decision to retire.

2. Many potential politicians find
the lower house of the state legislatures a good place to experiment with politics.

Most state legislatures have limited
sessions, and this allows a potential
politician to minimize the interruption
from a full-time occupation when experi-
menting with politics. Additionally,
a legislative district of the lower house
is frequently small enough for a newcomer to conduct a campaign without necessarily incurring the major expenses
needed for other state, or even state
senatorial, positions. Thus, the lower
house of the state legislature is frequently well-suited for young and am-
bitious legislators to experiment with
politics without seriously jeopardizing
their full-time careers or incurring
major debts when running for office.
If they find legislative politics reward-
ing, they will probably remain in the
lower chamber only temporarily, since
they seek to move up politically. As
they see it, the lower chamber is their
initiation into politics and not their
final destination /1, pp. 67-115; 8,
pp. 147-200/. Thus, these legislators
also rank compensation of slight importance when they consider leaving the
lower chamber.

CONCLUSION

This research offers no general support to the
belief that a close relationship exists between
compensation and turnover. Generally speaking,
states with higher levels of compensation do not
have lower voluntary turnover than do states with
lower levels of compensation; nor do the results
indicate that states which increase compensation
will ipso facto reduce their rates of turnover.
In the states for which comparison data were available, compensation levels increased in all of them,
but turnover both increased and decreased. In some
states, compensation increases may possibly have
helped to lower turnover, but in others, despite
major increases in compensation, voluntary

154

retirement increased. Turnover is a complex phenomenon induced by numerous factors of which compensation is only one, and to many considering retirement, it may be of relatively slight importance.

NOTES

1
When the word turnover is used by itself in this
paper, it applies only to voluntary turnover.

2
Reapportionment figures are taken from Book of
the States, 1968-69, p. 67.

REFERENCES

1. Barber, James David, The Lawmakers, (New Haven:
   Yale University Press, 1965).

2. Book of the States, 1975-76, (Chicago: Council of State Governments, 1976).

3. Modernizing State Government, (New York:
   Committee for Economic Development, 1975).

4. Herzberg, Donald, and Rosenthal, Allan, eds.
   Strengthening the States: Essays on Legislative Reform, (Garden City, N.Y.: Double-
   day & Company, 1972).

5. Hyneman, Charles, "Tenure and Turnover of
   Legislative Personnel," Annals of the American Academy of Political and Social Sciences,
   1938:21-31.

6. Keefe, William, and Ogul, Morris. The Amer-
   ican Legislative Process: Congress and the
   States, 3rd ed. (Englewood Cliffs, N.J.:
   Prentice Hall, 1973).

7. Lockard, Duane. "The Legislature as a Personal
   Career," in Strengthening the States, edited
   by Herzberg and Rosenthal.

8. Oxendale, James R., Jr. "An Exchange Model of
    Voluntary Legislative Withdrawal: A Case of
    the West Virginia House of Delegates." Ph.D.
    dissertation, West Virginia University, 1974.

9. Rae, David. "Membership Stability in Three State
    Legislatures: 1893-1969." American Political
    Science Review, March 1976 pp. 106-12.

10. Rae, David. "Voluntary Retirement and Electoral
    Defeat in Eight State Legislatures." The Jour-
    nal of Politics, May 1976 pp. 426-33.

11. Rosenthal, Alan. "Legislative Turnover in the
    States." State Government, Summer 1974
    pp. 148-52.

12. Van Sant, Jan. "How Much Are State Legislators
    Paid?" Research Memorandum 18 (September,
    1975) Englewood, Colorado: The Citizens Con-
    ference on State Legislatures, 1975.

13. Wahlke, John C.; Eulau, Heinz; Buchanan, William;
    and Ferguson, Roy C. The Legislative System
    (New York: Wiley, 1962).

14. The Nebraska Nonpartisan Legislature
An Evaluation*

John C. Comer

The Nebraska Legislature is, in a sense, an experiment in politics. It is the only unicameral (one house)
legislature and it is nonpartisan; that is, candidates
run for the legislature without party labels appearing
on the ballot, and partisan groupings do not elect legislative leaders or, in general, oversee the operation of
the legislature. It has been forty years since the change
to a nonpartisan unicameral legislature--time enough to
begin to assess the impact of these changes on the operation and performance of the legislature. Have the
reforms lived up to the expectations of proponents, or
have they undermined the legislative process as predicted
by opponents.

Unicameralism is far less controversial today than
it was when it was adopted in Nebraska. There appears
to be little reason to return to a bicameral arrangement.
Whether or not a state has a one- or two-house legislature seems to be more a function of tradition and accident than of superior performance. Nonpartisanship,
however, is another matter. It remains controversial,
and there are periodic attempts to return the Nebraska
Legislature to a partisan basis. These attempts very
often are politically motivated, but some stem from the
belief that nonpartisanship fundamentally alters the
political process in a way that undermines the capacity
of the legislature to serve the people of the state.
This article evaluates the Nebraska Legislature and as-
sesses the prospect that a return to partisan politics
would improve it.

EVALUATION CRITERIA

What criteria of evaluation are to be applied here?
One set is suggested by Leroy Rieselbach. He notes that
legislatures, in particular the Congress of the United
States, can be judged on the criteria of responsibility,

* Reprinted from State and Local Government Review, Vol.
XII, No. 3, September 1980, pp. 98-102 by permission
of the Institute of Government, University of Georgia.

157

responsiveness, and accountability [2]. Responsibility, according to Rieselbach, concerns problem solving-- whether or not the institution can deal effectively and efficiently with public problems. One measure of this, although perhaps not the best, is the degree to which citizens support the legislature. Are they satisfied with its performance, or are they dissatisfied? Responsiveness focuses on legislative operations. Does the institution take into account the preferences of those it serves? Is it an open institution, one that responds to the appeals of interested parties? Accountability concerns control. Are there sanctions for failing to perform, that is, can the voters turn out a legislator or party that fails to perform?

Thomas Flinn builds on this list [1]. He too observes that legislatures should be accountable. For him, this means facilitating "rational choice." Voters should have a reasonable opportunity to know what the consequences of their voting decisions are likely to be. The operational standard is whether or not there is structure to voting in the legislature. Are there discernable blocs which enable the voter to cast his vote in such a way as to increase the strength of one bloc if the candidate he votes for wins? Rational choice might also include the degree to which electoral competition exists between candidates contesting for office. Choice can only have meaning if there is reasonable prospect that all candidates can win.

Another criterion, among the several suggested by Flinn, that is relevant here is a leadership structure capable of insuring that the job of the legislature gets done. Do leaders possess the requisite skills to enable them to do their job? Is leadership defined in such a way as to enable leaders to direct the legislative operation in an administrative as well as a policy sense?

These criteria are sufficiently general to facilitate comparisons across states as well as between the Congress and state legislatures. They reflect to some extent the tenets of democratic theory (e.g., responsiveness and accountability). They also capture some of the main elements in the literature of organization theory which reflect a concern for performance and efficiency.

AN EVALUATION

At the time of its adoption in 1937, a number of arguments were heard in favor of the nonpartisan plan. Some argued that freeing elections from partisan influences would restore power to the people to choose their representatives. Little known and irresponsible party leaders would be unable to determine candidates for public office. Furthermore, "better" people would be attracted to government service--people motivated by the public interest rather than by partisan politics.

Opponents of the plan were also heard. Some felt the change unnecessary since parties were merely electoral conveniences anyway, paper tigers hardly worth the effort to eliminate. Some felt that nonpartisanship would increase the influence of private interests and lobbyists; others felt that it would destroy the leadership structure of the legislature. A major argument, however, was that the removal of party labels from the ballot would destroy what little accountability there is in the legislature. While the parties may not present distinct and clearly defined programs, they do provide the voter with important information. In the absence of more specific information, party performance can serve as a valuable cue for the voter.

These claims and counterclaims, some of which can be heard today, warrant investigation. The analysis that follows applies the Rieselbach and Flinn criteria in an assessment--from the perspective of the nonpartisan argument--of the Nebraska Legislature.

1. RESPONSIBILITY

Here the concern is the legislature's performance. Has it dealt effectively and efficiently with public problems? One measure is the degree to which citizens are satisfied with the institution. Are they supportive of the legislature in terms of its performance as well as its place in the institutional structure of state government?

With respect to job performance, citizens in Nebraska responded very much like citizens in other states. As indicated in Table 1, 47 percent of the statewide sample responded that the legislature is doing a good job. Of these, 3 percent felt that the

TABLE 1

Citizen Support of the Legislature

	Nebraska [a]	Comparative States Election Project [b]
Legislature is doing a good job	47	50
Better for governor to take law into own hands than wait for legislature	34	33
Would make no difference if powers of legislature were reduced	19	19
Even if one disagrees, one should obey laws once passed by the legislature	89	96
Number of respondents	(886)	(8276)

a   Data from a statewide telephone survey of adults in 1978 by the Bureau of Sociological Research at the University of Nebraska-Lincoln.

b   Data from statewide surveys conducted in 1968 as part of the Comparative States Election Project. The states included were Alabama, California, Florida, Illinois, Louisiana, Massachusetts, Minnesota, New York, North Carolina, Ohio, Pennsylvania, South Dakota, and Texas.

legislature is doing an excellent job. This compares reasonably well with the response from the thirteen states included in the Comparative States Election Project; 50 percent of these citizens responded that the job being done by their state legislature was "good," with 5 percent of these responding "excellent." The unique nature of the nonpartisan legislature appears to make little difference with respect to citizen evaluations of job performance. Nor are differences significant with respect to perceptions of the place of the legislature in state government. Nebraskans do, however, show a somewhat greater tendency to disagree that one should obey a state law even if one is opposed to it.

To the degree that these items reflect citizens' perceptions of the problem-solving capability of the legislature, little difference seems to exist between Nebraska's nonpartisan approach and the partisan approach of the thirteen states for which comparative data are available. On the criterion of responsibility there appears to be little that opponents of nonpartisanship can point to in support of returning to a partisan plan.

2. RESPONSIVENESS

Here the focus is the degree to which the legislature responds to the appeals of interested parties. One measure is the degree to which citizens feel they can influence the legislative process of the state. One third of those surveyed in Nebraska responded "no influence" to queries concerning their personal influence in pressuring the legislature to change an unfair law; another 40 percent responded "little influence." Thus, three out of four see little chance to influence the state legislature.[1]

Perhaps more telling in this respect are the responses of legislators themselves regarding the activity and involvement of interest groups in the legislative process. If one assumes that interest groups lobbying the legislature reflect the interests in the state, receptivity of interest groups on the part of legislators should be a fair approximation of responsiveness. Table 2 reports legislator's orientations toward interest groups in five states including Nebraska. The orientations reflect both knowledge of and feeling toward

161

interest group activities. Legislators were categorized "facilitators" if they knew about interest group activities and responded positively toward them, "resisters" if they knew of but were negative toward them, and "neutral" if they were unaware of interest group activities or aware but neither positive nor negative toward them.

From the table, one can observe that, in terms of this classification, Nebraska is quite open to interest group activity and responsive to interest group appeals. Indeed, compared to the other states, Nebraska is extraordinarily open. Some would say, however, that this openness does not extend to unorganized interests or individual citizens. Proponents of this argument view political parties as a countervailing influence to special interests--as institutions that in some sense protect the general interest, especially those segments of the population who are unorganized and have no one to speak for them. The Nebraska Legislature is open, but this openness may extend only to those interests that take the initiative in pressing their claims.

It is problematical, however, how much the mere presence of political parties in the legislature guarantees protection of the general interest. Moreover, whereas unorganized interest may be disadvantaged in Nebraska, legitimate organized interest may have difficulty in states less responsive to interest group activities. Regardless of the structural features of the legislature, citizens interested in protecting their interests need to organize. Here too, there is little the opponents of nonpartisanship can point to in defense of their claims that a partisan legislature would necessarily be an improvement.

3. ACCOUNTABILITY

Accountability or rational choice refers to whether the voter can be sure how his vote for a particular candidate is likely to influence decisions on issues that come before the legislature. What bloc or group of legislators is going to be strengthened or weakened by the election of a particular candidate? To the extent that the voter can know this, he can make a rational choice. Satisfaction of this criterion obviously requires the presence of discernable voting blocs in the legislature. Most legislatures have partisan divisions or blocs that structure voting and provide the voter with an important piece of information on the probable behavior of a candidate once elected, as well as on the bloc or group in the legislature that will be strengthened by his election.

In Nebraska, what little structure to roll call voting that existed has declined significantly since the adoption of nonpartisan elections. Table 3 reveals that the number of roll call votes on which the alignment of legislators correlated with the alignment on at least four other votes was slightly more than 25 percent of all votes in 1969, a decrease of nearly 50 percent from the partisan and early nonpartisan years. Table 3 also reveals the degree to which structured voting in those years reflected partisan alignments. Here too a decline is visible from the partisan to nonpartisan period.

In Nebraska, it appears that party groupings are missing in legislative voting. Structure may, however, be achieved through other discernable groupings, such as ideological groups, occupational groups, or regional groups. One writer observes, however, that a certain randomness characterizes voting in the Nebraska [3, pp. 101-15]. That is, legislators do not form blocs. They do not consistently vote together, but form coalitions which change from issue to issue.

What does this mean in terms of accountability? It means the voter cannot see how his vote is going to bear on legislative majorities. First of all, he cannot know which group he would like to control the legislature--there are none--and second, for the same reason, he cannot know which group will be strengthened by his voting a particular way. Accountability, it seems, suffers under such an arrangement. To the degree that the situation results from the nonpartisan nature of the legislature, and evidence seems to support this, the finding represents a severe indictment of nonpartisanship.

Not only is structure missing from the legislature, competition in legislative elections, a related phenomenon, seems to have declined also. This too follows the change from a partisan to a nonpartisan legislature. The percent of uncontested primaries increased from 27 percent for the period 1924-72 to 29 percent for 1936-46 and 46 percent for 1962-72. Uncontested general elections for the same periods were respectively 8, 14, and 14 percent. Declining competition is revealed in terms of the margin of electoral victory also. For the period 1924-34, 63

TABLE 3

Voting in Five Sessions of the Nebraska Legislature

| | Partisan | Nonpartisan | | | |
	1927	1937	1947	1959	1969
Percent of roll calls correlating with four others	47%	48%	43%	35%	27%
Number of respondents	(217)	(131)	(145)	(172)	(282)
Relatonship of corre- lating roll calls to party [a]	.34[b]	.15	.16	.19	.11
Number of respondents	(19)	(9)	(9)	(8)	(11)

a Data from Susan Welch, "The Impact of Party on Voting Behavior in the Nebraska Legislature," in Nonpartisan-ship in the Legislative Process, edited by John C. Comer and James B. Johnson (Washington, D.C.: University Press of America, 1978).

b 1.00 represents a perfect positive association.

percent of the electoral contests for the legislature were won by 55 percent or more of the vote; this increased to 65 percent for 1936-46 and 71 percent for 1962-72 [4, pp. 29-38]. Clearly competition in terms of the number of candidates contesting as well as the division of the vote has declined and the trend parallels the change from a partisan to nonpartisan legislature. The trend also parallels increasing electoral success of incumbents, a success ratio that exceeds patterns in other states over the same period [4]. On the accountability criterion, the Nebraska Legislature clearly falls short.

4. LEADERSHIP STRUCTURE

A final criterion to be examined is whether or not there is a well defined leadership structure with power, authority, and expertise to direct the legislature in the efficient operation of its functions. Issues include the basis on which leaders are selected and the tasks they are expected to perform. Are leaders selected on the basis of knowledge and expertise, and are they expected to use these in directing the legislature toward particular ends? In the Nebraska Legislature, the important leaders are the Speaker and committee chairmen. What are the criteria by which legislators are selected for these positions? Table 4 summarizes responses of members regarding selection criteria. With respect to both the Speaker and committee chairmen, experience and expertise stand out. In particular, experience and expertise dominate references to selection criteria for committee chairmen. Friendship and seniority, important in the selection of Speaker, are much less important with respect to committee chairmen.

The experience and expertise, however, relate only to the operation of the legislature. For example, the role of the Speaker is defined largely in terms of the position's administrative duties. The Speaker is expected to keep the process moving. He is expected to keep order and to know the rules. The position is also honorific. Speakers serve only one term (by custom), and the position is seen by many to be a reward for service in the legislature.

The pattern is basically the same for committee chairmen. They are expected to maintain order and expedite the process. They are expected to lead and guide

TABLE 2

Interest Group Orientations

	Nebraska	California	New Jersey	Ohio	Tennessee
Facilitator	61[a]	38[b]	41%	43%	23%
Resister	2	20	27	22	40
Neutral	37	42	32	35	37
Number	(41)	(97)	(78)	(157)	(116)

a Data from James B. Johnson, "The Nebraska Legislative System:
   Legislative Roles in a Nonpartisan Setting," (Unpublished
   Ph.D. dissertation, Northwestern University, 1972).

b Data from John C. Wahlke et. al., The Legislative System
   (New York: John Wiley and Sons, 1962).

TABLE 4

Factors in Formal Leadership Selection
in the Nebraska Legislature

| | Percentage of Repondents Indicating this factor as a Selection Criterion for Leadership Position | |
	Speaker	Committee chairmen
Ability, experience, expertise	62%	65%
Friendship, personality	60	13
Seniority	45	28
Good leader, expedites	43	28
Dependable, fair	26	10
Number of respondents	(42)	(40)

Data from James B. Johnson, "Selection and Task Definition: Leadership in the Nebraska Legislature," in Nonpartisanship in the Legislative Process, edited by John C. Comer and James B. Johnson (Washington, D.C.: University Press of America, 1978).

167

but not dictate. They are expected to be fair and
impartial.

The administrative expectations for both the
Speaker and committee chairmen are not unlike what one
finds in other legislatures. What is different, however, is that both positions are defined largely, if
not exclusively, in these terms. There is little responsibility for the Speaker or committee chairmen with
respect to the policy direction of the legislature. It
appears that the kind of leadership desired of formal
leaders in the Nebraska Legislature is clerkship--lead-
ership concerned primarily with organizational and administrative affairs. Formal leaders provide little
policy leadership.

The effect of nonpartisanship on legislative leadership has been a recurrent theme in studies of the
Nebraska Legislature. Some maintain that the absence
of organized political parties destroys leadership; they
see each member of the legislature as an independent
agent to be reckoned with on his own. Others note that
leadership exists, but that it changes from session to
session and issue to issue. To be sure, the absence
of political parties and party organization in the
Nebraska Legislature results in a diminished policy
role for the formal leadership; this may have implications for the policy direction as well as the operation
of the legislature.

CONCLUSION

Where then does the Nebraska Legislature stand with
respect to responsiblity, responsiveness, accountability,
and leadership structure? What is the prospect that a
return to partisan politics will have any influence on
these criteria?

In terms of responsibility, defined here as the
capacity to deal effectively with public problems, the
Nebraska Legislature does about as well as any one of
a number of American state legislatures. If citizen
reactions to job performance as well as the place of
the legislature in the institutional structure of state
government are the operational standards, one can conclude that the Nebraska Legislature performs as well
as most other legislatures. There is little here that
critics of the nonpartisan plan can point to in support

168

of their charges. Nor does the Nebraska Legislature
fall short in terms of responsiveness. A sizable majority of Nebraska legislators are positive in their assessment of interest group activities and the role of interest groups in the political process. Here too, critics
have little to be enthusiastic about.

Some improvement can, however, be made with respect
to accountability. The absence of structured groupings
in the legislature, whether partisan, ideological, or
geographical, makes it difficult for citizens to know
who controls the legislature and how their vote for legislative candidates relates to that control. By this
standard, the Nebraska Legislature fares poorly. Another
area where the legislature falls short is leadership
structure. Leadership in the Nebraska Legislature is
defined almost exclusively in terms of administration.
The Speaker and committee chairmen are organizers and
expediters but not policy leaders. An effective functioning legislature requires, it seems, that someone be
charged with setting the legislative agenda and directing
consideration of it. Neither the Speaker nor committee
chairmen serve in this capacity.

Finally, one can consider what the impact of return
ing to partisan elections and organization in the legislature might be. Clearly, accountability might improve.
Parties do organize the legislature and structure voting
to a degree; Democrats have a tendency to vote with
Democrats and Republicans with Republicans. This is
the kind of bloc structure that enables the voter to
know who controls the legislature and how his vote will
affect control. There is the prospect, however, that
introducing political parties in an otherwise weak party
system would not have this effect. Legislators might
contine to respond in terms of loose, free-floating coal-
itions--at least, in the short run. Furthermore, improved
accountability might undermine legislative responsiveness.
Legislators who respond to the pressures of partisan politics are not free to entertain special appeals from organized interests.

A more effective leadership structure may also be
possible with partisan divisions in the legislature,
particularly if the majority party leadership is given
responsibility for overseeing the substantive direction
of the legislature. This would most likely mean that
the majority party leadership would appoint committee
chairmen and be responsible for committee assignments,

changes that would also facilitate accountability. Responsibility, at least in terms of the indicators here, is unlikely to be affected by a change to partisan politics.

In the final analysis, one has to attach priorities to each of the above criteria and opt for either the status quo or a change based on one's individual rankings of the criteria.

NOTE

1. Data are from a statewide telephone survey of adults conducted in 1978 by the Bureau of Sociological Research at the University of Nebraska-Lincoln.

REFERENCES

1. Flinn, Thomas, "Evaluation and Relevance in State Legislative Research." Paper presented at the American Political Science Association meeting in Washington, D.C., 1969.

2. Rieselbach, Leroy. Congressional Reform in the Seventies, (Morristown, New Jersey: General Learning Press, 1977).

3. Welch, Susan. "The Impact of Party on Voting Behavior in the Nebraska Legislature," in Nonpartisanship in the Legislative Process, edited by John C. Comer and James B. Johnson. (Washinngton, D.C.: University Press of America, 1978).

4. _____. "Election to the Legislature: Competition and Turnout," in Nonpartisanship in the Legislative Process, edited by John C. Comer and James B. Johnson. (Washington, D.C.: University Press of America, 1978).

15.   State Legislative Oversight of Federal Funds*

Carol S. Weissert

What difference does legislative involvement make
in the decisions relating to and uses made of federal
funds coming into states? Since 1976, legislative
oversight of federal funds has become a front-burner
issue in many states. A number of states have adopted
procedures to appropriate these funds; others have
moved to participate in the applications process and
to "track" federal dollars coming into the state. The
courts have been active with at least one major
decision in Pennsylvania upholding the legislature's
right to appropriate federal funds.

Legislative oversight of federal funds can be
justified in several ways. The primary one--cited by
the Advisory Commission on Intergovernmental Relations
(ACIR) and others--is that in order for state legislatures to fulfill their constitutional responsibility
for the proper and effective allocation of state
revenues, they must consider federal funds in their
appropriation process. To ignore these funds greatly
undermines the legislature's traditional power over
the purse strings, since federal funds now constitute
a significant portion of state expenditures.

A strict interpretation of this would mean that:

· When there is discretion involving how federal
grant dollars should be allocated, the legislature, not
state executive branch agencies, should make the
decision.

· When state legislatures refuse to provide state
funds for certain programs or projects, they should not
be established by using federal funds, unless the
legislature consents.

· There should be a legislative role in decisions
relating to both the organizational placement of a
program and its functional relationship with existing
or planned programs or policies.

---

*Reprinted with permission from State Government,
Vol. LIII, No. 2, Spring 1980, pp. 77-80.

171

• Even in federal programs that require no immediate state commitment or match, there should be legislative involvement since the state is generally expected to assume some or all of the costs of continuing the project in later years--sometimes at a price higher than the legislature would pay for its own programs. Once the program or project is "established" with employees and a constituency, it becomes increasingly difficult for the legislature to terminate it.

These specifics--relating to discretion, substitution, organization, and implied commitments--along with the size of federal aid (nearly 40 percent of total state own-source revenues in 1978) have led to a number of state legislatures assuming a stronger oversight role in the use of federal funds. Oversight can follow three patterns: legislative appropriation of federal funds, legislative review of agency applications for federal funds, and legislative tracking of federal dollars coming into the state.

APPROPRIATIONS PROCESS

According to a 1979 survey by the National Conference of State Legislatures (NCSL), nine states exercise a "high degree" of appropriations control over federal funds or their budgetary processes, usually characterized by specific sum appropriations at the subprogram level and reappropriation of such funds necessary in the next fiscal year. Included in this category are Alaska, Florida, Maryland, Montana, New Hampshire, North Carolina, Oregon, Pennsylvania, and Washington.

On the other hand, six states have automatic (or nonspecific) appropriation of federal funds--a system with little legislative oversight. These states are Alabama, Delaware, Indiana, Iowa, Tennessee, and Texas.

Most states fall in between--many have adopted one or two of the three patterns involved in "active" designation; others are only studying possibilities of more legislative involvement.

The approaches taken vary considerably. In 1976, Pennsylvania enacted legislation requiring immediate state appropriation of federal funds. In 1978, California called for a more measured approach by phasing in implementation over four years.

APPLICATIONS AND APPROPRIATIONS

Several states initiated efforts to appropriate federal funds only to find that the decisions regarding the content and scope of the programs had already been made.

"Major decisions are frequently made when applications are submitted," said Bill Hamm, California's legislative analyst. "By the time the legislature gets it, it is a fait accompli. The legislature must refuse the funds or go along with the program as is." He cited as an example Title II of the Public Works Employment Act, where the application identifies specific priorities developed by state agencies--not the legislature.

Several other states have developed procedures which mesh the legislative involvement in both the appropriations and applications processes. Like California, some of these legislatures discovered that involvement in the appropriations process is often too late to effect change or set priorities. Thus, they have enacted procedures whereby the legislature can review or approve state agency applications for federal aid, sometimes through OMB Circular A-95.

Legislative involvement in the applications process is not without risk. In South Dakota, the process had to be abandoned when the paperwork threatened to overtake the rest of the legislative agenda. The South Dakota approach required that applications for federal funds be processed through the A-95 review process.[1] One staffer in the legislature received copies of the applications and matched them with legislators who would be interested in those submissions. Senator Harold Schreier, former chairman of the Senate Appropriations Committee and cosponsor of a bill setting up the review system, and his house counterpart volunteered to do much of the paperwork involved, but they were soon "totally inundated" by it. They eliminated federal education grants from their review the first week; then federal dollars going to local governments; then the whole idea. "After a year we couldn't hack it," Senator Schreier said. "Two part-time legislators can't deal with all federal activities in South Dakota."

Oregon has established a procedure for reviewing applications which differs from most states in several ways. It includes the constitutional authorization for an interim emergency board to both appropriate funds and approve applications, the ability to deny a request for an agency to submit an application to the federal government, and the practice of having the Ways and Means Committee or the emergency board review the grant request early in the process--usually before submission to the A-95 clearinghouse.

An important element in the apparent success of the Oregon approach may well be the close working relationships that have developed between executive and legislative branches.

Another factor in the Oregon model relates to the amount of time members of the Ways and Means Committee and the emergency board spend on oversight of state agencies and the federal funds they receive. The emergency board meets approximately every six weeks for a two-day session. The Ways and Means Committee spends most of its six months in session reviewing budgets of the agencies in its six substantive subcommittees.

According to Leo Hegstrom, director of the Oregon Department of Human Resources, the Subcommittee on Human Resources knows the agency's budget backward and forward. But, he added, "If the legislature wants to make these decisions on their own, they must have this kind of knowledge." Representative Vera Katz agrees: "If we didn't have the experience and knowledge of the budget process, it would be useless to attempt this kind of oversight."

TRACKING FEDERAL DOLLARS

In many states, methods used to appropriate federal funds and procedures involved in the application process give legislators a good idea of how many federal dollars are coming into the state and how those dollars are used.

In 1977, the Illinois legislature enacted a measure requiring state agencies under the governor to submit all applications for federal aid to the Bureau of the Budget for approval. The bureau is required to send copies of this information to the Commission on Intergovernmental Cooperation. Similarly, awards of federal funds and changes in grants must be forwarded to the bureau, then to the commission. Agencies excluded from this notification process include state colleges and universities, agencies of the legislative and judicial branches, and elected officials other than the governor. However, they must submit summaries to the commission of all federal funds applied for, awarded, and received.

The system, which has been on-line since January 1978, is "still struggling," according to Dave Griffith, senior associate with the commission. The problem has been with the completeness and accuracy of the data. "We're just not sure how accurate our information is," he said. "And, it's hard to assess how much is being missed." The staff is currently attempting to determine why there are gaps and delays in receiving information.

JUDICIAL OVERVIEW

Over the past three years, the courts have been extremely active in the area of state legislative appropriation of federal funds. At issue have been both the general question of the legislature's right to appropriate funds and the more specific questions about what constitutes public funds and the ability of the legislature to delegate authority to a committee to appropriate funds when the legislature is out of session.

Key among the decisions was *Shapp v. Sloan*, a case involving the Pennsylvania legislature's right to appropriate federal funds. The case went through two state courts and was appealed to the U.S. Supreme Court. The Commonwealth Court and the Pennsylvania Supreme Court held that the state law defining the role of the legislature was not invalid under the federal or state constitutions. An appeal to the U.S. Supreme Court was dismissed "for want of a substantial federal question."

Two primary questions relating to state legislative appropriation of federal funds have surfaced in the courts:

175

• What constitutes "public funds" (or similar word-
ing used in many state constitutions to describe the
scope of the legislature's appropriation power)?

• Is delegation of the appropriation power to a
committee when the legislature is out of session
constitutional?

The courts have reached widely divergent rulings
on those questions. In 1978 decisions, for example,
Alaska and Massachusetts judges reached opposite
conclusions as to whether the legislature had the
right to appropriate federal funds.

The second question has been resolved with more
consistency. Most attorney general rulings and court
decisions have called statutory legislative delegation
to an interim committee with the power to appropriate
federal funds an unconstitutional delegation of authority.

The variety and discrepancies of these court
decisions are due to differing political climates,
varying state judicial history, and variations in
constitutional and statutory language. The situation
is complicated still further by the fact that most
grant-in-aid statutes do not mention the role state
legislatures are to play.

WHAT DIFFERENCE DOES IT MAKE?

There has been considerable commentary as to the
"rightness" of state legislative oversight of federal
funds. The basic argument relies on the state constitutional doctrines of separation of powers, checks and
balances, and the importance of the legislatures'
constitutional roles relating to power of the purse and
of oversight.

But the question remains: To what end? For
example, does state legislative oversight of federal
funds:

(1) Assure that legislative priorities and intent
are not deviated from by the executive branch?

(2) Reduce the incidence of implied commitment of
future state dollars for federal programs without

approval of the legislature?

(3) Improve the delivery and effectiveness of federally funded programs?

Instances where legislative intent is ignored or circumvented by the governor or state agencies are apparently frequent and have been cited in a 1977 report of the New York State Assembly Ways and Means Committee and by others. While these activities may continue to occur, state officials feel there is less opportunity for them to happen when the legislature becomes aware of the circumventions and has a way to prevent them (through appropriations or applications procedures).

Interestingly, sometimes legislative scrutiny leads to improved relationships between the legislature and the executive branch. In Pennsylvania, where an executive legislative disagreement was put to a court test in 1977, there are indications that reasonable accommodations have been reached.

In South Dakota, Senator Schreier feels that they have "maintained a better balance with the executive branch since we have been able to adopt, reject, or alter expenditure authority for federal funds." In Oregon, spokesmen of both executive and legislative branches have "developed a strong feeling of cooperation and confidence in each other," according to Rick Burke, legislative fiscal officer.

One of the most frequently cited concerns of legislators who pursue legislative oversight of federal dollars relates to the future use of state dollars.

In the past, federal dollars were frequently viewed as "free" money to states--subject to little scrutiny or attention. "The next best thing to a rainfall" was the term used at least once in South Dakota to describe legislative feelings about federal dollars. California, too, tended to think of acceptance of federal dollars as a "no lose" situation.

Yet, many state legislators now realize that these "free" dollars are not really free. The apparent peaking of the flow of federal aid to state and local governments has heightened their concern, for with the slowdown in aid has come the realization that federal dollars for existing programs might be cut back or eliminated--thus, potentially leaving the state to pick up part or all of their federally funded programs. A number of states would find assuming federal programs particularly burdensome due to recent enactment of taxing or spending limitations. There could be fewer federal dollars going into innovative demonstration projects and perhaps more "strings" on programs that are funded.

One way to eliminate or reduce this implied commitment, say proponents, is legislative oversight of incoming federal dollars. Sometimes this means turning down "free" money for programs which may end up being funded with state dollars.

Michael Hershock, executive director of the Penn-sylvania House Minority Appropriations Committee, cited as an example a 100 percent federal match program to the state to assist in relocating Indonesian refugees. When legislators discovered that the funds would be used to hire 15 people, they refused the money and told the agency head to administer the refugee program with the people he had.

Bill Hamm reported a similar instance where the legislature refused federal funding for an aging program which would employ only two people who would be added to the state's payroll.

While several such instances were cited of a state legislature refusing federal dollars, most of the examples were LEAA programs or small project grants that could set up a demonstration where the state already had an existing program. Does the small number of turndowns then undermine the case for legislative appropriation of federal dollars? In one sense, per-haps yes. Legislatures have a strong tendency to accept federal dollars, and turndowns are rare.

However, one could argue, as does Representative James Ritter, Democratic chairman of the Pennsylvania Federal-State Relations Committee, that the legislature must first establish the process, fix the responsi-bility, and go into the "deep water" one step at a time. "We will get to the large ones," he said. "It's the principle of the thing that's important. The principle that the legislature, given the information, will make the decisions that are best for that state."

The hardest question to answer is the measurement of improved delivery or program effectiveness. There is little doubt that legislative oversight of federal dollars increases the visibility of federal grants in a state and an awareness of where the grant dollars are going and for what purpose. It also may encourage legislators to more closely examine federal and federal-state programs to make sure they meet the needs perceived by the elected officials. Two examples from Oregon may be cited here. One involves the rejection by the state legislature of a federal child nutrition program that called for a survey of information which the state had already compiled. The application was approved when the program was modified to meet the concerns of the legislature.

A second example was the state's refusal of $20 million in federal aid to dependent children funds in 1979. According to Representative Vera Katz, a member of the emergency board and former co-chairman of the Joint Ways and Means Committee, the federal dollars were refused because the federal requirements prevented the state from shaping the program the way it wanted. The legislators felt that the program could be provided in the way that best met the state's needs at half the cost of the federally assisted program, so they decided to operate the program solely on $20 million in state funds that would have gone to match the federal dollars.

The result was a "better program" according to Jerry Brown, deputy director of the state's Department of Human Resources, who worked with the legislative fiscal office prior to joining the department. "Without legislative oversight, they would not have been able to deal with the program and its options so well."

Senator Schreier and Representative Ritter see legislative appropriation of federal funds as only one element in a larger commitment to legislative oversight which could help improve program effectiveness.

Representative Ritter would like to have state legislatures conduct in-depth analyses of federal programs as a cooperative agreement with Congress to assist it in making decisions. He feels such oversight would assure Congress that federal program intent is carried out and not subverted by bureaucratic maneuvering--at the federal or state levels. This oversight would ideally be accompanied by more state flexibility in determining the use of the federal dollar.

OTHER CONSIDERATIONS

There are many who feel that legislative appropriation of federal funds makes a difference--but a difference that is not generally desirable. The most commonly cited problems are that legislative appropriation allows legislatures to substitute their priorities for those of Congress--thus subverting the concept of programs or ideas "in the national interest" --and that it impedes the ability of state agencies to respond in a timely fashion to possible grant awards, thereby losing federal dollars.

Dr. John P. Mallon, director of government relations, American Association of State Colleges and Universities, cited both of these reasons in testimony before the U.S. Senate Intergovernmental Relations Subcommittee in June 1977. "Does Congress generally want a state legislator to be able to kill a grant for whatever reason after Congress has approved it?" he asked. "Once Congress has decided to make such money available for such a purpose, should local legislative leaders or state leaders have the power to veto or delay such a grant?"

In an effort to see if these things were happening, the Senate Appropriations Committee directed the Department of Health, Education, and Welfare (HEW) to investigate and report to the committee any misdirection or delays in distribution of federal funds caused by state statutes calling for legislative appropriation of federal funds. The HEW report, issued in February 1979, found "surprisingly few instances of serious delay or other problems" due to state legislative appropriation of federal dollars. They found no evidence that state legislatures were misdirecting or misusing federal funds.

The few examples of delay, said the report, suggest "that the state reappropriation process does not currently present a serious impediment to the effective and efficient operation of our grant and contract system."

"Furthermore," the report said, "the strongest concerns that have been expressed to us by state and federal program officials, and by interested agencies and organizations, relate to potential problems that could result from the state legislatures' exercise of their authority under these statutes, not to actual problems that have been experienced in the past."

CONCLUSION

In the last three years, there has been considerable activity in legislative oversight of federal funds in both the legislative and judicial arenas. Many questions have been raised; a few answered. Studies now under way by NCSL, the General Accounting Office, and ACIR, among others, may help answer the most nagging question of all: What difference does it make?

NOTE

1. Part I of OMB Circular A-95 establishes a process by which state, regional, and local governments are given the opportunity to review and comment on proposed applications for federal grants that affect physical development and human resources.

16.   Chief Executives and the Budget:
       Controlling the Controllers*

Deirdre A. Zimmerman

Writers on executive budgeting stress that legislative intent should be respected, but they also
generally assume that the chief executive is solely
responsible for budget execution subject, of course, to
review by the legislative body. It also was recognized
that legislative oversight of administration during the
course of the fiscal year might result in modifications
for the next year.

The federal executive budget system was developed
with the enactment of the Budgeting and Accounting Act
of 1921. In New York State, the executive budget
system was established by means of a constitutional
amendment (Article VII), and the assumption was made
until 1980 that a constitutional amendment would be
required to change the system significantly.

A major source of congressional irritation with
presidents over the years was executive impoundment of
appropriations. By the early 1970s, presidential
impoundments were becoming more common, and there was
concern about the large and growing gap between
authorizations and appropriations, growth in continuing
appropriations and the determination of spending in a
given fiscal year by prior statutory authorizations.

President Richard M. Nixon's request in July 1972
for discretionary authority to establish a $250 billion
spending ceiling for fiscal 1973 induced Congress to
establish the joint study committee on budget control
which developed a plan that, with modifications, was
enacted as the Congressional Budget and Impoundment
Control Act of 1974 (P.L. 93-344). The act provided
for congressional determination of national budget
policies and priorities, and for review of impoundments
of appropriated funds. In effect, the act established
a legislative veto, by one or both houses of Congress,

---

*Reprinted with permission from the National Civic
Review, July 1981, pp. 356-60.

within a specified number of days, of policy decisions by the President and/or an agency administrator.

This type of legislative veto is traceable to a 1932 act of Congress which authorized the President to submit plans for reorganizing the executive branch to Congress, to become effective at the end of 60 days unless disallowed by a concurrent resolution or a resolution of one house. An analogous type of legislative veto is found in the War Powers Resolution.

Between 1932 and 1975, a total of 193 bills containing a legislative review and veto mechanism was enacted into law, and more than 150 laws enacted during the Carter administration contain a similar mechanism. President James E. Carter became so concerned about the proliferation of laws authorizing the legislative veto that he sent the first special message on the subject to Congress on June 22, 1978.

The constitutionality of the legislative veto has never been established clearly. There is no specific reference in the United States constitution, or in The Federalist Papers, especially numbers 47 to 51 by James Madison dealing with separation of powers.

The major argument advanced to support the constitutionality of this type of legislative veto is based on the "necessary and proper" clause of Article I, Section 8: "To make all laws which shall be necessary and proper for carrying into execution the foregoing powers, and all other powers vested by this constitution in the government of the United States, or in any department or officer thereof."

The United States Supreme Court to date has not addressed the issue. Justice Byron White, however, in a separate opinion in Buckley v. Valeo (424 U.S. 1 at 284, 1976) wrote that "a statutory provision subjecting agency regulations to disapproval by either house of Congress" is not constitutionally infirm since the provision originally was presented to the President for his approval.

In December 1980, the United States Court of Appeals for the Ninth Circuit held that the House of Representatives violated the separation of powers

principle and unconstitutionally sought to require the
Immigration and Naturalization Service to deport an
immigrant. The House action was taken under a law
authorizing the use of a one-house legislative veto to
override a decision of the service to suspend the
deportation of an illegal alien. Writing for the
three-judge court, Judge Anthony M. Kennedy maintained
that the use of the one-house veto bypassed the
bicameral check, encroached on the function of the
President to execute the law, and intruded on "a central function" of the courts. This decision undoubtedly will be appealed to the United States Supreme Court.

President Carter objected to a newer use of the
legislative veto--the requirement that the President
and agency administrators transmit to Congress in writing a decision or regulations. The President maintained that the sharp increase in the use of this type
of legislative veto "threatens to upset the constitutional balance of responsibilities between the
branches of government . . ." and ". . . represents a
fundamental departure from the way the government has
been administered throughout American history." The
President's position was supported by The New York
Times which noted in an editorial on June 26, 1978,
that "backwards runs the governmental process when
Congress insists on what has become known as the
'legislative veto.'"

In his special message to Congress, President
Carter suggested an alternative--"report-and-wait."
This provides that the President will "report" a proposed action to Congress and will "wait" a stipulated
number of days prior to implementation. Should
Congress disagree with the proposed action, time is
available for negotions on a compromise. If a compromise cannot be agreed on, Congress may enact a bill to
stop or modify the proposed action, subject to a
presidential veto. The President urged that his proposed approach be used sparingly because it "consumes
resources and causes delays . . ."

During 1975, President Gerald R. Ford impounded
$25.3 billion in appropriations, but Congress forced
the President to release $11.3 billion. This suggests
that, during its first year, the impoundment procedure
functioned well.

Concerning impoundments made by the President on
January 23, 1976, however, the Comptroller General
notified Congress that "the President's impoundment
message does not contain adequate information on proposed rescissions. We found that two . . . reported
the rescission of budget authority that had already
been deferred and was still in effect--not rejected by
either House of the Congress. As a consequence, the
combined amount of budget authority reported being
impounded in these two cases exceeds the amount of
budget authority provided by the Congress."

A second problem was the failure of the President
to report budget rescissions promptly to Congress; a
27-day delay was cited. The Comptroller General also
stressed that "the late reporting of these withholdings
is particularly troublesome because it may operate to
deny to the Congress the expected consequence of its
rejecting a rescission proposal--the full and prudent
use of the budget authority."

In New York, the 1927 amendment to the state constitution providing for the executive budget system and
the submission of the first such budget in 1929 led to
a legislative challenge to the governor in the form of
a law requiring that previously appropriated funds
could not be spent without the approval of the chairmen
of the two fiscal committees of the legislature. In
People v. Tremaine (252 N.Y.27, 1929) the state Court
of Appeals ruled that the law violated the provision of
the constitution that members of the legislature may
hold no other office.

A minor attack on the executive budget system was
launched by the legislature in 1930, and in 1939 the
legislature amended the executive budget bill by
deleting nearly every item and substituting a lump sum
appropriation for each department and agency. The
legislative action was challenged, and the Court of
Appeals in People v. Tremaine (281 N.Y.8, 1939) ruled
in favor of the governor.

Interestingly, the legislature has not challenged
the authority of the governor to impound appropriated
funds. A challenge to the power of the governor to
"freeze" appropriated funds, however, was made by
Oneida County. In his fiscal 1977 budget, Governor

Hugh L. Carey recommended that $12 million be appro-
priated for the sewage works reimbursement program.
The legislature added $14 million to the program and
the governor approved the $26 million. On October 7,
1976, the director of the division of the budget
impounded $7 million.

In upholding the position of the petitioners that
"they have been improperly denied state reimbursement
for the operation and maintenance of sewage treatment
works," the Court of Appeals in County of Oneida v.
Berle (49 N.Y.2d 515, 1980) held: "However laudable
its goals, the executive branch may not override
enactments which have emerged from the law-making
process. It is required to implement policy
declarations of the legislature, unless vetoed or
judicially invalidated. This the executive failed to
do." The court made clear that there is no constitutional basis for the governor, acting through his
budget director, to impound funds that have been
appropriated by the legislature.

On the federal level, impoundments by the President induced Congress to enact a law to control such
actions. In New York, the legislature did not seek to
exercise a veto power over impoundments made by the
governor, but a legal challenge by local governments
resulted in a court ruling that the governor lacks the
power to impound funds under the current state
constitution.

In a state such as New York where the governor has
the power to veto appropriation items, there is less
need for an executive impoundment power since the
governor can protect himself against legislative riders
that are attached to appropriation bills. A case can
be made for granting the President the impoundment
power in order to enable him to defeat legislative
riders. The Impoundment Control Act provides for a
system that retains executive responsibility and
flexibility in implementing the budget, but also allows
the Congress to make the final determination concerning
the "freezing" of appropriated funds. In other words,
the act ensures that the intent of Congress in preserved yet allows for flexibility in budget execution.

A system providing that the chief executive report budget rescissions to the legislative body works well on the national level since Congress is in session throughout most of the year. This is not true, however, in New York, and several modifications would be needed.

The New York State finance law currently recognizes that emergencies may necessitate the expenditure of unappropriated funds when the legislature is not in session. The law authorizes the governor to allocate money from the governmental emergency fund upon issuance of a certificate of intent to recommend an appropriation at the next session of the legislature signed by the temporary president of the Senate, the speaker of the Assembly, and the chairmen of the Assembly Ways and Means Committee and the Senate Finance Committee. A New York State impoundment control act could establish a procedure similar to the federal one while the legislature is in session and also provide for the interim.

17. Financing Gubernatorial Election Campaigns*

Herbert E. Alexander

The 1970s have witnessed noticeable shifts in state election campaign financing. Changes have been stimulated by election reform which affects the laws governing political finance in most states;[1] by a growing tendency for more candidates to use personal funds, brought about in part by escalating campaign costs resulting from more use of television and the new campaign technologies; by the growing influence of national parties and political action committees; and by the need to gear strategy increasingly toward the more independent voter, coincident with the spread of two-party competition.

These and related changes have affected the entire political environment in most states. New bookkeeping and public reporting requirements are causing a growing campaign professionalism, with lawyers and accountants hired to help candidates and political committees cope with comprehensive and complex election laws. New or additional sources of campaign funding are necessary when state laws limit contributions (as 25 now do) or restrict or prohibit corporate, labor, or other traditional sources (as 40 do to some degree). Professional fund raisers and direct mailers have joined campaign and computer specialists. The roles of political party committees have changed, in some states strengthened through the use of tax checkoff funds made available to them by state laws.[2] The rise of political action committees and single-interest groups has affected state as well as national politics. All of these changes have affected volunteerism and citizen participation.

---

*Reprinted with permission from State Government. Vol. LIII, No. 3, Summer 1980, pp. 140-43.

PUBLIC FUNDING

Changing Attitudes

At present, 17 states have some form of public
funding. In 1978, Michigan, Minnesota, Wisconsin, and
Massachusetts offered public subsidies to gubernatorial
candidates. Because expenditure limits are often imposed
on candidates accepting state subsidies, there is a change
in attitude toward accepting these funds.

In Michigan, the major party candidates received
$75,000 each, triggering a $1 million general election
expenditure limit,[3] part of an effort to equalize receipts
and expenditures in elections. Governor William Milliken
won by approximately 400,000 votes; the equality of
expenditures benefited the incumbent more than the
challenger. In addition, Michigan is the only state providing substantial public funds in primary campaigns,
and some $1.3 million was distributed to four Democratic
candidates while one Republican received $161,400.

In Minnesota, in contrast, Republican Albert Quie
succeeded in part because he did not accept general
election public funding. Incumbent Governor Rudy
Perpich accepted the public monies which restricted him
to a $600,000 spending ceiling for the general election
and provided only $190,316 in public grants.[4] Yet Quie,
who raised private funds, spent $1,026,425 and won
against the incumbent. The drama in Minnesota was
complicated because former Governor Wendell Anderson
resigned from office in 1976, which resulted in Perpich
filling his unexpired term. Perpich, as governor, then
appointed Wendell Anderson to a U.S. Senate vacancy.
This did not sit well with the electorate. Though the
campaigns were very expensive, the overall effect was an
upset victory for Independent Republicans who swept the
gubernatorial and senate elections.

Wisconsin has a unique gubernatorial election system which imposes expenditure limits for both the
primary ($184,325) and the general election ($430,075),
but provides public funding only in the latter period.
Neither major party candidate accepted public funds
in 1978, which would have been $76,500 split between
them (or all to one if the other refused to accept).[5]
In the general election, Governor Martin J. Schreiber,
the incumbent, spent more ($858,704) than Lee S. Dreyfus,

the challenger ($557,073), but Dreyfus won. Limitations on amounts actually spent, if added to candidates for lieutenant governor, would have increased limitations ($61,450) and public grants ($9,189) somewhat, since candidates run as teams. The reasons state funding was rejected were the low limits, the small amounts of money available, hotly contested primaries in which spending exceeded the limits, and the fact that the tax checkoff had been in operation for only one year, not the four years necessary to accumulate more money as will be the case in future elections.

Massachusetts has a surcharge system in which the taxpayer can add $1 and $2 to his or her tax liability (as distinguished from the tax checkoff in which the $1 or $2 consists of tax payments which would have to be paid in any case, but can be earmarked for a political fund for distribution to political parties or candidates). Massachusetts provides minimal funding in gubernatorial campaigns in both the primary and general elections. In 1978, three primary candidates received $12,152 each, and two general election candidates received $27,406 each.[6] The general election funding did not go far toward the spending totals, which were not readily available for the general election but, combining primary and general election, were $1.4 million for Edward J. King, Democrat, who won, and $1.4 million for Francis W. Hatch, Republican, who lost.

Defining a Limit

The New Jersey gubernatorial general election in 1977, publicly funded for candidates who could qualify, illustrates the problem of finding an equitable spending limit. Both major party candidates raised up to the maximum in private contributions (about $500,000 each) and received public funds (a little more than $1 million each) which brought them close to the spending limit ($1,518,576 each).[7] This gave an advantage to the incumbent, Brendan Byrne, who, although burdened with responsibility for an unpopular state income tax, was better known. The limits worked to the disadvantage of his challenger, state Senator Ray Bateman. When Bateman wanted to change strategies and revise campaign themes late in the campaign, he was unable to do so and still stay within the limit. Spending limits in this case rigidified the system. In general, spending limits give advantage to candidates who are better known and who have the backing of superior party organization, celebrity status, or the ability to enlist volunteers.

After the 1977 election, a majority of the commission administering New Jersey's law recommended continued limits on contributions and loans and a cap on the amount of public funds available to the candidate, but with no overall spending limit. This recommendation was passed by the New Jersey legislature, with the surprising support of New Jersey Common Cause, but was vetoed by Governor Byrne. The vetoed bill also would have extended public funding to primary campaigns for governor.

PRIVATE FUNDING

Texas

Money is often a decisive factor in Texas statewide elections, primarily because of the state's size. In one of the most significant upsets in Texas political history, William Perry Clements, a multimillionaire from Dallas, in 1978 became the state's first Republican governor in 105 years. A former deputy secretary of defense in the Nixon-Ford administration, Clements spent $7.2 million to defeat John Hill, the state attorney general, in the general election. Although Clements spent more than twice as much as Hill, he won the election by less than 1 percent out of 2.3 million votes cast. More than $4.5 million of Clements' funds came from personally guaranteed loans from several Dallas banks.[8] The advantage gained from the ability of a candidate to borrow large sums on his or her own name is immense, and is indicative of one of the major trends affecting gubernatorial campaigns across the country.

Louisiana

In Louisiana in 1979, an historically expensive and controversial contest concluded with the election of the first Republican governor in more than a century. In the nonpartisan primary, six major candidates spent $16 million, and in the general election runoff, the two candidates receiving the most votes spent another $4.7 million, for a total of $20.7 million to elect a

governor. Combined primary and runoff spending by the
winner, David Treen, totaled $5.9 million, while that of
Louis Lambert, the loser, amounted to $4.8 million. All
the candidates and campaigns taken together spent $9.8
million--or nearly half the total--for producing and
placing mass media advertising.[9] About $2.5 million was
expended for other consultants and professionals, including strategists, attorneys, accountants, pollsters, and
those managing computers, telephone banks, and research.
Pollsters billed nearly $690,000 for their services.
Even adjusting for inflation, the Louisiana amounts exceed
previous costly gubernatorial campaigns of Nelson
Rockefeller and his opponents in New York, including the
costliest in 1970.

In the Louisiana primary, the six candidates spent
$8.17 for each registered voter. In spending per vote
received, amounts ranged from $19.79 for Mouton to $8.65
for Treen. In the general election, Treen and Lambert
spent an average of $2.49 per registered voter, or $3.51
per vote received.

Alaska

On a cost-per-vote basis, the Alaska gubernatorial
campaign in 1978 was probably the most expensive in the
nation. Only 106,307 Alaskans voted in the Democratic
and Republican primaries, but $2,100,990 was spent by
seven candidates to influence the outcome--an average of
$19.76 per primary vote. Walter Hickel spent the most
money but, on a cost-per-vote basis, the most expensive
campaign was mounted by former state Senator Ed Merdes
who spent an average of $41.23 per vote; one third of
that amount was self-financed. Though general election
campaign expenditures were lower--an average of $8.96 per
vote--this figure is still extraordinarily high
compared with other states.[10]

TRENDS IN COSTS: A CASE STUDY

The California Fair Political Practices Commission
surveyed various statewide campaigns in California over
a 20-year period to observe trends in campaign costs.
The study revealed that while California campaign costs
are increasing in terms of actual dollars, once inflation is factored out, the cost of gubernatorial campaigns has remained relatively unchanged over the last

20 years when expressed in terms of constant 1958 dollars.[11]

Total constant dollar spending (primary and general election campaigns) increased from 1958 to 1962 and increased again in 1974, and then dropped in 1978. In actual total dollar spending, there was an increase from 1958 to 1962 and again in 1966, a significant drop in 1970, and then an increase in 1974 and in 1978. (See Table 1.)

Table 1

ACTUAL AND CONSTANT DOLLARS SPENT IN
CALIFORNIA GUBERNATORIAL CAMPAIGNS: 1958-1978*

| Year | Combined expenditures of both major parties | | Status of election |
	Actual dollars	Constant dollars	
1958..............	$ 2,655,292	$2,655,292	Open
1962..............	4,542,195	4,272,966	Incumbent
1966..............	6,904,654	6,072,313	Incumbent
1970..............	4,882,356	3,616,560	Incumbent
1974..............	10,563,509	6,265,426	Open
1978..............	13,481,678	5,889,768	Incumbent

*Source: California Fair Political Practices Commission, Campaign Costs: How Much Have They Increased and Why?: A Study of State Elections, 1958-1978.

The pattern of expenditures for both major parties is exhibited in Table 2. In general elections, both Democratic and Republican candidates increased expenditures in 1962 and 1966. In 1970 both declined, although the decrease was far greater for the Democrats. Then in 1974, Republican expenditures continued to fall, and the Democrats' began to rise. Both parties recorded increased expenditures in 1978, the first gubernatorial year in the past 20 years in which the Democratic candidate outspent the Republican candidate in the general election. However, the relative rise and fall of campaign costs over the years is the result

Table 2

PRIMARY AND GENERAL ELECTION EXPENDITURES IN
CALIFORNIA FOR GOVERNOR, BY PARTY: 1958-1978*

| Year | Republican | | Democrat | | Total |
	Primary	General	Primary	General	
1958...	$ 564,171	$ 915,949	$ 403,307	$ 789,865	$ 2,655,292
1962...	952,499	1,656,126	497,750	1,435,820	4,542,195
1966...	1,684,661	2,759,290	386,760	2,109,943	6,940,654
1970...	917,854	2,584,779	474,980	904,743	4,882,256
1974...	1,168,013	2,055,586	5,730,612	1,609,298	10,563,509
1978...	6,397,822	2,274,772	1,374,050	3,435,034	13,481,678

*Source: California Fair Political Practices Commission, Campaign Costs:
How Much Have They Increased and Why?: A Study of State
Elections,1958-1978. Data for the years 1958 through 1970 are
taken from John R. Owens, Trends in Campaign Spending in
California, 1958-1970: Tests of Factors Influencing Costs
(Princeton, N.J.: Citizens' Research Foundation, 1973).

of many factors: the candidates, personality, incumbency,
open seats, and the state of the economy and of the parties.
These changing political climates are sometimes more responsible for escalating campaign spending than inflation. Of
particular note is that the Republicans in 1978 and the
Democrats in 1974 spent more in the primary than in the
general election.

NATIONAL PARTY INFLUENCE

Another change in practices occurred in 1978--the
organized effort on the part of the Republican National
Committee (RNC). Though a post-Watergate rebound helped
Republicans to gain seats in state legislatures and in
Congress, RNC Chairman Bill Brock also was concerned about
the possibility that Republicans would be severely gerry-
mandered after the 1980 census unless state elections
were won by Republicans in 1978 and 1980. He expanded
the Republican Governors' Association (RGA) and energized
its Campaign Services operation. RGA contributed a total

of $530,000 to 1978 gubernatorial campaigns. Of these contributions, which ranged in amounts from $32,000 in New York to $700 in Georgia, 53 percent went to winning races. According to John Bibby:

> The RGA role in gubernatorial races ranged from paying the salary of a campaign staffer to extensive involvement in campaign planning, selecting consultants, financing, and carrying out selected aspects of the campaign plan.[12]

The 1978 elections resulted in a net gain in six Republican governorships, and the RNC can claim some credit for this gain.

In addition to supporting gubernatorial candidates, a new unit was established to help recapture state legislative seats. Called the Local Election Campaign Division, it spent approximately $1.7 million on 1978 legislative elections--more than three times as much as on gubernatorial campaigns. It organized candidate/campaign manager training sessions and, with the aid of state party committees, co-sponsored 65 seminars reaching 2,800 legislative campaigns, as well as targeted selected campaigns for special assistance.

RNC's efforts were upgraded in 1979 by the establishment of a political action committee. In November 1979, the GOP Action Committee (GOPAC) announced a goal of $1 million to provide money to 650 legislative candidates in the 1980 election year. In 1979, GOPAC gave an average of $460 to 41 Republicans.[13] Republican efforts in 1980 gubernatorial and legislative campaigns will be even greater, seeking to capture more seats in order to influence the reapportionment that will occur starting in 1981 in the states. For example, the Local Election Campaign Division will have a $2.7 million budget in 1980.

Hoping to exploit anti-Carter sentiment during off-presidential year elections in 1979, Republicans believed they could win at least one of the governorships in Mississippi or Kentucky, and the Republican national party poured tens of thousands of dollars into each state, with disappointing results. In Kentucky, millionaire John Y. Brown, Jr. (D) beat former Governor Louie B. Nunn (R), and in Mississippi, Democrat William Winter was victorious over Republican

Gil Carmichael, despite RGA and RNC combined contributions of $150,000.[14]

In many parts of the south, the growing incidence of independent voters is causing changes in campaign tactics. In Alabama in 1978, for example, leading Republican candidates systematically omitted party affiliation from advertising materials. Radio messages on the Republican side explained the virtues of "voting a split ticket" even though Republicans contested most statewide offices.

In addition, in 1980, RNC is sponsoring a $5 million national television campaign which, while focusing mainly on federal elections, should have some impact on elections at the statewide and local levels.

CONCLUSION

Significant trends and events have affected gubernatorial campaigns in recent years. While money is only one factor in electing governors, as in electing public officials at any level, it is an essential ingredient in most successful campaigns.

Realistically, the present policy of fiscal restraint makes the extension of public funding in the states unlikely in the short run. However, any new campaign finance scandals could generate new enthusiasm which could outweigh opposition as well as consideration of fiscal policy. Public funding is not a panacea, but it is a new and significant element in certain state elections.

NOTES

1. For an overview of state election reform, see Herbert E. Alexander, Financing Politics: Money, Elections and Political Reform, 2nd ed. (Washington D.C.: Congressional Quarterly Press, 1980), pp. 127-44; Karen J. Fling, "The States as Laboratories of Reform," in Herbert E. Alexander (ed)., Political Finance (Beverly Hills, California: Sage Publications, 1979), pp. 245-69; and Herbert E. Alexander (ed.), Campaign Money: Reform and Reality in the States (New York: The Free Press, 1976).

2.   Ruth S. Jones, "State Public Financing and the State Parties," in Michael J. Malbin (ed.), Parties, Interest Groups, and Campaign Finance Law (Washington, D.C.: American Enterprise Institute for Public Policy Research, 1980), pp. 283-303.

3.   Michigan's Gubernatorial Public Funding (Lansing: Michigan Department of State, 1978).

4.   Public Financing Report, (St. Paul: Minnesota State Ethical Practices Board, 1980). Candidates for lieutenant governor run jointly with candidates for governor in the general election, and the given amounts are joint figures.

5.   1979 Disbursement Levels for Gubernatorial Candidates Elibible for Grants from the Wisconsin Election Campaign Fund (Madison: Wisconsin State Election Board, undated).

6.   Charles J. Doherty, Limited Public Financing of Campaigns for Statewide Elective Office in Massachusetts 1978 (Boston, Mass: Office of Campaign and Political Finance, 1978).

7.   Public Financing in New Jersey: The 1977 General Election for Governor (Trenton: New Jersey Election Law Enforcement Commission, 1978), pp. 1, 43. Independents or minor party candidates could get funding if they qualified, but none did.

8.   Rhodes Cook and Stacy West, "1978 Gubernatorial Contests: Incumbent Winners Hold Money Advantage" Congressional Quarterly Weekly Report, August 25, 1979, p. 1755.

9.   The Great Louisiana Campaign Spendathon (Baton Rouge: Public Affairs Research Council of Louisiana, Inc., 1980), Table 1, p. 2, and Table 7, p. 5. No dollar value was assigned to in-kind contributions, which were considerable and would increase the total.

10. Cook and West, "1978 Gubernatorial Contests," p. 1758.

11. Campaign Costs: How Much Have They Increased and Why? A Study of State Election, 1958-1978 (Sacramento: California Fair Political Practices Commission, 1980).

12. John F. Bibby, "Political Parties and Federalism: The Republican National Committee Involvement in Gubernatorial and Legislative Elections," Publius, p. 232.

13. Jack W. Germond and Jules Witcover, "Conservatives Want Helms as No. 2," The Washington Star, November 25, 1979.

14. Bill Peterson, "Democrats Capture Governorships in Kentucky, Mississippi," The Washington Post, November 7, 1979.

18. Kean's Freshman Year as Governor:
     Budgets, Taxes and a Ton of Mail*

I never realized the amount of paper work that a
Governor has to deal with. You don't think of things
like personal appeals to the Governor for commutations
or pardons.

I look at those things as coming from human beings
directly to the Governor, and therefore I think I ought
to read them personally. It can be as long as a legal
brief--sometimes they've been to the law library--or a
short handwritten note. I get three a week. Then
there are extraditions; I get 30 to 40 of those a week.

Then there is the paper work from counsel's office,
from the various authority minutes and the 2,000 or so
bills passed in a legislative session. I also have
to decide whether this department or that department
should make a proposal in a particular area, or whether
we as an administration should do something.

For some reason, I get a lot more mail than
Brendan did. I don't know why. I was told he would
get 150 to 200 letters a day. We get 400 to 600, and
sometimes it will average 1,000 letters a day over a
period. No big issue, usually. People recommend
spending cuts, but there's a tremendous misunderstanding
of state revenues. They say you've got to use gambling
revenues to balance the budget, not knowing it's
dedicated to programs for senior citizens and the
handicapped.

PEOPLE WITH PROBLEMS

Most of the mail is just from people with problems.
I believe if someone writes the Governor they should
get an answer, and I'm always disturbed when I go some-
place and a person tells me, "Hey, I wrote you and you
never answered me."

---

*The New York Times, January 29, 1983, p. 26. © 1983
by The New York Times Company. Reprinted by permission.

You get a flurry of mail on an issue like the death penalty or the moment of silence in the classroom, but most of the mail is not legislative. It's from people with individual problems.

People sometimes write just pouring out their heart, saying they don't feel well and they've been to see a doctor and he hasn't found anything wrong with them and they can't sleep at night, so they write the Governor.

I received thousands of letters when I was in the hospital with my back problem, most of it offering advice on how to cure it.

PROBLEMS

We had so many problems, and we tried to attack them one by one. Obviously there was a problem with the prisons. When I came into office, it was a problem that had been simply neglected for the past eight or 10 years.

Everybody recognized the fact that prisons were getting more and more crowded, and the Legislature aggravated the situation by passing bills that put more people into prison--and nobody had planned for the beds. At the time I came into office, judges were releasing prisoners in some cases and putting them back on the streets simply because there was no place for them in the prisons.

We gave it our immediate attention and came up with a six- or seven-point program that included not only the building of cells but also a program for those people who perhaps shouldn't be incarcerated. It included things like intensive probation and parole reform, and it suggested there were other ways of dealing with people who were not violent than putting them in a cell. We've gotten a majority of that package through.

Whether we keep pace with the overcrowding problem depends on whose figures you believe. If the population increase keeps up to the extent that was predicted over the next five years--double the present population --we'll barely keep pace with the problem. If the increase gets any greater, we won't. If the increase is less, of course, we will.

Now I've always worried about building toward those kinds of projections. That's one reason we've gone so heavily into modular facilities. They're temporary. We don't expect them to last more than 10 or 15 years, but we'll get a handle on what these figures mean by then. To build permanent facilities to meet the kind of figures we have now, I'm reluctant to do that.

EXTENT OF BUDGET DIFFICULTIES

Then there was the whole budgetary question. We went around the campaign debating an opponent for six or eight months about what the two of us were going to do and whether we had a $100 million budget problem or a $200 million problem.

We didn't know it was really a $700 million problem. If we knew the fiscal problem was much worse, the debate would have changed, because I said quite clearly--and there was no question--that if the problem was $100 million or $200 million, we could take care of it through efficiencies and economies. But no one envisioned a $700 million problem.

There were two things that happened that increased the problem. The first was that the early Federal budget cuts were supposed to be much smaller than they eventually became. There were things we had to make up--mass transportation, Medicaid--things we feel responsible for that the Federal Government did not make up.

The other thing, of course, was the recession. We had not been hit by the recession as early as the Midwest, but when it hit we lost close to $200 million.

It started hitting in February or March. When we passed the budget finally at the end of last summer, we had a conservative budget that was going to tide us over for the year. Then along about late August, I began to get these nervous blips from the Treasurer saying revenues aren't quite what we anticipated. And by early September, not only was our $50 million-to-$60 million budget surplus gone, but another $30 million to $40 million had begun to disappear. The

economy went down so fast that $100 million disappeared
over a two-month period.

TAXES

The tax solution we finally enacted wasn't what I
proposed. My feeling was strong that we shouldn't
touch a broad-based tax unless we were going to do it
as part of an overall reform of the tax system--the
spending part of the budget as well as the income side.

I think using both the sales and income tax to
solve a short-term problem will make it more difficult
for me to get real reform in the future. There is no
more room in the broad-based taxes. We have a sales
tax that is still competitive, but we can't raise it
again. We have to have a relatively low income tax in
the region, and we're now right on the border.

I was amazed at the legislative position on the
other taxes. It wasn't public resistence to them; it
was the forces that work on the Legislature. No
legislator told me he received any mail against the
alcohol tax. They told me the mail said, if you have
to tax, that's a good one to tax. But the lobbyists
were so strong. The liquor interests are so strong in
the halls of the Legislature that we never even got
started on it. I would much rather have gone in that
direction.

TRANSITION

The vote recount that delayed our transition
caused a tremendous problem. We had very little time
to fill important posts and pick 20 Cabinet managers.
We hired an executive search firm to help fill some
important posts, and when we asked them how long they
took to conduct a search, they said six months. We
had to interview people, asking them to leave their
jobs and join us over the holidays. It was very
difficult. I was preparing a budget without three
Cabinet members in office.

LEGISLATURE

I didn't have a Legislature of my own party, and
that created some problems, particularly when some
people in the Legislature feel the best thing they can

do, politically, is to oppose whatever the Governor proposes. I don't believe it is a wise strategy, but they think it is something that ought to be done, and it has created some difficulties.

I don't think it's possible to have a government without partisanship, and I'm not sure I would even want one. Partisanship is fine, but there's a place for it. There are a good many issues that are not partisan and shouldn't be partisan. And those are things I talked about in my annual message.

If you can pass a bill to bring down insurance costs, that shouldn't be a partisan matter, or pass a law to reform the Civil Service system, or bring jobs into the state, or what have you. My own feeling is the Legislature is going to be judged on whether or not they addressed every area covered in my message.

I remember that some of the most successful things that happened when I was a legislator didn't come out of the administration. They came out of the Legislature. I know that because I did some of them. The largest scholarship program in the state I wrote, the Educational Opportunity Fund. The Coastal Protection Bill was my bill, my idea, and I wrote it with a law student at Rutgers.

These and other things came from the Legislature, including the final form of the state income tax, whether you agreed with it or not.

I think the Legislature will find it's to their best interest to find solutions to some of the state's worst problems. If they are not solved, the public will blame someone, and I'm not running this year. Some problems have been festering too long.

THE STATE'S IMAGE

The Governor has to be a promoter in two ways. He has to go out looking for jobs. I spend a lot of time on the telephone calling company presidents who are thinking of locating in New Jersey. I called one the other day who was making a decision between New Jersey and Connecticut, and I told his secretary it was Governor Kean and she said: "Who are you kidding? Who is this really?"

It's been very effective. We are going to have
some jobs because of the calls. The executives were
surprised, and they believe if I was interested enough
to make the call, now they will be able to reach out
if they come into the state.

The other role is as a promoter for New Jersey.
We've got a lousy image, and it's an image I feel is
totally undeserved. We've got to go out and change
that image and talk about the good things of New
Jersey. And that means talking about two areas.

I tell groups we have a history that's got any of
the New England states beat and nobody knows it.
Washington spent one winter at Valley Forge. So what.
He spent two in New Jersey, and they were tougher
winters. Let's talk about our history. Let's make
New Jersey that kind of tourist area.

And we have the best seacoast in the Northeast,
and we have mountains, and two-thirds of New Jersey is
farms and woods, and nobody knows that about the state.

And, finally, we've got to get over this image
that somehow people in government in New Jersey are
less than honest. Let's face it, it's out there. I
would hope to have an administration that doesn't have
some of the problems that existed in the past. It's
a terrible thing for the state when state senators
get indicted and municipal officials get in trouble.

We have to get over that kind of reputation, and
point out this is a state where government can be run
as cleanly and as well as any state in the country.
It's a state where 99 percent and more of the people
in government are decent and trying to do a good job.
And those are the people we have to feature.

19. Appointments Mixture of Skill, Chance*

Robert de la Vega

Just how do people get appointed to top posts in state government? "There is no sure way in. There is no single way in," said one speaker.

It is good to know the governor, said another, but even better if the governor knows you.

The more than 100 persons who were at the House of Hope Church in Saint Paul for the December 2 CL seminar on the appointments process heard from officials of the Anderson, Perpich, and Quie administrations, as well as a candid talk from Tom Triplett, who is working on Governor-elect Perpich's transition team.

Triplett said the transition team is working on filing the more than 400 key appointments at the same time it is trying to put together a new budget.

For the very top positions, Triplett said, Perpich is looking for generalists, not specialists. The administration will consider non-physicians to run the Department of Health, and nonschool-superintendents to run the Department of Education, he said.

Who is excluded from consideration is just as important as who is included, Triplett said, adding the Perpich team is looking outside the Legislature and the staff of Governor Quie for people. It is vital that the new governor have total confidence in the new people, according to Triplett.

Moving quickly to fill vacancies is important, and the transition team had begun to consider people even before the election, Triplett said.

Although the Perpich team is not using a committee-based system to fill key posts, Triplett said the team is listening to the media, the public, and the legislators about choices for major posts.

*Reprinted with permission from CL News (Citizens League, St. Paul-Minneapolis metropolitan area), Vol. XXXI, No. 25, December 7, 1982, pp. 1 and 4.

Former Supreme Court Justice James Otis asked Triplett what process would be used to name people to the new Appellate Court, adding he was concerned that Perpich would not seek outside advice about selections to the new court. Triplett replied that Perpich will develop his own merit-selection process, and will not use the committee-based system developed by Governor Al Quie. Triplett said the selection group for court appointees may not even have a majority of lawyers on it.

Tom Kelm, former top aide to Governor Wendell Anderson, echoed Triplett's view that the top appointees need to have the complete confidence of the governor. In addition to any qualifications deemed important by outside groups, Kelm said, the ability to work with the governor is crucial.

For the very high-level posts, the open appointments process is "a sham," according to Kelm.

"The open process is the worst process to use at the commissioner level," Kelm said, because top applicants will not apply if their names will become public. Top people do not want their employers to know they are looking for a new job, and do not want anyone to know if they are not selected, he said.

The same is true for the Metropolitan Council, the Pollution Control Agency and metropolitan agency appointments, he said.

The open process was very good for the various advisory boards and committees, Kelm said.

Ronnie Brooks, former special assistant to Rudy Perpich in his previous administration agreed with Kelm.

"The open process may inhibit a strong staff relationship with the governor," she said. The open process is entirely dysfunctional for major, full-time administrative functions, according to Brooks, but works well for judicial, advisory, and rulemaking appointments.

Brooks said the governor chooses people he is comfortable with for those posts which are central to his administration. She cited the post of Commissioner of Labor and Industry as one which had not in the past been seen as especially influential and important, but that in the new Perpich administration is critical because of the importance of the workers compensation issue.

The views of a major constituency is also important in some posts, according to Brooks such as the Commissioner of Finance, an agency which is important to the business community.

There is a "healthy touch of irrationality about the appointments process," Brooks said, and the "kinds of appointments vary quite radically."

In contrast, Jean King, former administrative assistant to Governor Quie, said that administration followed a careful, open process in making virtually all of its appointments. She said Governor Quie liked the process of using selection committees because it was open and because he had been out of state for many years and was not personally familiar with many of the potential office holders.

The open process helped find good people, King said, because it drew in the applications of people who might not have applied otherwise, and because it revealed negative things about a person's history, removing those persons from consideration. Other practical considerations for the open process are that it helps the governor learn about the way state governments works by interviewing many of the applicants, it takes some of the pressure off the governor's staff, and it allows someone other than the governor to say no to applicants, according to King.

On the negative side, the process of using selection committees and openness is time consuming, scares off talented people, and is a strain on the some selection committee members, King said.

Not having many key posts filled during the first weeks of the Legislative session was a real handicap for the Quie administration, King said. She suggested moving the starting date for the Legislature back so that the new governor would have time to select people to run the administration and to work on crucial tasks like developing a budget in the few weeks between the election and the governor's inauguration.

Brooks, Kelm, King and Triplett focussed on the view from the governor's office but Sam Grais, former chairman of Governor Perpich's Appointments Advisory Committee, a member of Governor Quie's Appointments Advisory Committee, and a member in many advisory agencies and committees, took the view of the citizen interested in participating in the appointments process and making it work well.

Hundreds of important part-time posts are filled by gubernatorial appointment, and Grais directed his comments to the selection process for those slots.

Communication skills and local community involvement are important Grais said, but it is critical to have a working knowledge of the subject over which the board or committee will have jurisdiction. Grais said potential applicants should not be worried if they are not chosen quickly. Frequently, those applicants who are not chosen at the time they first apply are chosen later, when new openings occur. He said most boards and committees keep the applications on file once they know the person is interested.

20. Innovations in State Cabinet Systems*

Lydia Bodman
and
Daniel B. Garry

The past two decades have witnessed a dramatic change in the role the nation's governors perform in state management and policy development. An important contributing factor in the enhancement of the governor's power has been the growing phenomenon of a three-tiered cabinet structure--with considerable variation--in the states.

In 1969, only 26 states had cabinets, whereas today, 40 states have incorporated this advisory mechanism into their organizational structure. Cabinets are defined as a system whereby state agency directors are grouped together into an organizational structure to advise the governor and to perform other functions. Membership is usually comprised of those agency and department heads appointed by the governor, but may also include directors who are either elected or appointed by a state board or commission.

In addition to the surge of cabinets in state governments, 25 of the 50 states have established sub-cabinet systems. Under such arrangements, most of which were implemented in the past decade, agency and department heads are assigned to broad issue groups, such as natural resources, human resources or executive management, to provide advice to the governors on management and policy issues and for other purposes.

Subcabinets are not to be confused with task forces which are ad hoc groups generally made up of top resource people and agency and department heads gathered to analyze a specific problem and make recommendations. Following the issuance of a report or assessment, the group generally disbands.

---

*Reprinted with permission from State Government, Vol. LV, No. 3, 1982, pp. 93-97.

These three advisory systems--cabinets, subcabinets and task forces--make up a three-tiered
structure identified by a state census recently conducted by the National Governors' Association Office
of State Services. The responses from this survey on
state cabinet systems, which was completed in February
1982, serve as the foundation for this article on
innovative state management practices. The 52 responses
(American Samoa and Puerto Rico included) were, for the
most part, completed by executive assistants to the
governors and were detailed enough to provide a clear
picture of the changes in state cabinet systems. This
essay will outline the following trends reflected in
the Office of State Services efforts:

. The establishment of cabinets.
. The implementation of subcabinets.
. The formation of ad hoc task forces.

CABINETS

Historically, there has been a dichotomy of views
on cabinet effectiveness. In the 1930s, A.E. Buck
reported that Governors Al Smith and Franklin D.
Roosevelt of New York and Frank Lowden of Illinois had
viewed cabinet meetings as useful. Conversely,
Governor Vic Donahey of Ohio said that cabinet meetings
accomplished nothing. In the NGA publication,
Reflections on Being Governor, former Governors
Michael Dukakis (Massachusetts) and Blair Lee III
(Maryland) spoke enthusiastically about cabinets. Lee
described his cabinet as, "probably the chief source
of both warning, information and help in developing
programs."

Despite these conflicting views on cabinets, more
and more states are reorganizing their structures so as
to accommodate, in some manner, the cabinet mechanism.
In 16 of the 40 states with cabinets, the authorization
for existence is either constitutional or statutory;
13 are created by governor's directive or executive
order; and the remaining have their roots mainly in
tradition or a combination of the above sources.

The NGA State Services census found that the types
of agencies and departments most frequently having
cabinet status are: Corrections and Public Safety (27
states); Administration and Finance (27 states);

Health, Human and Social Services (26 states); Transportation and Public Facilities (25 states); Food and
Agriculture (18 states); Natural Resources (18 states)
and Labor (16 states). Other agencies and departments
having cabinet status range from Education, Economic
Development and General Services to more specific areas
such as Computer Science/Data Processing, Toxic Wastes
and Vocational Rehabilitation. Cabinet size varies
from five to 33 members (with an average of 15 members).
No correlation was found between the size of the cabinet
and the size of the state.

The operational procedures that govern cabinet
meetings vary with regard to meeting frequency,
formality and authority. All 40 states with cabinet
systems conduct meetings at differing time intervals:
18 states hold meetings at the call of the governor;
nine states conduct sessions monthly; eight states hold
meetings weekly or biweekly; three states hold meetings
on an ad hoc basis; and the remaining two states
schedule sessions quarterly or bimonthly. Twenty-four
of these states require mandatory attendance. In terms
of formality, the executive assistants indicated that
most cabinet gatherings have both formal and informal
characteristics. Only three states, Florida, Missouri
and Washington, hold formal meetings where the governor
chairs every meeting and there is a set agenda.

As for cabinet power, the authority is for the
most part advisory in nature, as only five of the 40
states (Colorado, Florida, Illinois, Ohio and Vermont)
have cabinets with binding decision-making authority.
Thus, the advisory feature of cabinet systems dominates
over their legal authority.

The variety of cabinet structures and composition
demonstrates their many forms in the states. One trait
standing apart from these variations is effectiveness.
To determine effectiveness, the purpose and function of
cabinets must be defined. In the states with cabinets,
a third of the executive assistants see the cabinet's
function as an advisory body; eight others see their
cabinet's function as a combination of advisory board,
issues forum and debate mechanism; six others view the
cabinet's main purpose as an issues forum; and the
remaining executive assistants varied with their
responses. Judging from the survey comments, the state
cabinets appear to fulfill the above responsibilities

and thus provide an effective form of government organization.

Several governors' assistants expounded on the strengths and weaknesses of cabinet systems. An assistant to Arkansas Governor Frank White maintained the strengths are that a cabinet "provides for a forum for comprehensive views of state government; enables the governor to act with a broad range of advice available to him and provides direct communication with key offices." Speaking about the weaknesses, the same assistant said a cabinet system is "often unwieldly, fragmented and slow to respond." A problem faced by many states as they attempt to use cabinet government was voiced by an assistant to Governor John Carlin of Kansas who said: "The only weakness of the cabinet system is that all aspects of state government are not under the governor's control and consequently are not represented on the cabinet; for example, education, agriculture and legal matters." One of South Dakota Governor William Janklow's assistants also pointed out the pros and cons by commenting that: "The strength of cabinets is that it allows the governor's directives to be adjusted if necessary to meet governmental constraints while still allowing for implementation. The weakness is that division and program managers do not participate in decision-making (at cabinet meetings)." Despite these underlying weaknesses, the successes of cabinets outweigh the weaknesses as exemplified by the number of states establishing these advisory bodies.

States dissatisfied with their cabinet systems should bear in mind a quote from the chief of staff to New Hampshire Governor Hugh Gallen who commented that: "If other governors have cabinets and complain, tell them it could be worse--it could be like our government (where 132 agencies report directly to the Governor) and not have any cabinet at all."

Several states, among them Delaware and North Carolina, have had great success with their innovative practice of holding cabinet retreats. The chief executive assistant to Delaware Governor Pierre du Pont describes the purpose of cabinet retreats as a way to:

. . . impress upon cabinet secretaries, whose ordinary priorities involve the

operation of a department, that they are
part of decision-making process for all
state issues. The collegiality developed
at these cabinet retreats significantly
contributes to inter-departmental cooperation as well as cooperation between the
Executive Office and the various cabinet
departments.

In North Carolina, Governor James Hunt conducts
day-long cabinet retreats semi-annually. These
meetings, away from the political arena and daily
pressures, are designed to exchange information,
discuss short- and long-term goals of the administration and of each department and to supplement team-
building on a continuing basis.

In the survey responses, many states cited jealous
agencies, limited follow-through, lack of accountability
and the cabinets' fragmentation as weaknesses of the
first tier structure. Both cabinets and cabinet
retreats attempt to alleviate these apparent faults
of the system.

SUBCABINETS

Recently, the most prevalent trend in state
cabinet systems is the development of subcabinets,
otherwise referred to as cabinet subgroups or the
second tier of the decision-making structure. In an
era of complex problems when decisions are no longer
straightforward, the need for continuous, broad issue
groups to advise the governors, improve communications
between agencies and marshall resources is evident.
Since 1971, 25 states have established groups of agency
and department heads aligned by broad issues, such as
management streamlining government (eight states),
criminal and criminal justice (five states), block
grants (four states), fiscal policy (three states),
economic development (three states), social services
(two states) and emergency management (two states), to
name a few. Authorization for these groups is based
primarily on executive orders or other gubernatorial
actions and directives in all but five states.

It appears that the major strengths of the subgroup system are the ability to: (1) zero in on major
issues--the "big ticket" items--with the key state

government actors; (2) improved coordination; (3) re-
align membership--adding new members as needed--
depending on current issues on the docket. Several
governors' assistants discussed the importance of subcabinet groups. The following are a sample of those
comments:

    . Idaho Governor John Evans is a strong supporter
of the subcabinet form of government and one of his
assistants said the most effective use of subgroups is
for "specific recommendations on narrowly defined
issues." He went on to say the subgroup system is
more useful than the cabinet as a whole because "small
groups are able to focus better."

    . An assistant to Illinois Governor James Thompson
said, "The main strength of the subcabinet system is
that there is a regular meeting at which agency
directors are able to converse about problems which
cut across agency lines or which potentially impact on
other agencies. It is a way that directors see problems
from a broader perspective than that of their own
agency and in which they become comfortable with one
another. . . . Directors have been questioned about the
use of the subcabinet system and uniformly believe
that, at the very least, the subcabinet system offers
them an opportunity to meet face to face on a monthly
basis and talk about any problems which may be con-
fronting the agencies collectively or individually."

    . An assistant to Iowa Governor Robert Ray said
subgroups of the cabinet are more effective than
cabinets, "because cabinets are so diffused in their
composition, they find it difficult to focus on a
problem. Cabinets would have to use 'subgroups' to
deal with particular problems." Additionally, he said
a key ingredient to the successful use of cabinet subgroups is to have "clearly defined, specific goals to
be accomplished or questions to be answered."

    . Speaking of the strengths of cabinet subgroups,
the assistant to Michigan Governor William Milliken
said such a system "gets relevant department heads
around a table on common issues." He added that subgroups were generally more beneficial than the cabinet.

    Areas of weakness cited by governors' offices
centered around large membership of subcabinets which

may be counter-productive and individual time commitments which may be too limited to allow full devotion to issues. The director of Government Operations for Governor Thompson stated that, "the weakness of the system is that frequently agencies are concerned about more immediate, pressing problems of their own administration of policy and find the more general policy discussions, surrounding broader issues, frustrating." The same comment was made of cabinet systems. Despite any weaknesses, a strong plurality--22 of 25 states-- said that the strengths of the subcabinet system far outweigh the weaknesses.

A number of states employ subgroups to deal with day-to-day administrative issues and problems that affect two or more agencies of state government. In this manner, the subgroup becomes the vehicle for focusing the collective wisdom of several agencies or department heads on a particularly difficult issue. Solutions will in turn, it is hoped, develop as a result of this debate. Finally, some states have experimented with using cabinet subgroups as a key component of their long-range planning activities.

Instead of further generalizing about the gamut of subcabinets, the following describes some of the state experiences. Governor George Ariyoshi of Hawaii has established subcabinets which include people from the private sector and individuals whose interests and expertise are essential to address problems and issues in the state. The Governor's Agriculture Coordinating Committee, for example, includes 10 members: the Special Assistant for Agriculture, the Director of Planning and Economic Development, the Chairpersons of the Board of Land and Natural Resources, the Board of Agriculture and of the Hawaiian Homes Commission, the Director of Transportation, the Dean of the College of Tropical Agriculture and three farmers. By including this diversity of experts and experienced persons in the subgroup, the Governor is not only enhancing the knowledge behind his policy-making, but simultaneously enriching the credibility of his policies to the public. This type of public involvement may become increasingly important in the future when cooperation and understanding between the public and private sectors is lacking.

The arrangement which Maine Governor Joseph Brennan

uses seems to represent a balance between the cabinets and subcabinets. His assistant made the following comments concerning their system:

> I would say that our cabinet meetings are used largely as a forum for airing problems, announcing policy and coordinating efforts on various issues. The full cabinet is not used as a policy developing or review group, primarily because of its size (approximately 20 members). The Governor feels that this is simply too large a group for the type of free discussion which is necessary for developing good policy.

In accordance with this view, Governor Brennan established a Human Resources subcabinet to deal with issues concerning health, human services and education. This is the only subcabinet group in Maine, although the cabinet format is used on an ad hoc basis to deal with specific problems or policy issues. Once again, Governor Brennan's assistant comments that, "the smaller groups work much better for policy development and can be given finite goals so that its meetings do not last forever." On the whole, this system has saved time for the individual members and introduced efficiency into the system.

Policy-oriented subcabinets are also found in states such as Idaho, Illinois and South Dakota. Each of these states has cabinet subgroups relating to the four areas of Executive Management, Economic Affairs (titled Economic Development and Employment in Illinois), Human Resources/Services and Natural Resources. In all three states, the use of these subcabinets is seen to be more effective than using the cabinet as a whole; although in Illinois, the four groups are effective in different areas. As reported by Governor Thompson's assistant: "The Management Sub-cabinet is most effective in implementation of policy; whereas the Natural Resources Subcabinet is most effective in conflict resolution among the agencies; and the Human Services Subcabinet is most effective in policy development."

Oklahoma views their system as oriented more toward management, rather than policy. The chief of staff for Governor George Nigh gave a brief description of the theory behind their "Mini-Cabinets:"

> The Governor's Mini-cabinets are management
> communication forums. . . . Through these
> meetings, communication can be improved by
> allowing the Governor to inform departments
> of his philosophies, his goals and objec-
> tives for all state government; allowing
> department administrators to inform the
> Governor of problem areas affecting their
> operations and/or ability to assist the
> Governor's efforts; and, providing a forum
> for discussion of specific programs or of
> broad philosophical concern affecting
> participating departments. . . . Experience
> with the mini-cabinets has proven validity
> of the theory, evidenced by examples of
> improved coordination, eliminated duplication,
> clarification or resolution of overlapping
> responsibilities, conflicting objectives,
> competition, etc. . . . . The mini-cabinets
> are not intended to replace the Governors'
> traditional liaison to an agency, but to
> supplement that communications linkage
> between the Governor and the department.

Vermont, on the other hand, has a development subgroup that meets for lunch every month. An agenda is
set up for the meeting by the State Planning Director
who assigns follow-up tasks for the group after the
meeting has concluded.

The states' experiences mentioned above show how
they use cabinet subgroups for different purposes:
policy-making, enhanced communications and improved
management capacity. With these functions, subgroups
become vehicles for efficiency in state government.

TASK FORCES

The third level of management tool is the task
force. In general, governors form these groups to deal
with one specific issue (youth unemployment, for
example) and then terminate their existence after the
issuance of a final report. Several combinations of
task force membership are possible: (1) citizens at
large; (2) agency heads or cabinet secretaries; or
(3) citizens and agency heads. Eight states, including

Nebraska, New Mexico, Utah and Kentucky use ad hoc task forces to manage block grant implementation and to prepare for disasters. Missouri, for instance, uses task forces to confront problems regarding block grants, mental health delivery, soil erosion and droughts. Governor Bond's assistant highlighted the success of the task force on block grants comprised of all departments having responsibility for a grant. Suggestions made by each department were by-and-large incorporated in plans used by other departments. These groups also tended to reinforce decisions made by individual departments concerning how to approach interest groups and assign priorities. As with cabinet subgroups, task forces are a good way for department directors to see that others have the same problem they do.

In a recent speech, Governor Milliken (Michigan) spoke of his success with a High Technology Task Force, created early last year, and comprised of business, education and government leaders. The governor reported that: "the task force is coordinating efforts of industry, state government and the academic community to achieve a greater high technology base for Michigan. It identifies both robotics and molecular biology as initial target industries for our new high technology development efforts." A task force in this situation, as in others, is preferable to an established subgroup due to the nature and timeliness of the issue.

CONCLUSION

Since 1965, the multi-tiered cabinet structure has for the most part replaced the large, one-tiered cabinet system. This pattern is exemplified by the fact that one-third of the states have established the full three-tiered cabinet structure, while one-third have two-tiered systems of either a cabinet supplemented by task forces (as in 13 states) or a cabinet and subcabinet combination (as in four states). There are only four states (Alabama, Arkansas, California and Florida) that depend solely on their cabinets for policy and administrative advice.

Of the 10 states without cabinets, five form ad hoc task forces when necessary; three depend on subcabinets and task forces and the two remaining states use a boards and commissions system.

Thus, in an era when increased demands are being placed on the states, the prevalent trends towards two- and three-tiered cabinet systems are designed to improve management capabilities and increase efficiency of state government.

21.   Rebirth of the Item Veto in the Empire State*

Joseph F. Zimmerman

A 1980 decision of the New York Court of Appeals--
County of Oneida v. Berle--has reactivated the item
veto, a device first adopted in 1874 to protect the
governor against legislative riders attached to
appropriation bills. The item veto allows the governor
to reject individual items in appropriation bills and
protect the public purse. This power first was
exercised by Governor Samuel J. Tilden in 1875 and
1876 when he disallowed 64 items totaling $705,865.
Between 1875 and 1931, New York governors disallowed
4,155 items.

Following the 1929 establishment by constitutional
amendment of New York's executive budget system, the
number of items vetoed decreased noticeably. Governor
Franklin D. Roosevelt, battling a legislative challenge
to the heart of the executive budget system, disallowed
275 items totaling $55,439,937 in 1929. In 1930, he
struck out 172 items totaling $12,258,734, but by 1932
he vetoed only two items totaling $211,000.

Governor Thomas E. Dewey, between 1943 and 1954,
vetoed only two items totaling $11,500, and Governor
Averill Harriman disallowed only three items totaling
$32,000 between 1955 and 1958. Throughout his 14-
year tenure in office, Governor Nelson A. Rockefeller
disallowed only eight items totaling $30,521,000. His
veto of two items in 1973 resulted from a policy disagreement with the legislature rather than a decision
that the items were unneeded. The legislature had
shifted two items of the appropriation for the state
university to the appropriation for the State Department of Education.

The decline in use of the item veto in New York
in the early 1930s and its relative disuse since then

---

*Reprinted with permission from State Government, Vol.
LIV, No. 2, 1981, pp. 51-52

are due to the executive budget system, which gave the
governor complete charge of budget administration and
let him impound appropriated funds during the interim
between legislative sessions. Even impoundment of
appropriated funds during the annual legislative
session was not challenged by the legislature, which
apparently assumed that the state constitution made
the governor completely responsible for overseeing the
expenditure of appropriated funds. In 1980, however,
the challenge by local governments of the governor's
power to impound appropriations was successful. The
result was the immediate resurrection of the item veto
as an important tool in the arsenal of weapons employed
by the governor to defend his fiscal program against
legislative extravagance in the form of items added or
increased as the result of log-rolling.

COUNTY OF ONEIDA v. BERLE

Governor Hugh L. Carey included in his 1977 executive budget a $12 million item for the sewage works
reimbursement program. Believing that the item was too
small, the legislature added $14 million, which the
governor did not veto. However, the director of the
Division of the Budget in 1976 "froze" $7 million of
the appropriation.

The local government petitioners maintained that
they had been "improperly denied state reimbursement
for the operation and maintenance of sewage treatment
works," and the Court of Appeals agreed.

The state budget director argued that the governor
has a constitutional obligation throughout the fiscal
year to maintain a balanced budget and consequently
possesses the implied power to impound appropriated
funds. The director also argued that the appropriation
act granted him discretionary authority to reduce
appropriations.

In the opinion of the court, the governor lacks
the constitutional power to impound funds and has a
responsibility only to propose and not to maintain a
balanced budget. In an earlier case--Wein v. Carey,
41 N.Y. 2d 498 at 504--the court stressed that "it is
unattainable for any budget plan, perfectly and
honestly balanced in advance, to remain in balance to
the end of the year." The court added that the

executive branch is not required to raise additional
revenues to maintain a balanced budget and obviously
lacks the unilateral power to reduce an appropriation
item.

Contrary to the budget director's contention that
the appropriation act allowed him to reduce payments,
the court quoted the mandatory directive language in
Section 17-1905(2) of the Environmental Conservation
Law: "Within the limits of the annual appropriation
made by the Legislature, the Commissioner shall
apportion and approve for payment state assistance to
each municipality which . . . is responsible for
operations and maintenance of sewage treatment
works. . . ."

The court held that the governor and his budget
director must execute every item in an appropriation
bill unless the governor vetoes items and the vetoes
are upheld or unless the courts invalidate the items.

As long as the governor was free to impound funds,
there was no need to veto appropriation items unless
the governor wished to deliver a public rebuff to the
legislature or the sponsors of the items. Since the
governor needs the active cooperation and good will of
the legislature, the impoundment of appropriated funds,
which receives relatively little publicity, is
preferable to an open confrontation with the legislature in the form of item vetoes. Almost immediately
following the court decision, Governor Carey vetoed
158 items, totaling $240 million in the 1981 executive
budget appropriation bill.

GUBERNATORIAL-LEGISLATIVE COOPERATION

New York can boast of a long-standing policy of
gubernatorial-legislative cooperation. The senate
sends bills to the governor on Thursdays to allow him
an extra day--Sundays are not counted--to analyze bills
during the 10-day bill consideration period, and the
governor sends, at the request of legislative leaders,
"Messages of Necessity" suspending the three-day aging
requirement for bills.

The state constitution--Article VII, Section 1--
provides for cooperative gubernatorial-legislative
relations in the appropriations process by directing

222

the governor to furnish copies of the budget requests
of departments and agencies to the legislature's fiscal
committees and by entitling the committees to attend
the hearings on budget requests held by the governor.

In approving the governor's budgets, the legislature makes modified "lump sum" appropriations which
are segregated by the Division of the Budget.   In
addition, the legislature often authorizes the governor
to impound appropriations.   To provide added flexibility
in budget execution, the State Finance Law authorizes
a department or agency with the approval of the
Director of the Budget to transfer funds with the
limitation "that the total amount appropriated for any
program or purpose may not be increased or decreased
by more than five percent."

CONCLUSIONS

Prospects are slim that the New York State Constitution will be amended to place the governor
completely in charge of budget execution.   The legislature, however, may decide that some additional
flexibility in budget execution is desirable and may
adopt an impoundment control procedure similar to the
federal procedure under which the president must report
impoundments to the Congress, which may vote to override the impoundments.

No legislative action is anticipated in the near
future to adopt an impoundment control procedure.   But
the governor likely will employ the item veto more
frequently in the immediate future to disallow items
or increases in items he has recommended.   Of course,
the item veto in fact may not be used often if the
threat of its use--the gun behind the door--is
sufficient to convince the legislature to accept the
governor's spending limits, thereby protecting the
integrity of his fiscal program against what he deems
the extravagance of the legislature.

22. PARTY REPRESENTATION ON STATE SUPREME COURTS
"UNEQUAL REPRESENTATION" REVISITED*

Francis Graham Lee

The events of the past twenty years have radically
transformed the face of American politics. They have
eliminated many traditional notions concerning political behavior and changed countless others to such an
extent as to render them almost unrecognizable.[1] Out
of the process, new trends are gradually taking shape
that in all probability will give order and meaning to
the politics of the future.

In the meantime the changes that have already
occurred have had considerable impact upon American
political life. Among the developments that seem for
the present most important are the gradual but steady
erosion of Republican strength in the states of northern New England and the Midwest and the almost simultaneous breakup of the once "Solid South." The result
has been an appreciable decline in the number of one-
party or "safe" states. The causes for these changes
are many. A sharp falling-off in traditional voter
loyalty to political parties, the diminishing role
played by the race issue in southern politics, and the
increasing urbanization and industrialization of what
were until very recently primarily rural states are
surely among the major reasons.

Whatever the cause, however, the consequences for
state politics have been dramatic. Republican governors have been elected in Arkansas, Florida, and
Virginia, and Democratic chief executives have been
elected in such formerly Republican bastions as Vermont, Maine, and North Dakota. Similar shifts in
congressional and state legislative voting have also
been apparent of late in these states.

EARLY RESEARCH ON THE PARTISAN MAKE-UP OF
STATE SUPREME COURTS

The goal of this article is to determine the
degree to which these changes have affected the political complexion of state appellate courts of last

*Reprinted from State and Local Government Review, Vol.
XI, No. 2, May 1979, pp. 48-52 by permission of the
Institute of Government, University of Georgia.

224

resort, courts that have assumed increasing importance as the United States Supreme Court under the leadership of Warren Burger has tended toward a more conservative line and given greater leeway to the states and to the state judiciaries in particular (9). Writing in the *Journal of the American Judicature Society* in 1961, Stuart Nagel reported that despite overall figures showing the numbers of Republican and Democratic judges approximately equal, state by state analysis showed that most courts were under one-party control. Few Republicans sat on southern supreme courts--southern defined by Nagel as all the slave-holding states in 1860 plus the Oklahoma territory--and almost as few Democrats held posts on the highest courts of the remaining states (7, p. 63). By the mid-sixties, the situation had changed only a little. In a survey of the 479 judges who served on state supreme courts during the period 1961-68, Bradley Canon was able to identify the party affiliation of 300. (An additional 2 were classified as Independents.) Of the 300, Democrats outnumbered Republicans by about a 3:2 ratio (60.8 percent to 39.2 percent), an advantage that can be attributed largely to the former's near monopoly of southern courts (2, p. 34). Only two Republicans were to be found on southern courts, both on the Florida bench.

The vast majority of states employ methods of judicial selection that are open to some degree of political manipulation. Only eleven states use the Missouri or A.B.A. Plan whereby the governor fills judicial vacancies based on nominations from a nonpartisan committee: the others either elect their judges (by partisan or nonpartisan ballot), vest the appointment power in the governor (subject generally to senate approval), or allow the state legislature to choose the judges. It would be very surprising to find that the developments that so altered other aspects of state politics had no effect upon the judiciary and that the earlier findings of Nagel and Canon remain unchanged.

PARTY REPRESENTATION ON STATE SUPREME COURTS IN THE SEVENTIES

In 1973 there were 322 judges sitting on the fifty state supreme courts. Using both national and regional editions of *Who's Who* (11), various state government manuals (the most helpful being that of Ohio (8)), and

the *Directory of American Judges* (3), it was possible to
determine the party affiliation of 240 judges.
Questionnaires were sent to the remaining jurists.
The response from this mailing was excellent, furnish-
ing additional evidence to support Becker's claim as to
the rich possibilities of judicial interviewing (1).
Sixty-two of the judges who replied gave their party
affiliation.

Another step was necessary to determine the
partisan allegiance of the remaining 20 jurists who
either failed to reply, refused to give any information, or claimed that by state law they were required
to be independent or nonpartisan. Letters were sent to
the political editor of the state capital's largest
daily and to the United States senators from the
judge's state. This last step, combined with those
described above, produced positive party identification
for all judges as either Democrats, Republicans, or
Independents. Only 5 of the 322 fell into the latter
category, confirming once more the hypothesis that the
more politically active people are the more likely they
are to belong to a political party (5, pp. 54-5).

The events that have taken place since the publication of the Nagel article appear to have had
considerable impact upon the party composition of state
supreme courts. The number of Democrats has increased
sharply. Indeed, it is possible that the differences
in Democratic strength between 1955 and 1973 might be
even greater than indicated in Table 1.

The reasoning for this is as follows: Nagel
reported 33 judges for whom no party preference was
given in any of the sources he consulted (7, p. 63).
Though some of these judges were undoubtedly Independents, it seems likely that the vast majority of those
unidentified jurists were either Democrats or Republicans. It is also very possible, despite findings on
judicial role perception reported by Kenneth Vines
(10, pp. 478-82), that Republicans are more apt to view
the judicial role as foreclosing to them any type of
political party activity, even mere membership, and
thus are more likely than Democrats to refuse to state
their party affiliation. In this regard, it is useful
to note that of the 20 judges for whom no information
was available in the published sources consulted and

226

TABLE 1

Party Affiliation of State Supreme Court Justices

Party	Number		Percentage of Total		Percentage of Democrats and Republicans	
	1955[a]	1973[b]	1955	1973	1955	1973
Democratic	153	195	50	61	56	62
Republican	118	122	39	38	44	38
Independent		5		1		
No party given in the sources consulted	33		11			
Totals	304	322	100	100	100	100

[a]All statistics for 1955 in this and following tables are taken from Stuart Nagel, "Unequal Party Representation on the State Supreme Courts," Journal of the American Judicature Society 45 (1961): 62.

[b]This article's 1973 statistics include Alaska and Hawaii. Their inclusion, however, does not alter any of the above percentage by more than 1 percent.

who either did not reply to the questionnaire or claimed they were forbidden by state law to engage in party activity, 12 turned out to be Republicans, 7 Democrats and 1 Independent. If somewhat the same ratio held for the 33 judges for whom Nagel was unable to ascertain party identification (or the 177 in the Canon study), this would significantly increase the percentage of Republican judges serving on the bench in 1955 (or in the sixties) and make the Democratic inroads of recent years that much more dramatic.

As was true in 1955, many of the state courts remained under one party domination in 1973. Nagel had found twenty-five states--fourteen in the South and eleven in the rest of the nation--that had no members of the minority party serving on their supreme court in 1955. By 1973 this had changed significantly, as shown in Table 2.

TABLE 2

State by State Party Affiliation of State
Supreme Court Justices, 1955 and 1973

	SOUTH[a]				
	1955[b]		1973		
State	Dem.	Rep.	Dem.	Rep.	Ind.
Alabama	7	0	9	0	0
Arkansas	5	0	7	0	0
Delaware	1	2	2	1	0
Florida	7	0	6	1	0
Georgia	7	0	6	1	0
Kentucky	6	0	5	2	0
Louisiana	6	0	7	0	0
Maryland	3	2	9	1	0
Mississippi	8	0	9	0	0
Missouri	4	2	5	2	0
N. Carolina	7	0	7	0	0
Oklahoma	9	0	8	1	0
S. Carolina	5	0	5	0	0
Tennessee	5	0	5	0	0
Texas	9	0	9	0	0
Virginia	6	0	6	1	0
W. Virginia	5	0	4	1	0
Totals Raw	100	6	109	11	0
Percent	94%	6%	91%	9%	0%
	NON-SOUTH				
Alaska	–	–	4	1	0
Arizona	5	0	2	3	0
California	2	2	3	4	0
Colorado	3	4	2	5	0
Connecticut	3	2	1	5	0
Hawaii	–	–	4	1	0
Idaho	1	3	2	3	0

continued on next page

228

TABLE 2--continued

	1955[b]		1973		
State	Dem.	Rep.	Dem.	Rep.	Ind.
Illinois	2	5	4	3	0
Indiana	0	4	2	3	0
Iowa	0	9	4	5	0
Kansas	0	7	2	5	0
Maine	1	5	3	3	0
Massachusetts	2	5	2	5	0
Michigan	2	6	6	1	0
Minnesota	1	4	0	5	2
Montana	2	1	5	2	0
Nebraska	2	5	2	5	0
Nevada	0	1	4	1	0
New Hampshire	2	3	2	3	0
New Jersey	3	2	4	3	0
New Mexico	4	0	5	0	0
New York	5	2	2	5	0
North Dakota	1	3	0	5	0
Ohio	2	4	2	5	0
Oregon	2	5	1	6	0
Pennsylvania	2	5	3	5	0
Rhode Island	3	2	3	2	0
South Dakota	0	4	2	3	0
Utah	3	1	2	2	1
Vermont	0	5	0	5	0
Washington	0	4	5	3	1
Wisconsin	0	5	3	4	0
Wyoming	0	2	2	1	1
Totals					
Raw	53	112	86	111	5
Percent	32%	68%	43%	55%	2%

[a]South is defined as all of the slave-holding states in 1860 plus the Oklahoma territory.

[b]Nagel's data for 1955 do not include a state by state breakdown of judges who could not be classified as either Republicans or Democrats.

Only eleven states were now one party and eight of these were located in the South.

SOME CONCLUDING OBSERVATIONS ON PARTY
REPRESENTATION ON STATE SUPREME COURTS

The nationalization of the two-party system has
clearly not benefited the parties equally. Though
Republicans have scored breakthroughs in many parts of
the old Confederacy, these successes seem limited to
the major statewide offices and seats in the United
States House of Representatives. On the other hand,
while the Democratic party seems generally to have lost
ground in the South, such losses have not really
affected their hold on the state judiciary, minor
statewide posts, or local political offices. Data
showing changes in percentage of congressional vote and
number of supreme court justices for the Democratic
party are shown in Table 3. The percentage of Democrats on southern state supreme courts in 1973 was off

TABLE 3

Congressional Vote Compared with Supreme Court
Representation, 1955 and 1973

	Democratic Percentage of Congressional Vote		Democratic Percentage of Supreme Court Justices	
	1954	1972	1955	1973
South	76	62	94	91
Non-South	47	49	32	43

by only 3 percentage points from 1955. The story for
the rest of the country is quite different. Democrats
have increased the percentage of seats they hold on
nonsouthern courts by 11 percent. Having constituted
only 32 percent of the judges identified as either
Republican or Democratic in 1955, they made up fully 43
percent of the judges in 1973.

The underrepresentation of the Republican party on
southern courts becomes even more glaring when examined
from the perspective of the votes Republicans received
in southern congressional contests. The GOP took 38
percent of the vote in southern congressional races in
1972; it held only 9 percent of the seats on the
supreme courts of these same states. By contrast, the

Democrats had 43 percent of the slots on nonsouthern
supreme courts, a figure that more or less reflected
the 49 percent of the vote they picked up in the 1972
congressional elections in these same states.

Though much lower than the 1955 figures, it is
well to note that more than a fifth of the nation's
state supreme courts still do not have two-party representation. Nagel, in his 1961 article, proposed three
possible solutions: redistricting of judicial districts, the adoption of some form of proportional
voting, and bipartisan appointments. Though little
real progress appears to have been made in any of these
directions--the United States Supreme Court for
instance has refused even to review lower court
decisions upholding judicial election schemes that
clearly run afoul of the "one man, one vote" rule
(4, p. 43)--it should be pointed out that of the eleven
states that employed some variant of the Missouri or
A.B.A. Plan for selecting their judges, only one fell
into the one-party category. Of the ten other states,
nine had at least two judges from the minority party on
their high court. If, as Nagel contended, "promoting
party balance on the state courts, particularly the
state supreme courts, should be as high on the judicial
reform agenda as promoting party balance on the federal
courts" (7, p. 67), the use of the Missouri or A.B.A.
Plan for choosing judges might provide a possible means
for moving the states in this direction.

REFERENCES

1. Becker, Theodore. "Surveys and Judiciaries or
    Who's Afraid of the Purple Curtain." Law and
    Society Review 1 (1966) 133.

2. Canon, Bradley C. "Characteristics and Career
    Patterns of State Supreme Court Justices." State
    Government (1972) 39.

3. Directory of American Judges (Chicago: American
    Directories Corp., 1953).

4. Martin, Philip L. "The Courts and Reapportionment:
    The Exemption of Judicial Elections." Kentucky Law
    Journal 62 (1973-74): 43.

5. Milbrath, Lester. Political Participation
    (Chicago: Rand McNally, 1976).

6. Nagel, Stuart S. "Political Party Affiliation and Judges' Decisions." American Political Science Review 55 (1961): 843.

7. _____. "Unequal Party Representation on the State Supreme Courts." Journal of the American Judicature Society, 45 (1961): 63.

8. Ohio Official Roster of Federal, State, County Officials. (Columbus, 1972).

9. Porter, Mary Cornelia. "State Supreme Courts and the Legacy of the Warren Court." Paper presented at the 1977 annual meeting of the A.P.S.A., Washington, D.C.

10. Vines, Kenneth. "The Judicial Role in American States," in Frontiers of Judicial Research edited by Joel Grossman and Joseph Tannenhaus. (New York: John Wiley and Sons, 1969).

11. Who's Who in America 37 (Chicago: Marquis, 1972); Who's Who in the East 13 (Chicago: Marquis, 1973); Who's Who in the Midwest 12 (Chicago: Marquis, 1972); Who's Who in the South and Southwest 13 (Chicago: Marquis); Who's Who in the West 13 (Chicago: Marquis, 1973).

23.   THE ROLE OF THE
            SMALL-CLAIMS COURT*

"There is no country in the world in which
the doing of justice is burdened by such heavy
overhead charges...The delays of litigation, the
badly adjusted machinery, and the technicalities
of procedure cause an enormous waste of time."

A comment on today's judicial system? No,
it's a 1916 statement by Elihu Root, former
president of the American Bar Association. Things
may not have improved much since then. But one
good sign is that the small-claims court has
endured since 1913 as an alternative to the "badly
adjusted machinery" of the formal court.

A small-claims court is not so much a place
as a simple way of settling minor civil (noncrim-
inal) disputes. The cases are minor only in dollar
terms. The plaintiff (the person suing) asks for
money compensation for harm allegedly caused by
the defendant (the person sued), and there's a
dollar limit on the amount the plaintiff can ask
for. The limit varies from state to state.

An effective small-claims court system is
important to consumers because it provides a simple
and inexpensive way to have a complaint fairly
judged by an impartial third party.

Small-claims courts are usually divisions of
general courts, such as county, city, or district
courts. They can also be divisions of courts administered by justices of the peace. As in the general

---

courts, a case in a small-claims court is an "adversary proceeding." That is, the plaintiff and the defendant are each required to present the appropriate facts and their arguments to a judge. The difference is that the small-claims proceeding is much less formal and the judge plays a more active role.

The basic idea is to keep the procedure so simple that neither party will have to hire a lawyer. In fact, in nine states, lawyers aren't allowed to participate in small-claims proceedings.

HOW THE COURTS WORK

The first small-claims court was in Cleveland. Today, variations on the original can be found in almost every state.

A comprehensive study of small-claims courts was published in 1978 by the National Center for State Courts (NCSC), a nonprofit organization dedicated to improving state and local courts. According to the NCSC report, about three-fourths of the states have statewide small-claims court systems. The key provisions of state laws are summarized in the table /on the following pages7.

The NCSC study focused on courts in 15 metropolitan areas throughout the United States. The state laws and the courts were quite different from one another, but the researchers were nevertheless able to provide information on how, in general, the courts work:

Judges. Most small-claims judges are on temporary assignment from the parent court. Typically, a judge might spend every tenth week in small-claims court.

Because the procedures in small-claims courts and formal courts are different, the judges have to be fairly flexible. For example, in a formal court, it's up to the opposing lawyers to look up the relevant law and show how it applies to the case.

234

How small-claims courts vary

State	Claim limit	Informal proceeding?	Can lawyers participate?
Alabama	$500	Yes	Yes
Alaska	1000	Yes	Yes
Arizona [A]	999.99	No	Yes
Arkansas [B]	300 [C]	Yes	Yes
California	750	Yes	No
Colorado	500	Yes	No
Connecticut	750	Yes	Yes
Delaware [A]	1500	Yes	Yes
District of Columbia	750	Yes	Yes
Florida	2500	Yes	Yes
Georgia	300	Yes	Yes
Hawaii	300	Yes	Yes
Idaho	500	Yes	No
Illinois	1000	Yes	Yes [D]
Indiana	3000	Yes	Yes
Iowa	1000	Yes	Yes
Kansas	300	Yes	No
Kentucky	500	Yes	Yes
Louisiana	300	Yes	Yes
Maine	800	Yes	Yes
Maryland	500	Yes	Yes
Massachusetts	400	Yes	Yes
Michigan	300	Yes	No
Minnesota	1000	Yes	No
Mississippi [A]	500	Yes	Yes
Missouri	500	Yes	Yes
Montana [A]	1500	Yes	Yes

[A] No separate small-claims court.
[B] Small-claims court not statewide.
[C] $100 if nonbusiness
[D] Except in Cook County

State	Claim limit	Informal proceeding?	Can lawyers participate?
Nebraska	$ 500	Yes	No
Nevada	300	Yes	Yes
New Hampshire	500	Yes	Yes
New Jersey	500	Yes	Yes
New Mexico [B]	2000	Yes	Yes
New York	1000	Yes	Yes
North Carolina [A]	500	No	Yes
North Dakota	500	Yes	Yes
Ohio	300	Yes	Yes
Oklahoma	600	Yes	Yes
Oregon	500	Yes	No
Pennsylvania	1000	Yes	Yes
Rhode Island	300	Yes	Yes
South Carolina [B]	3000	Yes	Yes
South Dakota	1000	No	Yes
Tennessee [A]	3000	No	Yes
Texas	150	Yes	Yes
Utah	200	Yes	Yes
Vermont	250	Yes	Yes
Virginia [A]	5000	No	Yes
Washington	300	Yes	No
West Virginia [A]	1500	No	Yes
Wisconsin	500	Yes	Yes
Wyoming	200	Yes	Yes

The judge plays a relatively passive role. But in
a small-claims court, if the plaintiff and defendant aren't represented by lawyers, the judge has
to interrogate both parties to elicit the facts.
If one side is represented by a lawyer, the judge
may have to protect the other party from the consequences of not having a lawyer. To play this role
properly, the judge needs to be well versed in
consumer law.

     In a few courts, some or all of the cases are
heard by arbitrators--lawyers, for the most part,
who have been trained to assume the judge's role.
For example, during a typical small-claims session
in a New York City court, cases are divided among
a judge and seven or eight arbitrators. Cases
are assigned to arbitrators only with the consent
of both parties.

     Judges and arbitrators obviously have a lot
of control over the trial, which raises the question of whether the outcome will be fair. The NCSC
report noted, "It was our subjective impression
that most judges are able to achieve fair and even-
handed results even though their trial practices
differed widely."

     Burden of proof. Most judges follow the
"preponderance of evidence" rule. They often explain the rule by comparing it to a set of balance
scales, with the plaintiff's evidence on one side
and the defendant's on the other. The plaintiff
wins only if his or her evidence is heavier.

     Plaintiffs and defendants. Although cor-
porations and associations are excluded from some
courts, the NCSC researchers found that about
half of the plaintiffs in the 15 courts were
businesses, as opposed to private individuals.
About a fourth of the defendants were businesses.

     Types of cases. When the plaintiff is a
business, the business is usually a seller or
a seller's representative trying to collect money

237

from a customer. When the plaintiff is an individual, the most common type of case involves property damage. Other common types are disputes about purchases and landlord-tenant disputes.

Winners and losers. Plaintiffs have a very good chance of winning their cases. According to the NCSC report, about half the defendants didn't bother to show up, which usually meant the plaintiff won by default. In the contested cases, where both parties appeared, 92 percent of the business plaintiffs and 72 percent of the individual plaintiffs won.

The authors concluded that businesses were more successful than individuals not because the system favors businesses but because businesses come to court with stronger cases. Business plaintiffs are probably better at assembling evidence--contracts, receipts, and so on--and they probably don't file claims unless they have the evidence they need.

Lawyers. Although about one-third of the plaintiffs and a little more than one-third of the defendants contacted lawyers about their cases, very few plaintiffs or defendants were actually represented by lawyers in court.

Plaintiffs who had legal advice were no more likely to win than those who did not. On the other hand, defendants who had legal advice fared better than those who didn't.

Case costs. For about two-thirds of the plaintiffs, the cost of taking a case to small-claims court was $25 or less. (It's often only a few dollars.) Where the cost was significantly higher, the plaintiff had either hired a lawyer, lost wages while going to court, or both.

Collecting. Although plaintiffs have a good chance of winning, the winners don't necessarily collect their money. A lot depends on whether it's a contested case or a default

case, and whether the defendant is a business or
an individual.

In contested cases, about three-fourths of
the winning plaintiffs were able to collect.
In default cases, only about a third collected.
Winners collected more often when the defendant
was a business, not an individual.

HOW TO HANDLE YOUR CASE

Taking a case to small-claims court isn't
difficult, but you'll have a better chance of
winning and collecting if you anticipate potential problems and prepare your case carefully.
here are some guidelines:

Identify your opponent properly. Many small-
claims cases are dismissed because the plaintiff
hasn't correctly identified the defendant.

The defendant's legal name may not be the
same as his or her most commonly used name.
For example, suppose you have a TV repair problem.
The sign over the shop door says Mark's Radio/
TV, but the business is a corporation whose legal
name is Marconi Electronic Systems. If you sue,
use the legal name. The legal names of businesses
that are licensed can usually be found on certi-
ficates posted so they're visible to the public.
If not, check with the appropriate licensing
bureau.

Individuals are harder to identify. One
good source of information is a car registration.
If the person you want to sue owns a car, take the
license number and ask the state motor vehicle
agency to provide the registration information.

Sending a warning letter. Before you file
a claim in small-claims court, send the prospective defendant a warning letter. The tactic may
persuade him or her that it would be worthwhile to
settle the matter immediately.

The letter should be short, cool, and factual. State your claim--with all the appropriate dates, dollar amounts, and serial numbers-- and what you expect to be paid. State that you'll go to court if you don't have a satisfactory reply within, say, 10 days. Send the letter by certified mail, and ask for a return receipt.

Find the court. This is not always a simple matter, according to the NCSC report. Court administrators haven't made it very convenient to find small-claims courts. In some cities, small-claims courts are listed in the phone book under the name of the parent court-- usually a city or county civil court. Sometimes there's no listing. You might ask the state or local consumer affairs office for help.

File a claim. When you file a claim, you'll have to give your name and address, the defendant's name and address, a short description of the problem, and a statement of how much, in dollars, you're trying to recover. Once you've paid the filing fee (usually a few dollars), the clerk will schedule a hearing a few weeks after the date of filing. You're often entitled to recover the amount of the fee from the defendant if you win.

Notify the defendant. The NSCS researchers discovered that, in some courts, about half of the small-claims cases fail to reach trial because the defendants haven't been notified.

The notice is usually just a printed form indicating that the plaintiff has filed a claim against the defendant, that the defendant must appear in court at a particular time, that the case may be decided in the plaintiff's favor if the defendant doesn't show up, and that a favorable decision for the plaintiff may require the defendant to pay the amount claimed, plus court costs.

The court will usually notify the defendant by certified mail, requesting a return receipt. If the attempt is unsuccessful, the court will leave it up to the plaintiff to notify the defendant. For a fee, you can have the notice delivered by a marshal, a sheriff, or an independent process server. The court clerk can tell you how to get in touch with a marshal or sheriff. Process servers are listed in the Yellow Pages under that heading. Whoever handles the job will have to swear that the notice was actually delivered.

Assemble the evidence. Assuming you have a legitimate claim, whether you win or not will depend mainly on the evidence you can present to the judge. You should carefully assemble all the documents and papers that are related to the case—contracts, warranty statements, receipts, canceled checks, letters, repair estimates, and so on.

In most cases, your paperwork will make the difference. But don't overlook other kinds of evidence, such as photographs or witnesses. If you have a dispute with your landlord about a leaky roof, for instance, clear pictures of the damage might settle the question.

If your claim has to do with a particular object—a piece of clothing or furniture, for example—take it with you to court, if it can be carried. In one case recalled by Denver lawyer John Ruhnka, co-author of the NCSC report, the plaintiff carried an entire set of bedroom furniture into court: "They just dumped it down and said, 'Look at it.' The judge said, 'I'm looking—you don't have to tell me anything more.'"

If you don't have enough evidence on paper, perhaps you can call on a witness. Ruhnka says, "In a situation where it's your word against someone else's, the judge is in a very uncomfortable position. The question is, whom does be believe? Anything you can do to tip the scales in your favor—such as having a witness who's backing

241

your story--gives the judge a way out. Now two
people are telling him such and such, not one."

          If you want the witness to be present, but
he or she won't come voluntarily, the court can
order the witness to appear. That type of order,
known as a subpoena, can also be used to obtain
documents or records that the defendant or someone
else has.

          Consider settling out of court. When the
defendant is notified of the trial, he or she may
be willing to settle the matter, if only to avoid
the trouble of going to court. If you can make a
settlement satisfactory to you, write out the
terms on a piece of paper. Each of you should date
and sign it, and each should keep a copy. If you
have to reopen the case later, the written agreement can be used as evidence. In the meantime,
tell the small-claims clerk the case has been
settled.

          Present your case. In a typical trial, the
judge will begin by identifying the plaintiff and
the defendant and summarizing the complaint. Then
both parties will be sworn to tell the truth. The
judge will ask the plaintiff to tell his or her
side of the story. At that point, the judge will
examine any evidence the plaintiff offers. If the
plaintiff has a witness, the witness will be sworn
in and questioned about the facts. The defendant
then tells his or her side, presenting documents
and witnesses as necessary. Finally, each party
will have a chance to ask questions or challenge
the other's testimony.

          The process is quite informal, but it's easy
to overlook an important point. If you want things
to run smoothly, you should probably try presenting
your case in advance to a friend who knows little
or nothing about the problem.

          If your opponent doesn't appear in court,
the judge will ask you to tell your side of the
case. If your evidence seems persuasive, the

judge is likely to award a default judgment. In
contested cases, the judge will record the
decision after both sides have presented their
case. In some courts, the judge will inform
both parties of the decision immediately. In
others, the parties are separately notified by
mail a few days after the hearing.

HOW TO COLLECT

In small-claims court, winning isn't everything. If you as plaintiff receive a favorable
judgment, you still have to collect from the
defendant. In some cases, that may be very
difficult.

If the defendant is a business, there are
some fairly effective ways of putting the pressure
on. Here is what John Ruhnka suggests: "Give the
business seven days to pay. If they don't pay,
call them up and say, 'If I don't get a check within five days, I'm taking this unpaid judgment to
the business license bureau. I'm going to ask
them to revoke your license.' That will generally
do the trick."

If the defendant is an individual, you may
have to resort to more formal procedures, which are
often a lot of trouble. Here are a few you might
consider:

Bank accounts. For a fee, a sheriff or
marshal in the county where the defendant lives,
works, or owns property may be able to help you
collect your money. One source is the defendant's
bank accounts. If you do manage to collect, you're
entitled to add the sheriff's fee to the amount the
defendant already owes you. The small-claims clerk
can tell you how to get in touch with a sheriff or
marshal. The problem is to find out which bank
handles the defendant's savings or checking account.
If you've paid the defendant by check, look at the
back of your canceled check.

Wages. If the defendant is employed and you know the employer's location, you can ask the sheriff or marshal to arrange to have periodic payments deducted from the defendant's paycheck. (There are usually legal limits on how much can be deducted per paycheck.)

Real estate. If you can't arrange for payment from a bank account or from wages, you might look into a real-estate "lien"--a legal claim on property owned by the defendant. If there's a lien on the property, the owner can't sell it until that debt is paid off. You can apply for a lien at the county clerk's office.

Motor vehicles. If the defendant owns a car or truck, the sheriff or marshal can seize it and have it sold at auction. The defendant's debt to you will be paid from the proceeds of the sale.

However, this procedure raises a number of problems. First, you have to identify the vehicle by make, year, and license number. Second, you have to find out where it's usually parked. Third, if it's old, it may not be worth enough to cover what you are owed. Fourth, if the vehicle is collateral for a loan, the lender must be paid off before you are. Fifth, you'll have to pay the cost of seizing and disposing of the vehicle, in advance, though entitled to recover this expense from the sale proceeds.

License suspension. In some states, if the case involves damage resulting from the defendant's operation of a motor vehicle, you may be able to have the defendant's driver's license suspended until you're paid. Ask the small-claims clerk if this applies to your case.

ADVICE FOR DEFENDANTS

If you're named as defendant in a small-claims case, you have three options: settle before the trial, go to trial (and possibly settle during the trial), or default. Default is a poor option because the plaintiff will probably be awarded the full amount he or she has claimed. Then you'll be faced with the problem of paying it off immediately. If you don't pay, the plaintiff can collect in one of the unpleasant ways noted above.

If you think the plaintiff has a strong case against you, it would be a good idea to try settling out of court. You may be able to negotiate for a smaller amount than the plaintiff is claiming, and you won't have to pay court costs.

If you aren't sure of your position, or if you think you have a good defense, go to trial. One advantage of going to trial is that you can ask questions about the plaintiff's claim. Also, if you prepare your case carefully and produce the relevant contracts, receipts, or witnesses, you may find that the plaintiff's case is weaker than you thought. Remember that the plaintiff has to come up with enough evidence to tip the scales. If they balance, you win. But even if you lose, the fact that you appeared and disputed the case may persuade the judge to reduce the award. You may also be able to arrange terms for payment that will make it easier for you to pay off the debt.

IMPROVING THE COURTS

How well do small-claims courts work? Critics disagree. "Little Injustices," a 1972 report by the Small Claims Study Group, offered this conclusion: "For the vast majority of American consumers, small-claims courts are unavailable, or invisible." The recent NCSC report was more optimistic: "Overall, we found that the small-claims courts we examined were meeting the goals of speedy and inexpensive justice far better than the previous literature on these courts led us to expect."

Despite such widely varying assessments, there's general agreement that the small-claims system needs improvement. Here are several things we recommend:

1. Expand the system. At the moment, small-claims courts are far more accessible in some states than in others and far more accessible to certain segments of society than to others. As a matter of principle, these courts should be readily available to every citizen.

2. Publicize the courts. Both the administrators and bar associations have the responsibility to publicize small-claims courts, and, in many cases, both have failed to do so. Administrators have been reluctant to publicize small-claims courts, presumably because they don't want to encourage unnecessary lawsuits. But as the Small Claims Study Group pointed out, "Informing people as to how to exercise their legal rights is hardly inciting them to bring unworthy actions. Publicity simply puts people who do not know about the courts on the same ground as those who are already aware of them." Among other things, the telephone number of the small-claims court should be listed at all likely reference places in the phone book, including the "frequently called" sections of government listings.

3. Improve court schedules. With very few exceptions, small-claims cases are heard only during normal business hours (9 to 5) on weekdays. That forces many people--both plaintiffs and defendants--to make a choice between taking part of the day off (possibly losing income) and participating in a trial whose outcome is uncertain. The problem can be alleviated by scheduling some court sessions in the evening and on Saturday.

Many courts schedule all the day's cases for the same hour--say, 9 A.M. That means many people have to wait a good while for their cases to come up. It should be possible to schedule cases in batches, at half-hour intervals, for example. According to the NCSC report, seven of the 15 courts studies had instituted such scheduling methods.

4. <u>Use more arbitrators</u>. The NCSC report
indicated that only three of the 15 courts use
lawyers to settle small-claims cases. There are
obvious advantages in having lawyer-arbitrators
handle such cases: The court can hold costs down,
and backlogs can be avoided by expanding the
staff. Of course, since it would be hard to re-
cruit volunteers for service during normal business
hours, a court relying mainly on unpaid arbitrators
would probably have to schedule most of its cases
during the evening.

5. <u>Revise claim limits</u>. The upper limit
should be at least $1500, with periodic increases
reflecting the national inflation rate. That's
high enough to cover many common claims, but not
so high that plaintiffs with the larger claims will
be risking much by proceeding without legal counsel.

6. <u>Limit business influence on the courts</u>.
In some states, certain kinds of businesses are
specifically excluded from small-claims courts.
However, there is considerable disagreement over
whether or not this benefits individuals. The
argument for the exclusion of business plaintiffs
is that they substantially increase the caseload
and tend to overwhelm the courts. As a result, it
is said, the tone of the court and the attitude
of court personnel show bias in favor of business
plaintiffs. Individuals then become discouraged
from using the courts.

There's no doubt that caseloads increase
when business plaintiffs have access to small-
claims courts, yet in the 15 cities covered in the
NCSC study per-capita use of the courts by individual plaintiffs bore no relation to whether
business plaintiffs were excluded or not. Furthermore, there is an argument for allowing businesses
to use small-claims courts: When businesses can't
sue in such courts, they have to take their cases
to formal civil court. In that event, it will
cost defendants (usually consumers) a lot more to
defend themselves because they will have to hire
lawyers.

Nevertheless, there is still the nagging question of whether business use of small-claims courts discourages use by individuals. Over the years various proposals have been advanced for limiting the influence of business. Some critics have proposed that a business firm be allowed to bring only a limited number of cases during a certain period. Others have suggested that the courts be closed to businesses but that when an individual is sued in court for a sum within the small-claims court limit, he or she have the right to transfer the case to a small-claims court. That allows consumers to take advantage of the lower costs of the small-claims court, if they so choose.

Still another solution was initiated in Chicago in 1972. The Cook County Small Claims Court was split into two parts. Business plaintiffs are allowed in the regular court, but there is a separate "Pro Se" ("for oneself," meaning that the party is appearing without a lawyer) court, which only individuals can use. This system reduces the likelihood that the court will be perceived as geared to serving business plaintiffs.

CU strongly favors preserving small-claims courts as a quick, cheap, and fair way for consumers to have their complaints settled. If that can be achieved without total exclusion of business plaintiffs, so much the better.

7. Exclude lawyers. The presence of lawyers can affect the outcome of a trial, especially when one party is represented by a lawyer and the other isn't. Justice requires that lawyers appear for both sides or neither. Since the aim of a small-claims court is to resolve minor disputes without lawyers, and since it would be expensive for courts to provide lawyers for those without them, the most practical option is to exclude all lawyers except those who appear in their own behalf.

248

8. <u>Provide more pretrial help</u>. Well-train-
ed paralegal advisers should be available in
every small-claims court to tell plaintiffs and
defendants how the system works and what kinds of
evidence would be useful for a trial. This
advice should also be available in the form of
free booklets that can be given or mailed to plaintiffs and defendants on request. When the claim
is filed, both parties should be informed of the
pretrial help.

9. <u>Train court personnel in consumer law</u>.
The NCSC researchers found that judges and defendants are often poorly informed about consumer
laws that are revelant to small claims. For
example, a consumer might have purchased furniture
on an installment plan without having been properly
informed of the finance charges. If he or she
falls behind in the payments, the seller could take
the matter to small-claims court. In that event,
the defendant might be able to avoid an unfavor-
able judgment by demonstrating that the sale was
inconsistent with the Federal Truth-In-Lending Act.
If judges and paralegal advisers were thoroughly
familiar with such consumer laws, purchasers would
be more likely to get fair treatment in court.
Such familiarity is especially important where
parties appear without lawyers, since it's the
responsibility of the judge not only to know but to
apply the relevant law.

10. <u>Simplify identification of defendants</u>.
As noted earlier, many small-claims cases are dismissed because the plaintiff failed to identify
the defendant by a legal name. That's clearly
unfair if the defendant is commonly known by a
different name. In such a case, the plaintiff
should merely be required to provide evidence that
the defendant commonly uses the name indicated in
the original filing. A printed receipt, an entry
in a telephone directory, a photograph of a store
sign, or the testimony of a witness should suffice.
Plaintiffs should, of course, be informed of this
requirement well before the trial. New York

State recently passed a law allowing simplified identification of defendants.

11. <u>Issue clearly worded and neutral summonses</u>. The NCSC report shows that the printed notices mailed to defendants are sometimes very intimidating. They're hard to understand and may well convey the impression that the plaintiff has already presented evidence against the defendant. Also, the notices rarely advise the defendant that he or she can contact the court for more information.

Notices should be expressed in clear, non-threatening language and give the defendant the name, address, and telephone number of the person to call for additional information. It should indicate that both parties have the right to call on court personnel for guidance about how to get necessary evidence, and that both parties will have a chance to tell their stories at the hearing.

12. <u>Avoid hasty default judgments</u>. According to the NCSC report, default judgments are issued in some courts without verifying that the defendant was notified of the trial, without establishing that the defendant was liable as charged, and without examining the plaintiff's evidence of damage. Default judgments should not be issued unless these points can be confirmed.

13. <u>Announce the decision at the trial</u>. In some courts (four out of 15 in the NCSC study) the parties are notified of the decision several days after the trial. Announcing the decision at the trial has two advantages: First, it's an opportunity to explain to both parties the legal basis for the decision. Second, it means that the defendant has a chance to work out the terms of payment.

14. <u>Help plaintiffs collect</u>. One of the most prominent flaws in the small-claims system is that so many plaintiffs fail to collect the money they're awarded. That record might be substantially improved if the courts were to take responsibility for

collection. Losing defendants could be ordered
to make their payments to the court rather than to
the plaintiffs. Not only would defendants be more
inclined to pay, but the court would also be in a
better position than the plaintiff to take action
if the defendant didn't pay.

Collection might be further improved by
appointing a court official to handle the job of
extracting funds from delinquent defendants' wages
or bank accounts. Whenever a decision is against
the defendant, the judge could instruct the defendant, while still under oath, to fill out forms
identifying his or her employer and bank. If the
defendant later failed to pay, the court official
could then order the employer or the bank to divert
funds as appropriate.

A NIGHT IN MANHATTAN'S SMALL-CLAIMS COURT

The New York City small-claims courts handle
about 67,000 cases a year. In the Manhattan court,
hearings are held in the evening, Monday through
Thursday, between 6:30 and 10. About 170 cases
are scheduled for an average evening. In about
half those cases, neither party appears, often
because the matter has already been settled.

The court convenes in a large room with row
after row of wooden benches. Each session begins
with a reading of the evening's list of cases--
plaintiff first, defendant second. The clerk
announces that everyone is entitled to have his or
her case heard by the judge, but cases can also be
heard by lawyer-arbitrators who are as well qualified as the judge. The main difference is that a
case is likely to be heard earlier if it's assigned to an arbitrator. (Parties who want their
cases heard by a judge may have to come back on
another night.) Arbitrated cases can't be appealed,
but, in fact, very few cases are appealed.

About 85 percent of the cases to go arbitration. The arbitrators are unpaid volunteers, 800

251

in all, who typically have a lot of experience with small-claims cases. For example, lawyers Ernest Marmorek and Philip Greco each spend one night a month arbitrating cases, and each has served about 17 years.

Why do they do it? Marmorek says, "As Judge Edward Thompson discovered years ago when he set up this system, all lawyers want to be judges. But beyond that, I feel it's a privilege to be a lawyer, and this is something I can do in return." Greco concurs: "It's a way of giving something back to the community."

Arbitrators work in small hearing rooms off the main courtroom. The arbitrator sits at a table facing the plaintiff and defendant. Waiting plaintiffs and defendants sit around the room. The atmosphere is relaxed but serious.

Here is a sampling of cases recently arbitrated in the Manhattan court:

Personal injury: The plaintiff was a woman, the defendant a restaurant. The woman had cut her right hand on a broken glass when she reached under a counter for her handbag. She immediately went to New York Hospital and had five stitches. Her hand was bound for three weeks, and she now had a scar on the palm. Her claim was for $1000, covering medical expenses, loss of income as a demonstrator of cosmetics, and discomfort associated with the injury.

The woman offered medical bills as evidence and introduced as a witness a doctor who happened to be passing the restaurant as she left. The doctor hadn't treated the injury but acknowledged that she had seen it and that the scar would be permanent. No one representing the defendant appeared in court.

Resolution: Plaintiff awarded $627.

252

Tenant complaint about services. The
plaintiff was a man working at home as an
artist, the defendant was the building landlord.
The tenant claimed $1000 in damages because his
electricity had been off for 10 days. He offered
no evidence about the dates of the interruption
but submitted a list of losses, including income
loss, totaling $ 807. He said the remaining $193
was for mental anguish.

The landlord offered as evidence a paid
electrician's bill and a copy of the lease, which
specified that the apartment was to be used "for
residential purposes only." He also said that the
electrical problem had been caused by the tenant's
sewing machine and that the tenant had been a
troublemaker ever since he moved in, a couple of
months earlier.

The arbitrator asked whether there was any
room for settlement. The landlord said he would
be willing to return half the tenant's security
deposit if he would vacate the apartment immediately. The tenant refused. The arbitrator then
concluded the trial with the usual request that
both parties leave at the same time. He said they
would be notified of the decision in a few days.

Resolution: Plaintiff awarded $200.

Auto collision. The plaintiff was a cab
driver who claimed the defendant, a truck driver,
had pulled in front of him at the intersection of
46th Street and Ninth Avenue. The cab driver
produced a bill for $695 worth of repairs and
photographs of the cab taken immediately after
the accident. The truck driver, no longer
employed by the owner of the truck, was accompanied by a lawyer. He claimed the accident wasn't
his fault.

Resolution: Plaintiff swarded $347.

Camper's complaint about services. The
plaintiff was a man from Philadelphia who had

253

stayed at a camp in Jamaica, West Indies, with
a woman who was present in the hearing room.
The defendants were a man who managed the camp
and a woman who managed the camp's New York
office. The plaintiff claimed that the advertising brochures for the camp were misleading and
that the camp was so bad he stayed only two days
instead of the week he had paid for. The defendants had refunded his $278 payment in full.
But the plaintiff felt he was entitled to recover
an additional $308 for air fare and $150 for a
hotel room and miscellaneous food and travel
expenses, because he wouldn't have incurred those
expenses if he hadn't been misled by the camp's
advertising.

The plaintiff offered a typewritten description of his complaint, some 15 or 20 pages long,
but the arbitrator asked him to summarize it orally.
The plaintiff also offered in evidence the camp's
advertising brochures, various receipts, and an
article from The Philadelphia Inquirer confirming
that the camp's services weren't entirely satisfactory. The article had appeared a month and a
half before the plaintiff's visit to the camp.

Resolution: Plaintiff awarded $308.

Receipt for security deposit. In another
landlord-tenant dispute, the plaintiff said she
had moved into her apartment two years before but
wasn't given a receipt for her $250 security
deposit. The defendant was accompanied by a
lawyer.

The tenant had asked the landlord for either
a receipt or her money back. The landlord said
the tenant had been given a "verbal receipt."
The arbitrator asked, "But why can't you give her
a receipt right now?" The tenant offered a
booklet of receipt forms, the lawyer filled one
out in duplicate, the landlord signed it, and
the arbitrator handed the original to the tenant.
In tears, she said, "That's all I've wanted for
ten months."

Resolution: Case dismissed.

24. VARIATION IN THE OPERATION OF GRAND JURIES*

Donald M. McIntyre

One of the more viable features of criminal justice administration in this country is the use of grand juries. The most glaring example of this variation is that only twenty states, plus the federal system, make a grand jury indictment mandatory for the prosecution of serious crimes (with five additional states requiring it for capital crimes only). The other states allow the formal criminal charge to take the form of either an indictment or an information prepared by the prosecutor. As a rule, grand juries are used relatively infrequently in these "optional" states.

When grand juries are used, or are required, there is also wide variation in the law on such matters as the number on the jury (ranging from one to twenty-three), method of convening (i.e., only seven jurisdictions provide for calling a grand jury on petition of citizens), recording of testimony (only sixteen states require preparation of a full transcript of testimony), rights of witnesses (only six states recognize a witness's right to counsel inside the grand jury room), and the scope of the jury's investigatory power (i.e., eight states provide for statewide grand juries). Since the bulk of these kinds of provisions are covered by statute, the initial phase of the American Bar Foundation's project, a study of the actual operation of grand juries,

* Reprinted with permission from the American Bar Foundation Research Reporter, Winter 1977, pp. 1-2 and 6.

involved the preparation of a chart depicting
and outlining such provisions under state and
federal statutes.

The empirical part of the Foundation's study
focused on the hypothesis and frequent assertion
that the most traditional function of the grand
jury--providing a bulwark against unwarranted or
frivolous prosecutions--has little applicability
to current practice. Our study confirmed that
the typical "indicting" grand jury is very much
inclined to rubber-stamp decisions to charge when
the evidence presented to it by the prosecutor's
office relates to the large number of crimes that
can be best characterized as "hard core"--the
"index crimes" of unlawful homicide, assault,
rape, robbery, burglary, and other kinds of theft.
For at least these crimes, which constitute 95
percent or more of the felony caseload in the
states, complaints about excessive or unjustified
prosecutions are rarely made. Indeed the reverse
is true. Because of high caseloads, prosecutors,
to the extent they are to be criticized for their
charging decisions, are much more likely to be
called to task for not bringing charges in doubtful cases or for making too many concessions in
order to get guilty pleas. It is also understandable why grand jurors, who are not experts in
criminal law, are prone to rely upon the recommendations of prosecutors, who are experts, as to whether
there is enough evidence to charge and, more importantly, enough to win a conviction.

But it cannot be unequivocally stated that
the charging function of grand juries for routine
serious crimes is inefficient and wasteful, at
least when measured against the alternative of the
preliminary hearing. For when the grand jury is
not used, the law still requires the interposition
of a judicial officer between the accused and the
prosecutor. Hence, in lieu of a grand jury indictment in optional states, the prosecutor may file
an information only after sufficient evidence has

been presented to a judge at the preliminary
hearing to persuade the court that the defendant
should be bound over for trial on the felony.
Our study discovered that, in general, the preliminary hearing requires more time and incon-
venience than the presentation of similar evidence
to the grand jury. The time consumed at the hearing is often two or three times as long. Witnesses are subject to cross-examination, and in some
instances the defense presents its own evidence.
Continuances are often sought by the defense,
delaying the trial date and inconveniencing witnesses. In optional states the prosecutor's
practice, therefore, is to by-pass a preliminary
hearing by taking the matter directly to the grand
jury, in order to avoid the foregoing problems.
This procedure is also used when the state does
not wish to expose its case at an early stage.
These needs also seem to vary a great deal in
optional states. In metropolitan areas, where at
least one grand jury is always in session, the
percentage of felony cases referred to the grand
jury for indictment runs from as low as 1 percent
in Los Angeles to as high as 30 percent in Chicago.
A major advantage of the preliminary hearing in
all jurisdictions, and especially in those where
there is little or no intensive, systematic screen-
ing of cases by the prosecutor's office, is that
it constitutes a major point at which felony charges can be disposed of. That is, under judicial
supervision felony charges are reduced to mis-
demeanors or cases routed through other procedures
less severe than felony prosecution, thus reducing caseloads at the trial level.

It would appear, therefore, that the optional
approach, because of its flexibility, has the
advantage of permitting the state to select a
charging procedure tailored to accommodate such
needs as witness convenience, speed, and efficient case management.

The function of the grand jury to consider
evidence presented by the prosecutor, and then to
decide whether to indict, is only one of its

257

purposes, perhaps its least important. A much
more significant role is its power to issue sub-
poenas so that documents and crime suspects can
be examined. This power makes the grand jury a
vital investigatory agency for law enforcement
with regard to certain kinds of crimes, especially when it is used in combination with the prosecutor's prerogative to grant immunity to witnesses so that they can be compelled, under the
threat of being cited for civil contempt and
jailed, to tell all they know about a criminal
enterprise including identification of its per-
petrators. The use of the grand jury for investigatory purposes, however, typically is limited to
extraordinary criminals and the extraordinary
crimes they commit. It is not uncommon for special
grand juries to be convened for the express and
limited purpose of investigating unusual or special
crime situations.

The investigative role of the grand jury presents a serious dilemma. There are many who feel
that the process by which a person under suspicion
is subpoenaed to appear before the grand jury, is
granted immunity, and is incarcerated for refusal
to testify, smacks of a medieval European "inqui-
sitional" approach to criminal justice, a process
perhaps more abhorrent for its dangerous potential
than for the crimes currently investigated through
this process.

Equally abhorrent to others are the stealth-
ful, highly organized gambling, narcotics, and
other vice syndicate operators; corrupt officials
in government, labor unions and business; and
group "movements" aimed at achieving their ends
through violent disruptions. Undercover police
work frequently is either ineffective or impracti-
cal for such crimes because they involve tightly
knit groups engaging in sophisticated conspiracies.

State investigative grand juries do probe
such activity, but their emphasis in general seems

to be on vice operations. It is the U.S. Department of Justice, through its district attorneys' office, that increasingly is taking an active role, through the use of federal grand juries, to advance the suppression of vice crime syndicates as well as unlawful conspiracies to defraud, to steal, and to commit violence. This tendency has become increasingly apparent in recent years for several reasons. One is that such criminal enterprises often extend beyond state boundaries; the federal grand jury can subpoena witnesses outside of the state in which they are sitting. Another is that local prosecutors are "too close" to corruption in their immediate vicinities; state prosecutors, since they are politicans (in forty-five states prosecutors are elected), are not in as good a position to investigate and prosecute corruption of influential individuals, such as high public officials and prominent businessmen. Many unlawful conspiracy situations require highly trained experts in tax and accounting to discover evidence of the crime in subpoenaed documents; federal prosecutors have access to such experts--local state prosecutors frequently do not. Moreover, nationally organized movements to resist policies and practices for which the federal government has primary responsibility (such as the Vietnam War) have in the last several years spawned several noteworthy federal grand jury investigations.

Protests against the grand jury subpoena/immunity/incarceration process of course appear at the state level, such as recently in New York, where abuse of grand juries has been alleged because of their role in the highly publicized effort by a special New York prosecutor to unearth corruption in state and local government. But in citing examples of abuse, grand jury critics, such as the Coalition to End Grand Jury Abuse, focus their discontent overwhelmingly on federal investigations. It is not that the federal prosecutions are substantially increasing; the total number of federal prosecutions in 1970, for example, was 38,102 compared to 39,147 in 1976. Protests are aimed at the kinds of cases under federal grand jury investigation and the methods used in that process.

Agitations for changes in the law and practice
to curb the investigative power of the grand juries
and the prosecutor have resulted in U.S. congressional hearings and the introduction of several
reform bills, culminating in the bill (the
Federal Grand Jury Reform Act 1977) now pending
before Congress. This legislation at the federal
level provided the primary impetus for the ABA
Section of Criminal Justice, through its Grand
Jury Committee, to formulate some twenty-five
legislative principles to which grand jury reform
legislation, state and federal, should adhere.
All of these principles are aimed at restricting or
at least controlling the use of grand juries, nineteen of which specifically cover the jury's investigative function.

Finally, a point arguing for the desirability
of grand juries figured more importantly than
expected in the Foundation's study: that is the
attribute of citizen involvement in the criminal
justice process, beyond service as witnesses and
as petit jurors. In a system involving tremendous
discretion, a factor heavily influencing decisions
by all of the system's functionaries as well as
formulation of institutional policies, is an
awareness of public sentiment and expectations
about how vigorous or lax enforcement of each
criminal statute should be. Grand jurors, to an
inestimable degree, provide this awareness because
of the broad range of cases and circumstances presented to them. It was learned in New York, for
example, where indictments are mandatory, that
grand juries will often assess criminal behavior
as being less serious, because of extenuating
circumstances, than the literal application of the
law would allow. The result is that the jury, and
not the district attorney, will recommend charging
an "included" misdemeanor rather than indicting on
the felony even though the evidence, technically,
would support the more serious charge. While
decisions such as this are frequently made by

prosecutors and judges, the fact that they are made instead by ordinary citizens at the early charging stage lends support to difficult charging decisions. For some kinds of cases a decision to charge or not is more than should be expected from a public official. For example, whether to charge a police officer for having shot someone, when the evidence is borderline or weak, is likely to result in severe criticism of the prosecutor, whatever his decision. Here the grand jury proves to be valuable in sharing the responsibility.

It seems clear to me from the study that the grand jury is a desirable institution but that certain limitations on its role need to be recognized. Its usefulness as an independent charging agency for routine cases, in particular, is limited by time and caseload pressures. In jurisdictions with high crime rates the grand jury, of necessity, must cooperate with the prosecutor's office by reviewing the evidence of large numbers of cases and trusting the deputy prosecutor's judgment on the merits of going forward with an indictment.

Whether a criminal charge should be by an indictment, decided upon the secrecy of the grand jury room, or by the prosecutor's information after an open preliminary hearing, is determined by the many circumstances and needs of the system in which the decision is made. At least when a choice can be made, the processing of a case can be managed with a flexibility that efficiency often demands.

The separate and distinct problem expressed over the past seven or eight years concerning use of the investigatory power of grand juries, particularly at the federal level, has been recognized and dealt with by the American Bar Association's policies for grand jury use, by pending legislation in the U.S. Congress, and by law reform in a few states. None of the suggested reforms

suggests that the power of the grand jury to
investigate crime be withdrawn. Provisions for
greater control of the investigating grand jury
and for specifying greater rights of the witness/
suspect under subpoena will doubtless have the
effect of strengthening the grand jury institution.

25. BARGAINING AND LABOR RELATIONS: ISSUES AND TRENDS IN THE PUBLIC SECTOR*

Seymour Z. Mann

Having spent 30 years in academic research and service understanding how the local government system works and/or exploring the behavior of public service managers, and being now an executive with one of the largest and most influential public service unions in the nation representing upwards of 150,000 employees of the non-uniformed services in New York City, provides a unique vantage point from which to itemize or note some trends and issues in public sector collective bargaining and labor management relations. While the statistics on the growth of unionism in the public sector are now commonplace--and often cited since it is in that sector in recent years that any kinds of gains or growth in union affiliation can be claimed--it is worth making a quick summary and drawing a kind of moral with respect to them.

Loose employee affiliations and associations have become genuine unions at amazingly fast rates in all parts of the country. New unions have arisen and public service unions that had, only a few years ago, only small organization bases have grown rapidly. The American Federation of State, County and Municipal Employees (AFSCME), a general membership union representing state and local government employees, is an example. In 1956, AFSCME reported a national membership of some 125,000; today it totals 750,000.

In a labor relations environment in which provisions for an agency or union shop, full collective bargaining and union recognition are still

---

* Reprinted with permission from the National Civic Review, September 1978, pp. 354-57.

absent in most states, the number of workers public
sector unions actually represent far exceeds the
number of dues-paying members. This is in the face
of the fact that during the past 20 years union
membership as a whole has remained relatively stable
or, by some reports, has declined.

The latest figures would indicate that from
1948 to 1977 state and local governments' share of
total employment in the United States grew from 8.4
percent to 15.3 percent. During that same period
the share of the workforce engaged in service enterprises increased substantially, a large part of
which, obviously, was accounted for by the growth in
state and local government employment. By 1977 government production and expenditures accounted for
over a third of the G.N.P., with 15 percent attributable to the state and local levels. When one
realizes that in the decade of the sixties state and
local government payrolls alone jumped from just
over $2 billion to almost $6 billion, the rapid
escalation of state and local government impact on
the G.N.P. is understandable.

Payroll increases, of course, reflect the
growth in numbers of employees. But part of the
increase was and continues to be, even with the
severe fiscal restraints in many jurisdictions, a
reflection of the increased unionization and economic benefits gained from the expansion of collective bargaining rights. And what is the lesson
to be drawn as one faces these statistics and the
trends they connote? Remember that most of the
expansion of unionism in the public sector is
accounted for by organizing employees engaged in
service tasks and occupations--an area in which
union organization in the private sector has not
been notably successful. So, again, how come?
Surely it is not all attributable to the fact that
a union like AFSCME during these decades had dynamic
and wise leadership. Surely it is not all attributable to the political strength of the workers
in various state and local jurisdictions, or, if you

264

prefer the other side of that coin, to weak-kneed
and vote-hungry politicians. It seems, rather,
that a little bit of intellectual honesty and
applied common sense provides the answers: large
segments of the public service work force perceived
themselves as demeaned and without dignity; many
groups of public workers were highly indignant about
unsatisfactory working conditions; there were
literally hordes of employees who felt that they
were underpaid; civil service systems and protec-
tions weren't all perceived as what they were
"cracked up" to be, and there must have been something lacking in management, with consequent failures in, or the real absence of, labor-management
relationships.

It is important for the future to accept this
conclusion and the impressive numbers with respect
to the growth and economic impact of public sector
union development. Public sector unions are here
to stay, and if part of their coming on the scene
with the dramatic force and impact that they have
is in some part attributable to management fail-
ings we had better do something about it. But the
something we should do has to be done within the
context of the fact of the unions' presence, and
that the unions may be able to contribute something
to what we do about it. Among the improvements or
changes is to develop a core of managers that
understands unionism, understands the dynamics
which have resulted in its rapid expansion, and is
willing to give the time and attention to developing skills and gaining experience in collective
bargaining and the conduct of day-to-day labor-
management relationships.

With this kind of growth pattern in such a
short period of time it is clear that there is an
unevenness, too, in character and maturity of the
unions in different locales and in the various
kinds of jurisdictions, to say nothing of the differences between a federated body of 60-odd locals
like District 37, with a diverse membership

representing a complex and comprehensive span of
job titles, and a PBA or an isolated local composed
entirely of blue-collar workers in a small suburban
community or a rural county. Any generalizations
have to keep in mind this diversity and the youth
of the public service unions, and generalizations
have to be more concerned with what is emerging
than with what may be at present, and understand
that we still have many amateurs and greenhorns at
the bargaining table on both sides.

     Without a lot of documentation, then let's
accept that there is responsible, sensible and
intelligent unionism in the public sector. Unions
and union leadership exhibiting these qualities
will continue to emerge and develop as public
managers and public officials further recognize
and identify the community of interests between
themselves and a unionized workforce. And this is
a community of interests based on the mutuality of
their public interests commitments, especially with
respect to the patterns of responsiveness which
governance and public service ultimately demand.
The recognition of that mutual interest will come
in more places more frequently, with a consequent
diminution in the instability of labor-management
relations behavior as the parties gain more experience, as the collective bargaining processes
mature, and as there develop more uniformity and
consistency in the legislative guarantees and rules
of the game in the various jurisdictions.

     Aside from the issue of lack of experience and
maturity, we give too much attention to the differences between labor-management relations in the
public and private sectors. The alleged practical
differences are more mythical than real. By and
large the motivating forces for workers to join
unions, what they want their unions to do for them,
the social and psychic satisfaction that so many
union members feel as actors in a meaningful collec-
tivity are the same whether they are private or
public employees. (And so are their generalized
views or attitudes toward the employer or whomever

is identified as boss). More importantly, and this takes issue with what may be the mainstream of the prevailing views, there are not too many legal differentiations that ought to be made with respect to the unionized worker's rights and obligations. (Fortunately, the Supreme Court took a similar view on at least one matter--the agency shop application.) The main hang-up here has been with respect to the right to strike. With or without that right there have been strikes by public service workers-- unionized and otherwise--and disaster has not be- fallen us. Even where there have been lengthy teacher strikes there seems to have been little im- pact on the quantity or quality of the educational output. Which may be a less than complimentary comment on our public school educational establish- ments or on the values of our society or both. Of course there need to be special provisions in emer- gency and public safety services of various kinds. But, a better labor-management relations system and environment will be built and developed if we de- emphasize the differences and concentrate on the similarities.

Even with the right guaranteed, it is doubtful that the number of strikes would increase in inci- dence. What is important in this context is to realize that there is a growing trend toward the use of third party and tri-partite dispute settling mechanisms being set up through basic enabling legislation or agreed on among the parties through negotiated agreements. This trend will more than likely continue and burgeon in the future, and may, indeed, set a pattern for private sector dispute settlements. There is something inevitable in this trend because of the fiscal dynamics and other factors which are endemic or peculiar to the public sector. The force of these dynamics will be felt most positively, however, if we do not erect legal and political barriers which attempt to preserve and encourage the differences between private and public sector labor-management relations.

267

There are a few other items which should be
mentioned briefly (not that they are less significant than items or issues already addressed). They
are the kinds of matters and future implication
issues which probably will raise many questions and
differences of opinion.

First, there has been too much concern with
the alleged "evils" of the political action roles
of public service unions, and in this respect their
power in contrast to other active and organized
political interests (especially at local government
levels) is greatly overrated. What is important is
to grasp the contribution in this sphere that unions
can and do make through their organized political
action programs to the quality of representative-
ness and defining issues in an increasingly fragmented political scene.

Second, productivity and quality of work life
issues will in the present politico-economic environment increasingly become high on the labor-
management relations agenda, especially at local
government levels. Keep in mind, though, that the
process by which productivity and quality of work
life matters are approached is as important with
respect to the future of public sector labor-management relations as the short-run agreements that
may be reached on substantive items.

For example, the process that was developed
in New York City through agreements reached between
the municipal labor committee and the city in the
negotiations of June 1976 was, of course, in large
measure an aspect of the fiscal constraints that
were almost crushing at that time. But, that the
responsible city officials and a responsive union
leadership could squeeze and massage the then crisis
conditions into a positive accomplishment deserves
a lot of attention in and of itself. It is sufficient to make the point in addressing and dealing
with productivity and quality of work issues that
the process must encompass genuine labor participation and real labor-management cooperation

extending deep down into the ranks and agencies.

Third, bi-lateralism in public sector labor-management relations is going to increase in application and scope. There is no reason to fear this, but rather the public service unions should be viewed as vital elements and actors in the public administration and governance system.

There is much to be said for the role which public sector unions do and can play in seeking and implementing democratic goals. With the concern for justice and equality that has been the historic commitment of the American trade union movement--dimmed though some say it might be at this time--public sector unions with their current vitality and potential have the opportunity to energize the labor movement toward a restoration of that kind of commitment, and improve our capacity for local self-government under conditions as demanding as any the nation has ever faced.

PART IV

POLITICS OF LOCAL GOVERNMENT

The approximately 80,000 local governments, including 41,000 special districts, defy description in a
single volume. While the various types of local government have a number of similar characteristics, there
are vast differences between individual units. Readings
in this part deal with a variety of major local issues,
including patronage dismissals, state restraints on
local discretionary authority, the tax revolt of the
1970s, small towns, local charter drafting, alternative
electoral systems, evolving decentralization in New
York City, and metropolitan problems.

The subject of local government personnel is
examined in reading number 26 by Neil D. McFeeley of
the University of Idaho who focuses upon United States
Supreme Court decisions impacting upon the patronage
practices of local governments. In Elrod v. Burns, the
Court forbade the dismissal of non-policy making, non-
confidential county employees for political purposes
and in Branti v. Finkel the Court held discharged
assistant public defenders had to prove only they were
removed from office because of their political
affiliation. These decisions were based upon first
amendment rights of political association and belief,
and limit severely the ability of newly elected
officials to dismiss and replace patronage appointees.

State constitutions and statutes limit the discretionary authority of local governments as well as
court decisions. Jon A. Baer of the State University
of New York at Albany in reading number 27 describes
debt and tax limits constraining "home rule" and
examines in detail the impact of such limits upon
cities in New York State. In part, the fiscal problems
of New York City in the mid-1970s were a product of
the City's attempts to evade the constitutional
restrictions. Baer concludes the state legislature
and voters will not liberalize the limits and argues
the legislature should not impose costly mandates upon
a municipality without state reimbursement of the costs.

Reading number 28 reviews the literature on the
tax revolt that occurred in a number of states

271

commencing in the 1970s and offers an alternative explanation for the revolt. Noting a similarity to the free silver issue in the 1890s, David Lowery of the University of Kentucky offers a single-issue interpretation of the tax revolt and an interpretation of its impact upon public managers.

Robert J. Cline and John Shannon of the United States Advisory Commission on Intergovernmental Relations in reading number 29 examine the types of state limitations on the taxing powers of local governments and the various types of "escape hatches" employed by these units. In their judgment, the tax restrictions contain major loopholes but have served as a warning to officials to restrain spending.

The literature on local government tends to ignore small political subdivisions in spite of the fact that many prominent observers--Jefferson, de Tocqueville, Bryce--praised such units. The 1980 United States census revealed nonmetropolitan areas grew more rapidly in population than metropolitan areas during the decade of the 1970s. Alvin D. Sokolow of the University of California at Davis in reading number 30 examines the culture of small town government and administrative styles in such units. Sokolow points out voluntarism remains an important force in small communities and citizens tend to distrust experts. He concludes the article with advice for the newly arrived public administrator in a small town.

A charter is the fundamental law of a local government and citizens can play vital roles in drafting a charter by serving on a charter commission. In reading number 31, David K. Hamilton of Roosevelt University explores the influence of the personal goals of commission members on their structural change preferences and develops a framework of three structural change preference models and a typology of members' personal goals. The reading concludes with a case study employing the framework.

A local government charter typically provides for the types of voting system to be employed in local elections. Professor Zimmerman in reading number 32 presents criteria to measure the effectiveness of an electoral system in terms of producing "fair" representation. These criteria are effectiveness of

ballots cast, maximization of participation, responsiveness of elected officials, maximization of access to
decision makers, equity in representation, and legitimization of the governing body. Professor Zimmerman
criticizes voting rights decisions of the United States
Supreme Court which promote the use of the single
member district system and urges proportional representation as a better system.

Civil disorders in a number of large cities in the
1960s dramatized the growing dissatisfaction of
minority groups and raised questions with respect to
the ability of cities with their present structures to
improve the quality of life and eliminate the alienation existing between the city government and many
citizens. Cities responded to the disorders in a
variety of ways, including establishment of complaint
bureaus, ombudsmen, and neighborhood city halls.
While New York City employed some of these devices,
the City also restructured its system of community
boards, dating to 1947, and linked them to neighborhood
service cabinets. In reading number 33, Professor
Zimmerman examines evolving decentralization in New
York City and concludes that community boards in
higher income neighborhoods will be the most successful in achieving their goals.

The rapid development of metropolitan areas in the
post World War II period has been responsible for
numerous serious governmental problems. A major
problem is the mismatch between need and fiscal
resources within such areas. Many local government
boundary lines were established in the seventeenth to
the nineteenth centuries and clearly are not suitable
for the most economic and efficient delivery of
services in the latter part of the twentieth century.
Nevertheless, resistance to changing local government
boundary lines is strong. In reading number 34,
Professor Zimmerman describes the use of boundary
review commissions in nine states to cope with area-
wide problems.

Reading number 35 analyzes the impact of the
federal voting rights act upon annexation activity
and points out that the price to be paid for annexation
of territory by political subdivisions subject to the
act is a change in their electoral systems to the
single member district system. Professor Zimmerman

reviews the major United States Supreme Court decisions on voting rights in annexation cases and suggests that consideration should be given to alternative electoral systems.

Although a number of city-county consolidations occurred in the nineteenth century, such consolidations have occurred in only four areas--Baton Rouge, Indianapolis, Jacksonville, and Nashville--in the twentieth century. In recent years, metropolitan reformers generally have been pressing for the establishment of a two-tier system by converting the existing county government into an effective areawide unit. Los Angeles County became a metropolitan government incrementally. Dade County, Florida, became a metropolitan government upon voter ratification of a new charter.

Observers generally have been impressed by the Metropolitan Dade County Government, but Irving G. McNayr, the second county manager, in <u>reading number 36</u> believes municipal boundary lines impede service provision and concludes that consolidation of governmental units would facilitate resolution of major problems.

26. THE SUPREME COURT AND PATRONAGE:
    IMPLICATIONS FOR LOCAL GOVERNMENT*

Neil D. McFeeley

In recent years the United States Supreme Court
has made several significant decisions concerning
the system of patronage in general and local government patronage practices in particular. These
decisions affect the personnel management of public
organizations and are important for local government officials to understand.

Patronage is the power to appoint or dismiss
public officials on the basis of partisan political
reasons rather than professional qualifications or
merit. Patronage flourished in American states even
before the constitution was ratified, and soon
developed in the new federal government. Jefferson,
faced with a government composed almost entirely of
Federalists appointed by Washington and Adams, appointed only members of his political party to government posts. It was Andrew Jackson who justified
the patronage system; rotation in office was a means
to allow the common man to participate in government.
Later presidents extended this spoils system. State
and local governments were also engaged in extensive
patronage during this time.

Yet criticisms of patronage began to mount and
reform efforts at state and federal levels began.
The New York Civil Service Reform Association was
founded in 1877 and four years later the National
Civil Service League was organized. It had some
success at the local level. But when President Gar-
field was assassinated by a disappointed office

---

* Reprinted with permission from the National Civic
   Review, May 1982, pp. 251-58.

seeker in 1881, reform efforts intensified at the
federal, state and local levels. At the federal
level, the Civil Service Reform Act or Pendleton
Act, which set up a bipartisan civil service commission and was the beginning of the federal merit
system, was passed in 1883. Today more than 90
percent of all federal employees are covered by
some form of merit system. State and local governments followed the reform movement; New York and
Massachusetts passed laws similar to the Pendleton
Act in 1883 and 1884. By 1939 all states were required to have merit coverage for employees in
federally supported programs. By 1950, 75 percent
of all cities had some type of merit system. However, many state and local governments do not have
complete merit coverage. Robert Lee reports on a
1976 survey by the Civil Service Commission which
found that merit tests for appointments were used
in 79 percent of cities but only 35 percent of
counties, and that some "local personnel systems
may be nominally merit but practically political."[1]
It was in this situation--continuing although
lessened patronage--that the judiciary was asked to
decide on the constitutional validity of patronage.

Prior to the first major Supreme Court decision
on patronage in the 1970s, the lower courts had
faced the issue. Most had concluded that there were
no constitutional grounds on which to prohibit
patronage dismissals. In Bailey v. Richardson
(182 F.2d 46, D.C. Cir, 1950), the circuit court
for the District of Columbia rejected an early
challenge on First Amendment grounds on the basis
of the right-privilege doctrine of public employment. (By the early 1970s, however, the doctrine
that constitutional rights turn on whether a governmental benefit is characterized as a "right" or as
a "privilege" had been rejected by the Supreme Court
in such cases as Graham v. Richardson (403 US 365,
1971) and Board of Regents v. Roth (408 US 564,
1972). Alomar v. Dwyer (447 F.2nd 482, 2nd Cir.,
1971), a case involving a social worker's First
Amendment challenge to her political discharge was

decided on the authority of Bailey. The second
circuit held that non-civil service employment of
policy-making employees was "terminable at will
without notice or hearing," regardless of First
Amendment claims. And in <u>American Federation of
State, County and Municipal Employees v. Shapp,</u>
(443 Pa 527, 280 A.2d 375, 1971), the Pennsylvania Supreme Court considered the discharge of
some 2,000 state employees by a newly elected
governor of the opposite party. The claims of the
employees, all of whom were non-civil service
workers who had originally obtained their jobs
through political sponsorship, were rejected. The
court held that acceptance of patronage employment
constituted a waiver of constitutional rights:
"Those who, figuratively speaking, live by the
political sword must be prepared to die by the
political sword."

One court of appeals decision written in 1972
by then Judge John Paul Stevens held that patronage
dismissals of non-policy making officials infringed
First Amendment rights since no counterbalancing
vital state interests were proven. The case,
<u>Illinois State Employees Union v. Lewis</u> (473 F.2d
561, 7th Cir., 1972; cert. denied 410 US 928,
1972), involved the discharge of 1,940 of some
4,000 non-civil service employees by the newly
appointed secretary of state of Illinois.

Faced with these contradictory rulings on
patronage dismissals, the Supreme Court accepted
the case of <u>Elrod v. Burns</u> (427 US 347, 1976). In
1970, Richard Elrod, who had recently been elected
sheriff of Cook County, Illinois, discharged
John Burns and other non-civil service employees
on political grounds. The employees, who were in
the non-policy making positions of guard, process
server and chief deputy, had been appointed on a
patronage basis by the previous Republican administration. They were fired by the new Democratic
sheriff because they refused to affiliate with or
obtain sponsorship from the Democratic party of

Cook County. The employees filed suit, alleging that their First Amendment rights of association and political belief, as secured by the Fourteenth Amendment due process clause, had been violated by Sheriff Elrod, Chicago Mayor Richard Daley and the Cook County Democratic party. The Supreme Court accepted the case in order to decide whether public employees who were discharged solely because of their partisan political affiliation or nonaffiliation have been deprived of constitutional rights. A plurality of the court agreed that such dismissals were unconstitutional.

Although unable to agree on the specific opinion, five justices agreed that some patronage dismissals violated First Amendment rights, as guaranteed by the Fourteenth Amendment due process clause. Justice William Brennan, joined by Justices Byron R. White and Thurgood Marshall, announced the judgment of the court.

Brennan's opinion reviewed the government's claims for patronage and rejected them all. The claim that patronage dismissals ensured efficiency and effectiveness was belied by the inefficiency of wholesale replacement of large numbers of public employees when political offices change hands and by the fact that more qualified persons will not necessarily be found. In any event, less drastic means of ensuring vital interests of effectiveness and efficiency, such as merit systems and discharge for poor job performance, exist. A second interest advanced by Sheriff Elrod is the need for political loyalty to ensure that the electorate's wishes be carried out. Brennan rejected that argument for validation of patronage overall, holding that limiting patronage dismissals to policy-making positions is sufficient to achieve the goal of responsiveness. The third argument for patronage was that it preserves the democratic process by preserving the political parties. Justice Brennan was not convinced that the elimination of patronage dismissals would bring about the demise of party

politics, and in any event, held that such dismissals were not the least restrictive alternatives.
In addition, he argued that patronage may also
retard the democratic process by entrenching one
political party so any benefits are outweighed by
the loss of the constitutional rights.

Justice Potter Stewart, joined by Justice Harry
A. Blackmun, concurred in the result although they
did not agree with Brennan's "wide-ranging" opinion.
Stewart argued that the case did not require a
consideration of the broad contours of the patronage
system "with all its variations and permutations."
He reserved judgment about the constitutional validity of patronage hiring of some governmental employees and concluded: "The single substantive question
involved in this case is whether a nonpolicy-making,
nonconfidential government employee can be discharged from a job that he is satisfactorily performing
upon the sole ground of his political beliefs. I
agree with the Court that he cannot."

Justice Lewis F. Powell, Jr., joined by Chief
Justice Warren E. Burger and Justice William H.
Rehnquist, dissented, arguing that the plurality
decision, which held unconstitutional a practice
"as old as the Republic, a practice which has contributed significantly to the democratization of
American politics," neither is constitutionally
required nor serves the interest of democracy.

A majority of justices then, was willing to
strike down patronage dismissals of public employees in a non-policy making, non-confidential
position. Would a majority be willing to extend
that ruling? That question was answered four years
later.

The public defender of Rockland County, New
York, is appointed by the county legislature for a
six-year term. He in turn appoints nine assistants who serve at his pleasure. In 1978 the Democrats were in control of the legislature and

279

appointed Peter Branti as public defender, replacing the incumbent Republican. Branti immediately began to discharge six of the nine assistants, intending to replace them with Democrats. Republicans Aaron Finkel and Alan Tabakman, who had been assistant public defenders for several years, were among those who were to be terminated. They filed suit alleging that discharge solely for partisan reasons violated the First and Fourteenth Amendments.

In Branti v. Finkel (63 L Ed 2nd 574, 1980), a six-three decision written by Justice Stevens, the Supreme Court went further in striking down patronage dismissals. The court ruled that to prevail in this action the discharged employees need not prove that they had been coerced into changing their political allegiance but only to prove that they were discharged solely because of their private political belief.

Justice Stevens then considered Branti's contention that "even if party sponsorship is an unconstitutional condition of continued public employment for clerks, deputies, and janitors, it is an acceptable requirement for an assistant public defender." Elrod had recognized that:

> party affiliation may be an acceptable
> requirement for some types of govern-
> ment employment. Thus, if an employee's
> private political beliefs would inter-
> fere with the discharge of his public
> duties, his First Amendment rights may
> be required to yield to the State's vital
> interest in maintaining governmental
> effectiveness and efficiency.

Stevens examined whether political affiliation is a legitimate factor to be considered in the position of assistant public defender and concluded that it was not. His holding did not rest entirely on the "confidential, policy-making" character of the position, noting that under "some circumstances, a position may be appropriately considered political even though it is neither confidential nor policy-making in character," and also that "it is equally clear that party affiliation is not necessarily relevant to every policy-making or confidential position." "In sum, the ultimate inquiry is not whether the label 'policy maker' or 'confidential' fits a particular position; rather, the question is whether the hiring authority can demonstrate that party affiliation is an appropriate requirement for the effective performance of the public office involved." And it is manifest that the position of assistant public defender does not fit into the "political" category. The duties and responsibilities of the assistant public defender (and any policy-making or confidential information) relate to individual clients and not to any partisan political interests. Thus, employment as an assistant public defender cannot be "conditioned upon his allegiance to the political party in control of the county government."

Three justices dissented from the court's opinion. (Interestingly, Chief Justice Burger, who dissented in Elrod v. Burns, joined the majority.) Justice Stewart, relying on the dichotomy between "non-policy making, non-confidential" positions and confidential, policy-making responsibilities which he had made in his concurrence in Elrod, dissented. He argues that assistant public defenders were not "non-confidential" employees but were involved in a confidential professional association with the public defender.

Justice Powell, joined by Justice Rehnquist, again dissented, arguing that substantial governmental interests were served by the "long-accepted practice" of patronage.

These cases have some significant implications for public personnel administration in local government. It seems clear that a majority of the Supreme Court considers dismissals of public

employees based on political and partisan reasons
to be highly suspect. Such dismissals violate
First Amendment rights of belief and association
and may be justified only when party affiliation is
demonstrated to be "an appropriate requirement for
the effective performance of the public office involved." That is difficult to demonstrate for most
public jobs, and it appears that only a few top
"political" positions may remain within the patronage system of dismissal. After Branti v. Finkel,
even policy-making, confidential positions do not
necessarily fall within the patronage system.

Less clear is the constitutionality of other
patronage practices. In 1980, the fourth circuit
court of appeals in Delong v. United States indicated that patronage transfer and reassignment may
also violate the First Amendment, but the Supreme
Court has not so ruled. It does seem, however,
under the holding of Branti that such transfers and
reassignments of employees in "non-political"
positions would violate the freedom of belief and
association with no countervailing advancement of a
vital governmental interest. Of more importance
and more interest is patronage hiring. Elrod and
Branti will obviously limit the opportunities for
such hiring, yet vacancies will exist and may become more significant for the parties because of
their relative scarcity. Political hiring seems to
impose fewer burdens; an individual denied a job on
patronage grounds suffers less than one discharged
for political reasons. Yet patronage hiring still
may infringe First Amendment rights, especially when
employment is scarce, since individuals may subordinate their political beliefs in order to get a
job. It is also doubtful that the vital governmental interests in efficiency or effectiveness are
advanced by patronage hiring any more than by the
political discharges invalidated in Elrod. The
interest in responsiveness can be satisfied by less
drastic means, such as limiting political hiring
to "political" positions. The interest in the
preservation of the democratic process made by

partisan hiring is more difficult to assess.
Patronage appointments are of major importance to
political parties, and their elimination may have
some serious effects. Although the Supreme Court
has not decided on the issue of patronage hiring
(in Elrod the specific holding was that "the
practice of patronage dismissals is unconstitutional
under the First and Fourteenth Amendments,")
Justice Stevens' opinion in Branti seems broad
enough to cover such hiring and challenges to
patronage hiring may well be successful:

> Government funds, which are collected
> from taxpayers of all parties on a
> nonpolitical basis, cannot be expend-
> ed for the benefit of one political
> party simply because that party has
> control of the government. The com-
> pensation of government employees,
> like the distribution of other public
> benefits, must be justified by a
> governmental purpose.

There are some other barriers to successful
challenges to patronage practices. One barrier
arises from Mount Healthy City Board of Education
v. Doyle (429 U.S. 274, 1977), in which the
Supreme Court holding may require a patronage
challenger to prove that the government intended to
burden First Amendment rights and that discriminatory motives prompted the challenged action. If
all members of one party were discharged, as in
Elrod, then that mass firing could be used to infer
that the discharge was motivated by constitutionally
impermissible purposes. But the burden of proof
would be more difficult to sustain in a case of
alleged patronage hiring, for the employer could
argue that appointments were based on a multitude
of reasons and that political affiliation was not
the sole motivation. (This uses "Note--Patronage
and the First Amendment after Elrod v. Burns," 78
Columbia Law Review 488, 1978).

Another barrier to challengers is that of standing. In order to bring a suit to a federal court, a person must show that he or she had sustained or was in immediate danger of sustaining a direct and individualized injury from a constitutional violation that the court could cure. This may present an obstacle to those challenging patronage hiring because:

> When the plaintiff is simply one of many not hired or not granted a benefit, the grievance may be so generalized as to run afoul of the Supreme Court's holding that a harm shared in substantially equal measure by a large class of citizens normally does not warrant the exercise of jurisdiction. Furthermore, an alleged victim of political discrimination would presumably have to show that his inability to obtain the desired job or benefit resulted from constitutional infractions; that absent these violations he would have received the job or benefit. (Note, Columbia Law Review, 480).

These decisions on patronage may also affect another aspect of public employment: the restrictions on political activity of civil servants found in the Hatch Act and the "little Hatch Acts" in the states. The plurality opinion of Justice Brennan in Elrod v. Burns attempted to reconcile the court's previous decision in United Public Workers v. Mitchell (330 U.S. 75, 1947; reaffirmed for federal workers in United States Civil Service Commission v. National Association of Letter Carriers, 413 U.S. 548, 1973, and for state workers in Broadrick v. Oklahoma, 413 U.S. 601, 1973), which upheld restrictions on political activity, with the decision in Elrod striking down the political dismissals of public employees by arguing that the Hatch Act restraints on First Amendment activities were permissible to safeguard the core interests of individual belief and association from possible abuse. There indeed is a vital governmental interest in protecting public employees from political coercion and favoritism by limiting partisan political activities, but is the Hatch Act the "least restrictive" means for securing those interests? Since the "little Hatch Acts" vary widely, this indicates that more narrowly-drawn remedies which infringe First Amendment rights less might serve the governmental interests in an effective public service just as well as Hatch Act broad proscriptions of political activities.

> In theory and in practice, American politics has never developed a genuine alternative to the patronage system....

> Since the patronage has deep roots in every branch of legitimate American political life, it is unlikely that real changes can be made without accommodating in some degree to its traditions. Patronage is inevitable because of the existence of the two-party system, pressure groups, the vagaries of constitutional government, the human condition, and financial exigencies of campaigning.[2]

In the last few years the Supreme Court has made important decisions concerning the system of patronage, a two-century old part of our political system. Elrod v. Burns and Branti v. Finkel invalidated patronage dismissals for a significant segment of local public employment. Because of the adverse impact patronage has on First Amendment rights of political belief and association, the court concluded that any contributions to efficiency or political parties made by patronage dismissals were not enough to justify continuance of such dismissals. The broad language of the Branti decision also intimates the majority's negative views on the constitutional validity of

other patronage practices. Thus, in addition to
the immediate impact of the decisions, in the
future court decisions may affect a great many
other personnel practices in the public service.

NOTE

1
  Robert D. Lee, Jr., Public Personnel Systems
    (Baltimore, University Park Press, 1979), p. 26.

2
  Martin Tolchin and Susan Tolchin, To the Victor...
    (New York: Vintage Books, 1971), pp. 303 and
    307.

27. MUNICIPAL DEBT AND TAX LIMITS: CONSTRAINTS ON HOME RULE*

Jon A. Baer

Arguments for financial home rule focus on two aspects of state-local fiscal relationships: (1) state mandates without reimbursement to the municipalities for the costs of compliance and (2) debt and tax limitations imposed on local governments by state constitutions and statutes. Proponents of local fiscal authority contend that local elected officials should have wide discretion in establishing tax and expenditure policies since they are closest to the people, and, thus, the most competent to assess the needs of their constituencies. Moreover, debt and tax limits have been charged with severely hampering local governments' capacity to meet demands for increased public services, forcing local governments to pressure higher levels of government for increased aid, and spurring a wide variety of mechanisms to evade the limits.

On the other hand, debt and tax limits have been defended as protecting taxpayers from excessive deviations from local taxation norms and assuring investors as well as taxpayers that decisions on capital projects, and on the borrowing necessary to finance them, will be responsible ones. This view holds that a state has an absolute right to restrict the powers of local governments to levy taxes and incur debt whenever such action is deemed appropriate by the state.

State constitutional and statutory limitations on local debt generally take the form of a specified

---

Reprinted with permission from the National Civic Review, April 1981, pp. 204-10.

percentage of the total assessed valuation of taxable real property. These restrictions were a
reaction to overextension and waste in local borrowing during the last three decades of the nineteenth
century and to the default of about 10 percent of
all municipal bonds during the 1930s. Only four
states--Alaska, Colorado, Florida and Nebraska--
currently have no constitutional or statutory limits
on local authority to incur long-term debt.

Although debt limits may have been conceived
for noble purposes, many observers charge that they
have been fully circumvented. One evasive techni-
que is the issuance of non-guaranteed revenue
bonds to finance specific projects, since non-
guaranteed debt is not subject to limitation.
Another method is the creation of a special purpose
district. Since debt limits usually apply to each
unit of government, a city may establish a special
water district within its boundaries and thus
double its effective debt-incurring authority. In
this way, debt limits have contributed to the fragmentation of local governance. Still another cir-
cumvention is the long-term leasing of facilities
with the municipality assuming ownership on the
lease's termination. Such an arrangement is indis-
tinguishable from debt financing, but leasing is not
debt at law.

The fiscal plight of a number of America's
largest cities beginning in the mid-1970s has raised
the specter of defaults on municipal bond issues.
Obviously, this development has not strengthened
the case for elimination of municipal debt limits.
Furthermore, cities that do become overburdened with
debt face another problem: 44 states have constitutional provisions forbidding loans of state credit
to or on behalf of any corporation, including municipalities.

Property tax limitations on local governments
first appeared in the 1870s and 1880s, and were

adopted to shield property owners from exorbitant
tax rate increases during and after the Panic of
1870, and to limit local expenditures for private
road and canal construction. A new impetus for
such limits occurred when property values plummeted
and tax delinquencies soared during the depression
of the 1930s. A study conducted by the United
States Advisory Commission on Intergovernmental
Relations (ACIR) found that, as of 1976, 39 states
limited some or all of their local governments
relative to their capacity to raise revenue from
the property tax.

The most well-known tax limitation of recent
years is the Jarvis-Gann Initiative (Proposition
13), approved by the California electorate in June
1978. Proposition 13 has been credited by the
press with setting off a tax revolt, and indeed, a
new round of constitutional and statutory property
tax limitations swept the country in the wake of
its passage. Similar constitutional amendments
were approved in Idaho and Nevada, and, during
1979, seven states adopted limits on the authority
of their local governments to raise revenue and/or
to spend. (Many such limitation measures on the
1980 ballots, however, were defeated.)

Municipal tax limits have been charged with
encouraging the proliferation of special purpose
districts to obtain additional taxing power, stimulating debt financing, and necessitating special
legislation to alleviate the onerous burdens overall tax limits impose on individual municipalities.

A 1977 study by ACIR concluded that local tax
limits have little effect upon total state-local
expenditures. Additionally, Helen F. Ladd, in
"An Economic Evaluation of State limitations on
Local Taxing and Spending Powers" (National Tax
Journal, March 1978, pages 1-18), observed that
such limits yield little economic benefit but
carry significant costs in the form of service

level distortions. The existence of a substantial
state surplus prevented Proposition 13 from having
a disastrous initial impact on the ability of California municipalities to deliver public services,
but other states without such surpluses can expect
significant service disruptions if they adopt
similar measures.

Debt and tax limitations on municipalities in
New York State are embodied in the state constitution, and their early history parellels the
national trends discussed above. The limits are
based on percentages of the five-year average full
valuation of taxable real property, but these percentages vary for different types of municipalities
and even for individual municipalities. Debt limits
effectively range from 7 to 12 percent, and tax
limits from 1.5 to 4 percent. Debt and tax limits
apply to all New York municipalities, except that
there are no tax limits for towns.

After World War II, several factors led to an
increase in levels of taxation and indebtedness for
New York municipalities: national prosperity and
widespread demographic shifts; the creation and
growth of suburbs; and the accumulation of postponed
needs for public facilities and services, resulting
in a huge expansion of local government activity,
especially school and sewer construction. This
growth was restrained, however, by the debt and tax
limits, particularly in view of the slow rise in
assessed valuations and the dampening effect of
using the five-year average of assessed valuation.
Consequently, six constitutional amendments were
adopted by 1953 that involved changes in the com-
putation and application of the debt limits rather
than substantive modifications of the debt limitation principle. In particular, New York City was
granted three special exemptions involving school
debt service and capital spending for hospitals
and subways

Many localities, nevertheless, continued to
experience difficulty in financing sewage treatment

plants within their debt limits. Thus, a constitutional amendment was adopted in 1963 to permit the exclusion of indebtedness incurred by a municipality during the period 1962-1972 for such projects. In 1973, the voters approved another amendment extending this period through 1982. There have been no other amendments expanding the authority of New York's municipalities to incur debt.

Regarding tax limits, constitutional amendments adopted in 1949 changed the basis for tax limit calculations to full valuation of property assessments in order to eliminate artificial variations in taxing authority from jurisdiction to jurisdiction because of differing local assessment practices, and extended additional taxing authority to cities of less than 125,000 population that contain school districts. New York City was given more taxing power through a 1953 amendment establishing a combined tax limit for the city and its component counties (the five boroughs). Through this amendment, however, the possibility of a separate county tax within New York City vanished. No additional amendments modifying the constitutional tax limits have been adopted.

The debt and tax limits are alleged to have particularly exacerbated the fiscal problems of New York City. Frank J. Macchiarola, in "Local Finances Under the New York State Constitution with an Emphasis on New York City" (Fordham Law Review, 1966, page 263), observed in the mid-1960s that the city's failure to project accurate long-range budgets was not only a product of poor management practices but also a result of the constitutional limitations that encourage evasive and deceptive bookkeeping practices. One reason cited for the grave fiscal crisis that caused New York City to be closed out of the municipal bond market in 1975 was the gimmick of transferring $700 million in expenditures, properly belonging in the operating budget, to the capital budget. This device was designed to take advantage of the above-mentioned constitutional amendments that exempted certain capital spending

291

from the city's debt limit and to allow the presentation of a "balanced" operating budget.

Moreover, the city misused tax anticipation notes (TANs) and revenue anticipation notes (RANs), short-term debt instruments designed to bridge the shortfall between daily expenditures and tax and intergovernmental receipts that are received only on a quarterly or yearly basis. Such notes are exempt from the debt limit if repaid within the time period stipulated by statute. The city followed a practice of borrowing against tax revenues that on paper were due the city but in reality were uncollectible. The TANs and RANs had to be refinanced since the city's revenues were insufficient to pay them off. Thus the city's aggregate debt mushroomed, unregulated by the constitutional debt limit.

Additionally, New York City evaded the constitutional tax limit by including in its full assessed valuation figures parcels that were not realistically taxable. The constitutional exclusion of property taxes utilized for debt service was perversely used to justify increased taxes for the city's massive long-term and short-term borrowing. Although a number of fundamental factors was responsible for New York City's fiscal difficulties, such fiscal mismanagement--encouraged by the debt and tax limits--was the immediate cause of the 1975 fiscal crisis.

As one means of coping with the crisis, on November 15, 1975, the state legislature enacted the Emergency Moratorium Act for the City of New York, which afforded an opportunity for holders of the city's short-term notes to exchange them for long-term bonds issued by the Municipal Assistance Corporation (MAC). If these holders declined the offer, they were enjoined from initiating court action to enforce the city's short-term obligations for three years. However, in Flushing National Bank v. Municipal Assistance Corporation of the

City of New York (40 N.Y. 2d 731, 1976), the state
court of appeals held that the state constitution
prohibits the city from contracting any indebtedness unless the city's full faith and credit is
pledged for the payment of the principal and
interest thereon. (MAC bonds are "moral obligation"
not "full faith and credit" bonds.) Moreover, the
court took notice of the constitutional provisions
authorizing municipalities to exceed their tax
limits in order to pay for debt service and inferred
therefrom a "constitutional imperative" that a
municipality meet its debt obligations even if the
tax limit is exceeded. The court, however, realized
the disruption that would ensue--including a real
threat of bankruptcy--if it granted immediate relief to the plaintiffs and accordingly refused to
issue an order until the legislature and the city
were given time to prepare for the consequences of
the court's ruling.

Also in the fall of 1975, the state legislature enacted the Financial Emergency Act for the
City of New York, which established the Emergency
Financial Control Board to oversee the city's
fiscal management. The board is state dominated,
consisting of the governor, the mayor, the city
and state comptrollers, and three gubernatorial
appointees. Its powers include approving the
three-year financial plan, estimating revenues and
expenditures, approving major contracts and all
indebtedness, and disbursing city revenues only
after determining that the proposed expenditures
are consistent with the financial plan. Enactment
of this legislation effectively eliminated home
rule for New York City on the ground that the
city's fiscal trauma has a profound effect on the
financial stability of the state government as well.

For other municipalities, constitutional tax
limitations have been construed strictly in recent
court decisions. The most important of these is
Hurd v. City of Buffalo (343 N.Y.S.2d 950, 1973),

in which the appellate division of New York supreme court overturned a state statute exempting levies for pension and retirement liabilities from the 2 percent real property tax limit imposed on the city by the constitution. Though mindful that Buffalo was undergoing severe financial stress, the court declared: "The citizens of the State of New York, in establishing a constitutional tax limit..., presumably decided that this was the maximum tax which could be levied...without becoming oppressive, and it may not be circumvented by legislation." The court of appeals affirmed the decision (34 N.Y.2d 628, 1974).

In Bethlehem Steel Corporation v. Board of Education of the City School District of Lackawanna, Etc. (44 N.Y.2d 831, 1978), the court of appeals struck down the state's Emergency City and School District Relief Act on the ground that it was an unconstitutional evasion of the tax limit applicable to the cities of Buffalo and Rochester and to certain city school districts to allow these jurisdictions to exclude retirement and social security costs from their tax limits. The Hurd and Bethlehem Steel decisions have had very serious consequences for small cities nearing exhaustion of their tax limits, and have necessitated substantial additional state financial aid to school districts within such cities.

A New York Department of Audit and Control survey disclosed that counties' use of their constitutional tax limit in 1979 ranged from 4 percent to 77.3 percent and averaged 39.9 percent. We conclude that most New York counties are not experiencing major difficulty in keeping within their tax limits.

A different picture emerges when we look at cities. Three cities exhausted their tax limit in 1979: Buffalo, Rochester and Yonkers. Newburgh used 99.9 percent of its taxing authority. Three other cities used more than 90 percent of their tax limit, including New York City (93.3 percent).

Obviously, tax limits severely constrain the
ability of cities, especially the larger ones, to
raise revenue. Moreover, it has been and continues
to be alleged that other cities besides New York
engage in techniques to evade both the debt and tax
limits to the detriment of their financial stability.

Opinion as to the desirability of constitutional amendments that would remove New York's local
debt and tax limitations conforms to what one would
expect. Preliminary results from a survey conducted
by Joseph F. Zimmerman for the Advisory Commission
on Intergovernmental Relations indicate that state
officials feel such amendments would be undesirable.
County officials join in that assessment, not surprisingly, given that counties are largely unhinder-
ed by the restrictions. By contrast, mayors view
repeal of debt and tax limits as very desirable,
probably because the limits have greatly reduced
their range of fiscal options in meeting the service
delivery needs of their constituents.

It is clear that, although New York is a "constitutional home rule" state, the courts have consistently adhered to a narrow construction of the
powers of local governments, particularly when
"state concerns" are said to exist. Since the 1963
"home rule" amendment fails to extend local discretionary authority to finance, it can be safely anticipated that the courts will continue to uphold the
constitutional debt and tax limits to the letter.

To project the future of the limits in New York
State the following factors should be noted: (1)
Relative to the rest of the nation, New York has
entered an era of economic decline that will persist
for at least another decade. (2) The recent New York
City and Yonkers fiscal crises have stimulated calls
for more stringent monitoring of local finances by
the state to avert future crises. (3) The tax
limitation phenomenon will accelerate the rate of
relative slowdown in the growth of state and local
governments. We conclude from these considerations
that neither the state legislature nor the electorate

will approve a liberalization, much less the repeal, of constitutional debt and tax limitations in New York. However, these restrictions, especially those on the financially hard-pressed cities, provide a potent argument for establishing the principle that state legislation mandating local expenditures which must be financed out of the municipality's tax base or within its debt limit shall make provision for state reimbursement to the locality for such expenditures.

28. Interpreting the Tax Revolt: A Review of the
Literature and an Alternative Explanation*

David Lowery

Four years have passed since California's adoption
of Proposition 13. In that time, 17 states have conducted referenda on state and/or local taxing and
spending (29), and by 1980, 38 states had "moved to
reduce or at least stabilize taxes" (34). The revolt
obviously has major implications for those concerned
with state and local government. For citizens, the
revolt threatens the local provision of public goods
and services as restricted revenues lead to services
being cut back or shifted to other levels of government
(28). For administrators, the revolt signals a break
in conventional incremental decision processes and
thereby increases the uncertainty associated with
administrative decision-making (21, 12). Perhaps most
importantly, the revolt raises serious questions about
the workings of representative government. As Shapiro,
Puryear, and Ross have noted, "it should trouble
us . . .that within a stable democracy as ours, the
government could find itself so far out of line with
the desires of the governed" (36). The scope and significance of the tax revolt phenomenon has drawn
considerable research attention, and that attention has
taken two different directions--identifying methods to
cope with organizational decline and explaining causes
of the revolt.

Public managers are most directly concerned with
the "cutback management" literature that focuses on
"managing organizational change toward lower levels of
resource consumption and organizational activity" (22,
23). The sources of fiscal stress undoubtedly encompass more than the tax revolt and include such problems
as declining productivity, economic stagnation, inflation, and legal restrictions on economic growth. Yet
the tax revolt, routinely cited by cutback management
analysts, remains the most dramatic and drastic source
of fiscal stress (32). Cutback management literature

*Reprinted from State and Local Government Review, Vol.
XIV, No. 3, September 1982, pp. 110-16 by permission
of the Institute of Government, University of Georgia.

suggests a variety of strategies designed to cope with organizational decline, ranging from strategies that resist decline to those that smooth the process of decline (22, p. 21).

While cognizant of the managerial consequences of the tax revolt, other analysts have alternatively directed their research efforts to explaining why the revolt occurred in the first place. Unfortunately, social scientists have been largely unsuccessful in developing such an explanation or even in describing the tax revolt itself. Two bodies of empirical work have dominated the literature. The first addresses the question of voter expectations regarding tax-cutting referenda: would voters expect that services be cut or only trimmed of "bureaucratic fat?" Attempts to answer this question have proven inconclusive. Although they used similar data, Attiyeh and Engle reached a conclusion that is the polar opposite of those of Citrin and Mushkin (2, 10, 32). The second body of work attempts to explain the tax revolt using a conventional economic model that views the individual's demand for government services as a function of self-interest as inferred from demographic characteristics. When applied to tax revolt proposals, however, these narrowly defined rationality models have not worked well (10, 27, 14). The existing literature simply has not succeeded in explaining the tax revolt.

Unfortunately, the cutback management and explanation literatures have remained separate and distinct. Strategies adopted and decisions made by public managers faced with a tax revolt differ substantially, depending on the manager's own perceptions of the tax revolt. As George Break has noted:

> To a close observer of the Proposition 13 movement, both before and after the election, it is simply not clear whether it attracted votes mainly as a means of attacking Big Government, and taxes in general, as Howard Jarvis and others quickly claimed in the aftermath of the vote, or simply as a way of protesting the recent heavy overload of the property tax. . . .The differences between these two possible interpretations of what the public wants are critically important, as

298

the decisions following from the prevailing
one (the Jarvis view) will have far-reaching
consequences for the state (5, p. 43).

If the Jarvis view is accepted, cutback management
activities should be directed at smoothing the process
of scaling down public services. The property tax
explanation, on the other hand, should encourage
managers to maintain service levels and resist the
process of decline by, among other strategies, developing alternative revenue support systems. Thus, the
strategy recommendations of the cutback management
literature, as applied to the tax revolt, are meaningful only in so far as their selection is grounded on an
understanding of the cause(s) of the tax revolt. Without such a grounding, the strategy recommendations
remain a set of contradictory and conflicting proposals
that may lead to inappropriate and/or unnecessary
changes in the level and/or funding of public services.

The failure of the explanation literature
suggests, however, that such grounding is impossible at
this time. This paper attempts to begin the process of
resolving this problem. First, the existing explanation literature is reviewed and its limitations noted.
Then, an alternative explanation of the tax revolt as a
form of single issue politics is developed and its
ability to account for the failure of the contemporary
explanatory models is demonstrated. Finally, the
implications of this alternative research program for
both cutback management strategies and the study of tax
revolt causes are discussed.

CONTEMPORARY EXPLANATIONS OF THE TAX REVOLT

Two major approaches have been adopted in explaining the tax revolt. As we will see later, the two are
closely related; however, we will treat them separately
here for expository purposes as they are usually viewed
as discrete bodies of literature.

The first approach attempts to understand the tax
revolt by addressing the question of what voters
expected from tax revolt referenda. The importance of
this question cannot be overemphasized. The several
answers that are given are grounded on fundamentally
different models of the causes of the tax revolt. The

299

first is the excessive government or leviathan model which emphasizes the role of political and bureaucratic actors as strategic manipulators of fiscal institutions. The view of government as passive respondent to voter demands is rejected in favor of a view of politicians and bureaucrats as self-interested actors with a stake in the continued expansion of the public sector (6). Through a variety of mechanisms, including the use of indirect taxes to generate a fiscal illusion (17; 8, p. 129), public employee voting (13), and bureaucratic budget maximizing behavior (33), the actions of public officials lead to an expansion of the public sector beyond the size demanded by citizens. Since these officials exercise monopoly control of the institutions of government, citizens must resort to extraordinary means if they are to lower the production level of public goods. As Buchanan has observed, " . . .attempt to reduce the excessive governmental spending might be aimed at the motivational structure of bureaucracy rather than at aggregate budgetary and tax levels. On the other hand, if the bureaucracy is considered to be so firmly entrenched and its institutions so rigid that direct attack would be futile, alternative means may be required" (7, p. 5). From the perspective of this model, tax revolt referenda are viewed as extraordinary but necessary responses to the condition of leviathan government.

The second model takes a much narrower view of the causes of the tax revolt, viewing citizen support of tax revolt referenda as a response to excessively high taxes, especially property taxes. Citizens are viewed as being generally supportive of the size of government and opposed to any service cutbacks (with the possible exception of welfare). Taxpayer revolts are interpreted as voter reaction to their perceptions of waste and inefficiency in the public sector (32, 26). Taxes are considered to be too high relative to the benefits received from public goods and services, and tax limitation and/or reduction will place government on a diet to redress this imbalance.

The empirical work on the two dominant models, however, has produced ambiguous results.[1] Attiyeh and Engle examined the county level vote for Proposition 13 and found that high expenditure counties were more likely to support 13 and concluded "that in fact voters

did recognize the implication of substantial reductions
in government expenditures and voted to tolerate them"
(2, p. 140), that voters were acting to restrict the
leviathan.[2] However, analyses of individual level data
on tax-cutting referenda have tended to support the
efficiency explanation. Citrin, Mushkin, and also
Herbert and Bingham's analyses of both California and
national data on citizen expenditure preferences found
broad support for both general and specific policy
spending levels and found that California voters
expected only slight cuts in spending as a result of
the passage of Proposition 13 (10, 32, 18). Voters,
they argue, were concerned with the efficiency rather
than the size of government. An empirical resolution of
the question of what voters wanted from Proposition 13
has remained elusive given these conflicting results.
Moreover, as will be discussed at the end of this section, an empirical resolution is unlikely to be forthcoming.

The second major approach in explaining the tax
revolt is based on a narrowly defined rationality model;
the individual's demand for government tax-expenditure
levels are hypothesized to be a function of self-interest as inferred from demographic traits. The use of
such models to analyze tax and expenditure decisions is
quite common and has proven successful on a number of
specific issues (30, 35, 3). The application of this
approach to the study of the tax revolt is straightforward. As Mariotti notes,

> The basic hypothesis is clear: people cast
> their votes for or against (tax revolt ref-
> erenda) based on how they perceive their own
> narrowly defined economic self-interest.
> The model that is developed is based on the
> assumption of objective costs, i.e., that
> the voters--in aggregate--were motivated by
> purely economic and hence objectively meas-
> ureable factors (27, p. 17).

Several analysts have examined California and
Michigan tax revolt referenda using self-interest based
rationality models. Mariotti examined Michigan's 1976
vote on Proposal C, which would have placed a cap on
state expenditures. He had hypothesized that higher
income groups, government workers, nonminorities, rural

voters, homeowners, and those not receiving state subsidies would, in aggregate, be supportive of the Proposal (27). Courant, Gramlich, and Rubinfeld examined
Michigan's 1978 vote on the Headlee Amendment (similar
to Proposal C) and Tisch Amendment (similar to Proposition 13). Most of their hypotheses were similar to
Mariotti's, but they additionally hypothesized that non-
family, male, less educated, and Protestant voters would
support the referenda. Finally, in the most thorough of
these analyses, Jack Citrin examined California's vote
for propositions 8 and 13 as well as spending preferences on eight policy areas using many of the same hypotheses employed by Mariotti and Courant, Gramlich, and
Rubinfeld (10).

Given the previous successful applications of the
rationality model to tax-expenditure decisions and a
long history of theoretical and empirical support for
the specific hypotheses on self-interest contained
therein, it is surprising that the applications of the
model to tax revolt referenda largely fail. Each explains a low portion of the variance in the vote for the
referenda, and many of the specific coefficients were in
the wrong direction and/or insignificant. The analysts
reach rather pessimistic conclusions on the utility of
rationality models in explaining the tax revolt.
Mariotti notes that "the results indicate that a substantial portion of the Michigan Electorate voted for
reasons other than purely pecuniary ones" (27, p. 24).
More generally, Citrin concludes that "it is clear . . .
that a model that relies on these background and political variables provides an inadequate explanation of the
individual's preferences for public goods" (10, p. 127).
Like the first approach to understanding the tax revolt
which focused on voter expectations of the results of a
tax revolt, the narrowly defined rationality approach
has not proven very successful.

This is not meant to say that the contemporary
research on the tax revolt was poorly conceived or
naively conducted. The tax revolt occurred with little
advance notice. Social scientists, including myself,
naturally responded to it by applying conventional
models of social choice explanation. But it is time to
recognize that the tax revolt cannot be explained within
the context of the conventional models, particularly in
light of the policy consequences of being unable to
explain the revolt. The tax revolt is the most

302

important event to hit state and local government since the Great Depression of the 1930s. But with the substantial failure of these two initial approaches to explaining the tax revolt, no research program exists to guide either further efforts to explain the revolt or, more immediately, managerial decisions in response to the revolt. As Attiyeh and Engle have suggested, different explanations point to drastically different policies:

> The two extreme possibilities are that the vote (for Proposition 13) was a specific protest against the property tax as a means of raising revenue. The second is that the vote reflected a failure of local governments to represent adequately the wishes of the constituents in allowing expenditure and taxes to reach too high a level. The policy implications of these possibilities are of course very different. In the first case, the state should pick up the revenue raising functions through income or sales taxes and continue to "bail out." In the second case, the local governments should cut expenditures in a fashion best representing the wishes of their constituencies and the "bail out" should be terminated as soon as an orderly transition to a smaller public sector can be achieved (2, p. 132).

The problem, then, is how do we construct an explanation of the tax revolt that can guide progressive research on the causes of the tax revolt and reduce the uncertainty associated with managerial responses to the revolt? While an alternative explanation is presented in the next section of this paper, we can begin answering this question by identifying likely sources of model misspecification in the two unsuccessful approaches.

It would seem likely that the failures of the two contemporary approaches are closely related. Earlier, I suggested that an empirical resolution of the question of what voters expected from tax revolt referenda will probably not be forthcoming. Analysts who have worked in the research program predicated on answering this question have implicitly assumed that all voters have uniform expectations. The question is always framed in an either/or manner: either all voters expected

303

services to be substantially curtailed as hypothesized by the leviathan model or all voters expected service levels to remain the same as expected by the efficiency model. It seems unreasonable to expect all voters to perceive the tax revolt phenomenon as exactly the same thing either way. Even leaders of the tax revolt recognize that the revolt is composed of many discrete interests. Uhler and Stubblebine of the National Tax Limitation Committee, in explaining the continued interest in tax revolution, observed that, "the whole area of inflation, excessive spending, waste, corruption, inefficiency, and high taxes consistently commands the attention of between 70 and 80 percent of the people" (38). But not all those interested in governmental waste and inefficiency are necessarily interested in excessive spending. Both of the major answers to the question of voter expectations of the tax revolt could exist concurrently for different groups within the voting population. In this sense, the vote on Proposition 13 is not one message but a number of messages.

This reinterpretation of the first approach to understanding the tax revolt also suggests an explanation of the failure of the narrow rationality investigations of the phenomenon. If we assume that not all voters perceive the tax revolt in similar terms, it would seem unreasonable to expect that we could identify the focus and content of self-interest in the simple manner suggested by the rationality models. The meaning of self-interest may depend on perceptions of what the tax revolt is. For example, a voter with school-age children may take quite different positions on the tax revolt depending on whether he or she expects the tax cut to eliminate only waste or to severely cut educational services. Perceptions of what the tax revolt is must be identified before rational self-interest can be used to predict tax revolt referenda voting.

A SINGLE-ISSUE INTERPRETATION OF THE TAX REVOLT

An alternative explanation is based on viewing the tax revolt as a particular type of single-issue politics.

Clearly, the tax revolt has been viewed as single-issue politics and has several of the characteristics commonly ascribed to single issues. Political actors have linked many of their policy positions to the tax

revolt in fear of alienating supporters of the tax
revolt (36, p. 1). Other politicians have avoided
taking positions on the tax revolt at all in fear of
the consequences of alienating single-issue voters (12).
Other analysts have noted the potential political and
social costs of single issue voting on the tax revolt.
John Mikesell clearly expressed this position in "The
Season of the Tax Revolt" when he concluded that "there
are doubts concerning the social desirability of single
issue voting: The required majority of those voting can
inflict severe costs on the rest of society with dramatic consequences for the social fabric" (29, p. 128).
Politicians and academics have looked at the tax revolt
as a single issue.

But the identification of the tax revolt as a
single issue is not very useful without a well-developed
conceptualization of what single issues are and how they
differ from other kinds of issues. Such a conceptualization of single issues has yet to come forward. Most
of the literature on single-issue politics has assumed
that the substantive issue examined is a single issue
without defining what single issues are (19, 1, 9).
Before examining the tax revolt as single-issue politics, therefore, we must define single issues. In
comparison to other issues, single issues have one key
characteristic: they generate political behavior predicated exclusively on that issue. Single-issue voting
denotes support of a candidate on the sole basis of his
or her position on a single issue regardless of his or
her other policy positions. This zealousness generates
the political behaviors and fears for the social fabric
noted earlier about the tax revolt; other characteristics commonly ascribed to single issues are consequences of this inherent characteristic of single
issues.

But having defined single issues as those that
override all other policy concerns in electoral choice,
we must also realize that this override characteristic
can occur through at least two quite different processes. The type of issues generally thought of as
single issues (abortion, the Panama Canal Treaty, etc.)
override other policy concerns by ignoring them; a
person attentive to right-to-life concerns will vote for
or against a candidate on the basis of that one issue
without regard to the candidate's stand on any other
policy issue. These might be called particularistic

305

single issues as they are based on a discrete issue and policy choice. In contrast to particularistic single issues, a few single issues override other policy concerns by collapsing them onto a single dimension. A number of issues that might formerly have been viewed as distinct are collapsed into a single policy choice, a single yes or no query. These can be identified as comprehensive single issues as they link many policy issues together along one dimension and one policy choice. Single issues, then, can be viewed as occurring on a continuum from particularistic to comprehensive single issues where their position on the continuum specifies how the key definitionalcharacteristic of single issues, their override of other policy issues, is expressed: either through leading single-issue voters to ignore other issues or collapsing other issues onto a single-choice dimension.

Given this taxonomy of single issues and the critique of the existing literature on the tax revolt presented in the previous section, it should be apparent that the tax revolt is a comprehensive single issue. The revolt collapses questions of property tax administration, the size of government, bureaucratic efficiency, welfare, recession and inflation, and the responsiveness of representative institutions into a single yes or no choice. The two previous approaches to explaining the tax revolt failed precisely because they did not recognize this. If the tax revolt single issue is actually a fusion of other issues, we could not expect that efforts to single out one policy goal among supporters of the tax revolt or to identify the determinants of tax revolt referenda voting based on a simple understanding of self-interest to be very successful.

While interpreting the tax revolt as comprehensive single-issue politics is useful in explaining the lack of success in previous attempts to specify the cause(s) of the tax revolt, the concept of comprehensive single issues is essentially unimportant unless it can be demonstrated that comprehensive single issues are different from other single issues in ways that are substantively meaningful. Up to this point, even though it has been suggested that particularistic and comprehensive single issues are fundamentally different in their makeup, it has been argued that they have substantially identical political consequences: they both

306

generate political behavior that is characterized by extreme zealousness. Yet, we can expect the life cycle of comprehensive single issues to differ from that of particularistic single issues in several ways, each of which is a function of the conglomerate character of comprehensive single issues.

1. <u>Comprehensive single issues can be expected to be rare.</u> This rarity can be expected because each of the component issues of a comprehensive single issue operates under its own dynamic and, in times of political stability, the dynamics of each issue are likely to be carried out independently of other issues given the subsystem politics nature of American policymaking processes. The tax revolt is a popular movement that, at least temporarily, breaks the subsystem politics status quo, creating the opportunity to unite a number of diverse political issues under one policy choice. What transforms a condition of status quo politics into a popular movement is beyond the scope of this work. It might be suggested, however, that simultaneous frustration on the part of the public over a number of discrete political issues combined with the unique political leadership of Howard Jarvis rapidly transformed the California electorate from an unorganized set of specific issue oriented voters into a popular movement. Certainly Californians, and Michigan voters as well, had several opportunities to vote for tax revolt referenda during the 1970s and defeated each resoundingly before adopting tax revolt proposals. While economic conditions, particularly the availability of a large state surplus in California, had changed somewhat since the earlier proposals were defeated, the rapid and massive shift in support for the tax revolt is difficult to explain within the bounds of self-interest alone (15, p. 55). The popular movement linkage of several discrete issues does account for the reversal in public support. And, more to the point, comprehensive single issues are necessarily popular movements that break the bounds of status quo subsystem politics and, therefore, by definition can be expected to be uncommon.

Even though comprehensive issue politics are rare, the tax revolt is not unique. Stephen DeCanio has compared the tax revolt to the free silver movement of the 1890s. DeCanio's analysis of the free silver movement, which bears a strong resemblance to the tax

307

revolt interpretation presented here, can be considered
a second case of comprehensive single issue politics.
Like the tax revolt, the free silver movement was composed of a number of discrete issues. As DeCanio notes,
"According to the agrarian protestors of that era, the
farmers were suffering from falling prices of their
products, high interest rates, an appreciating currency
that increased the real burden on their debts, and
exploitation by railroads and other middlemen" (15,
p. 58). And like the tax revolt, the issue remained
obscure until a popular movement was generated around a
unique leader and a discrete policy choice that was
thought to be related to each of the component issues.

> A multitude of farmers' organizations and
> schemes for monetary "reform" flourished
> during the 1870s, 80s, and 90s without any
> of them having more than scattered electoral
> impact . . . . The program which finally
> united all the diverse agrarian and monetary
> reformers and became the central issue of
> the 1896 Presidential campaign was the
> demand for "free and unlimited coinage of
> silver at the ratio of 16:1." William
> Jennings Bryan was the Democratic-Populist
> candidate, and although he lost the election
> by 271-176 in the electoral college, he
> polled 47 percent of the popular vote
> nationwide (15, p. 59).

Like the tax revolt, the free silver movement compressed
the political issues of the day onto a single dimension
related to a single policy choice through a popular
movement led by a dynamic leader.

  2. Comprehensive single issues can be expected to
have severe implementation problems. The compression of
several issues onto a single policy choice is not without cost. A single, dramatic policy change is not
likely to resolve all of the issues that led to its
adoption. The policy change involved in comprehensive
single issues tends to be viewed as a cure-all solution
where the implementation linkage between the policy
change and issue(s) resolution is left vague. As
DeCanio notes of the free silver movement, "Regardless
of the underlying basis of the farmers' discontent or
the relative weight of economic and ethnocultural
influences on their political behavior, the most

remarkable feature of the demand for 'free silver' is
that it bore only the most obscure relationship to the
complaints articulated by farmers' (15, p. 59). Much
the same can be said about the tax revolt. While the
implementation linkage between tax-cutting proposals and
reducing the size and/or inefficiency of government can
be understood (though they were never precisely articulated), the relationship between the referenda and other
component issues is baffling. In particular, the precise relationship between limiting local property taxes
and reducing state welfare spending and the joint problems of inflation and unemployment remain unclear. And
even on the component issues where the implementation
linkage between adoption and issue resolution is
clearer, the simplicity of the comprehensive single-
issue policy choice will likely lead to rather severe
implementation problems, given inherently unanticipa-
table (because of the choice mechanism) consequences.
In California for instance, the adoption of Proposition
13 has led to severe problems in water resource
allocation (11), debt management (4), and labor-management relations (16).

3.   Comprehensive single issues can be expected to
be of relatively short duration. These issues are
relatively short-lived because of the unusual collapsing
of many separate issues onto a single policy choice.
After an initial period of rapid success, the movement
is likely to break down under the pressure of the individual dynamics of the component issues. Moreover,
after a period of time, the precise implementation
relationship between component issues and the single
policy choice become clearer and unanticipated consequences become anticipated; the mass enthusiasm
characteristic of comprehensive single issues, accordingly, can be expected to decline. For instance, Neil
Peirce (cautiously) predicted that Californians would
reject Proposition 9 because of a renewed attention to
the distributive impact of tax-cutting referenda (34).
The failure of five of the six tax revolt proposals on
state ballots in the fall of 1980 is understandable from
this perspective. While it is unlikely that the tax
revolt will disappear quite as rapidly as the free
silver movement did after 1896, the failure of Proposition 9 and the general decline in interest in the tax
revolt has led some to suggest that it has peaked and is
declining in importance (18, 24). The component issues,
however, can be expected to continue to command

attention, but as discrete issues rather than components of a comprehensive single issue.

4. Comprehensive single issues can be expected to
be associated with a particular type of choice mechanism. Popular referendum will be the preferred choice
mechanism among supporters of comprehensive single
issues. Eugene Lee has suggested that groups resort to
referenda for two reasons. First, referenda are used
if a legislature refuses to pass the measure of substantive interest to the group. Second, groups rely on
referenda if they feel that the give and take of the
legislative process will so modify a bill that it will
not achieve the purpose the group designed it to
achieve (20, p. 97). While both reasons lie behind
most referenda, they are especially salient to
supporters of comprehensive single issues. Because
comprehensive single issues are necessarily popular
movements, they are definitionally premised on the
expectation that the policy choice will not be accepted
by established political institutions. Additionally,
the simplicity of the comprehensive single-issue choice
and the obscuring of its relationships with the component issues leaves little room for the give and take of
legislative bargaining. It should not be surprising,
therefore, that the use of the referendum has characterized the tax revolt (29). Several state legislatures
have adopted tax revolt proposals, but many of these
proposals were adopted under the threat of a popular
referendum and/or were designed to head off a tax revolt
referendum (i.e., Kentucky's adoption of H.B. 44 in
1979). This characteristic of comprehensive single
issues raises severe problems for comprehensive issues
focusing on national policy. The lack of the referendum
at the national level leads to the linkage of the comprehensive single issue to a presidential candidate, as
in the case of free silver. Support of a constitutional
amendment and/or convention in the current drive for a
balanced national budget can be considered the national
adjunct of the tax revolt in the states.

In each of these ways, we can expect the life cycle
of comprehensive single issues to be substantially
different from particularistic single issues. Comprehensive single issues will tend to be very rare and of
shorter duration and will be characterized by greater
implementation problems and greater reliance on the
referendum. But because these issues are rare and of

310

short duration does not mean they are not worth studying. Even if the tax revolt has ended with the defeat of California's Proposition 9 and the decimation of the tax revolt proposals in the general elections of 1980, the tax revolt would have exercised a tremendous influence on state and local government.

IMPLICATIONS

The single-issue interpretation of the tax revolt seems to account for the poor empirical results of the two existing approaches to explaining the tax revolt. As such, it may offer a framework for future study of the tax revolt. Empirical assessment of the life cycle hypotheses are beyond the scope of this effort and, in any case, will be difficult. However, several suggestions can be made on the further study of tax revolt causes and on managerial cutback strategies in the face of the tax revolt.

The single-issue interpretation points to at least three research questions on the causes of the tax revolt. First, the individual rationality analyses of the tax revolt will be useful only if tax revolt referenda voting is decomposed according to voter objectives. Individual rationality in tax revolt referenda depends on a precise understanding of what the revolt is and what the consequences of a successful revolt entail; in the absence of an identification of each individual's precise interpretation of what the revolt is, individual rationality is meaningless. The tax revolt as a comprehensive single issue obscures the meaning of rational behavior by collapsing multiple objectives onto a single-choice question. If the individual rationality-based hypotheses are useful at all, that utility will be obtained only after the revolt referenda voting is decomposed into its component issues. The most important characteristic of comprehensive single issues is that they fuse several issues together. Therefore, the specific component issue to which a particular voter is attentive must be identified before individual rationality can be used to generate hypotheses about tax-revolt voting.

Second, research attention should be directed at explaining the origins of the tax revolt movement. It was earlier suggested that the tax revolt movement was initiated by the union of a charismatic leader with

311

voters who were simultaneously frustrated over a number of discrete issues. The underlying cause of the tax revolt, therefore, may have more to do with a decline in confidence and trust in government than with specific tax and expenditure issues. As Richard Musgrave has concluded, "The tax revolt may . . .be seen as a symptom, rather than a contributing cause, of the changing political climate" (31, p. 701). While empirical work is required, this understanding of the origins of the tax revolt can be viewed as an alternative hypothesis to the previous recommendation that tax-revolt voting be further decomposed. Both approaches are consistent with single-issue interpretation. Further decomposition may not be useful if the political movement character of comprehensive single issues so obscures the relationship between issue resolution and the referenda choice that rationality, as narrowly defined, is meaningless. In this case, we must give special attention to the process by which discrete issues are transformed into comprehensive single issues, which then become dangerous, if transient, phenomena in a political system. Fundamental institutional changes may be adopted with little or no consideration of the relationship between the change and its conglomerate objectives.

Third, the single-issue interpretation should draw research attention to the role of social choice mechanisms in the tax revolt. The life-cycle hypotheses suggest that the availability of the referendum is an important facilitating factor underlying the occurrence and spread of the tax revolt. The tax revolt may be an example of how the method for making choices determines the choices themselves (29, p. 128).

The single-issue interpretation has two major implications for public managers facing or trying to survive a tax revolt. First, the tax revolt should be treated as a symptom rather than a disease. The conglomerate character of comprehensive single issues means that the tax revolt has sent no single, clear message to public managers. Administrative attention should be directed instead to the component issues of efficiency, the joint problems of inflation and recession, and tax reform. Such efforts, if coupled with a revitalization of trust and confidence in government, would likely do more to prevent a tax revolt than the apparently unsuccessful negative campaign waged against Proposition

312

13 by public employees.

Such advice is not very useful, however, for managers in states and localities that have already experienced a tax revolt. These managers face the critical task of coping with the revolt; they must identify and adopt the cutback management strategies noted by Levine. At the broadest level, such an administrator must make a judgment about the durability and policy implications of the tax revolt in deciding whether to resist organizational decline or give up and make the process as smooth as possible. The comprehensive single-issue interpretation strongly implies that public administrators should resist decline for as long as possible. The lack of a clear policy message in the tax revolt in combination with its hypothesized short duration suggests that the revolt is more of a short-term constraint than a long-term rejection of current public service levels. Still, the impact of the revolt may be so constraining that cutbacks become necessary. And avoiding the effects of such cutbacks may be exceedingly difficult when taxing and spending constraints are placed in a state constitution. Under such conditions, the ingenuity of public employees in maintaining service levels and diversifying revenue sources will be sorely tested. From this perspective, public employees, rather than being spurned leviathans, may be the unwitting victims of an unfocused political movement.

NOTES

1. While these two interpretations of voter expectations of the returns from referenda choices have dominated the emerging literature on the tax revolt, other explanations have been suggested. For a review of these other explanations, see Lowery and Sigelman (25).

2. Every study that has found empirical support for this view uses aggregate data and, therefore, risks an ecological fallacy.

REFERENCES

1. Anderson, Roger. "The Ohio Alliance for Returnables: A 'Single Issue' Group in Action." Paper presented at the Midwest Political Science Association Convention, April 24-26, 1980, Pick-Congress Hotel, Chicago.

2. Attiyeh, Richard, and Engle, Robert F. "Testing Some Propositions about Proposition 13." National Tax Journal 32 (June 1979): 133-46.

3. Barkume, Anthony J. "Identification of Preference for Election Outcomes from Aggregate Voting Data." Public Choice 27 (Fall 1976): 41-58.

4. Beeba, Jack H. "Proposition 13 and the Cost of California Debt." National Tax Journal 32 (June 1979): 243-60.

5. Break, George F. "Interpreting Proposition 13: A Comment." National Tax Journal 32 (June 1979): 43-46.

6. Brennan, Geoffrey, and Buchanan, James. "The Logic of Tax Limits: Alternative Constitutional Constraints of the Power to Tax." National Tax Journal 32 (June 1979): 11-12.

7. Buchanan, James M. "Why Does Government Grow?" in Budgets and Bureaucrats, Thomas E. Borcherding, ed., (Durham, N.C.: Duke University Press, 1977), pp. 3-18.

8. Buchanan, James M., and Wagner, Richard E. Democracy in Deficit: The Political Legacy of Lord Keynes (New York: Academic Press, 1977).

9. Casey, Gregory. "Understanding Single Issue Politics Through Q-Methodology: The Case of Abortion." Paper presented at the Midwest Political Science Association Convention, April 24-26, 1980, Pick-Congress Hotel, Chicago.

10. Citrin, Jack. "Do People Want Something for Nothing: Public Opinion on Taxes and Spending." National Tax Journal 32 (June 1979): 113-29.

11. Cooley, Thomas F., and LaCivita, C.J. "Allocative Efficiency and Distributional Equity in Water Pricing and Finance: A Post-Proposition 13 Analysis." National Tax Journal 32 (June 1979): 215-28.

12. Cottman, Effie. "Few Officials Attack Tax Halving Initiative." Public Administration Times, April 15, 1980, pp. 1, 6.

13. Courant, Paul, Gramlich, Edward, and Rubinfeld, Daniel. "Tax Limitation and the Demand for Public Services in Michigan." National Tax Journal 32 (June 1979): 147-58.

14. _____. "Why Voters Support Tax Limitation Amendments: The Michigan Case." National Tax Journal 33 (March 1980): 1-22.

15. DeCanio, Stephen J. "Proposition 13 and the Failure of Economic Politics." National Tax Journal 32 (June 1979): 55-66.

16. Ehrenberg, Ronald G. "The Effect of Tax Limitation Legislation on Public Sector Labor Market: A Comment." National Tax Journal 32 (June 1979): 261-66.

17. Goetz, Charles J. "Fiscal Illusion in State and Local Finance." in Budgets and Bureaucrats, Thomas E. Borcherding, ed. (Durham, N.C.: Duke University Press, 1977), pp. 176-87.

18. Herbert, F. Ted, and Bingham, Richard D. "Public Opinion, the Taxpayers Revolt, and Local Government." in Fiscal Retrenchment and Urban Policy, John P. Blair and David Nachmias, eds. (Beverly Hills, Calif.: Sage Publications, 1979), pp. 131-48.

19. Jones, Judson H. "The Effect of the Pro- and Anti-ERA 'Single Interest' Groups on Voting Behavior on the Equal Rights Amendment in the Illinois General Assembly." Paper presented at the Midwest Political Science Association Convention, April 24-26, 1980, Pick-Congress Hotel, Chicago.

20. Lee, Eugene C. "California" in Referendums: A Comparative Study of Practice and Theory, David Butler and Austin Ranney, eds. (Washington, D.C.: American Enterprise Institute, 1978), pp. 87-122.

21. Levine, Charles H. "The New Crisis in the Public Sector" in Managing Fiscal Stress, Charles H. Levine, ed. (Chatham, N.J.: Chatham House Publishers, 1980a), pp. 3-12.

22. _____. "Organizational Decline and Cutback Management" in Managing Fiscal Stress, Charles H. Levine, ed. (Chatham, N.J.: Chatham House Publishers, 1980b), pp. 13-30.

23. _____. "More on Cutback Management: Hard Questions for Hard Times" in Managing Fiscal Stress, Charles H. Levine, ed. (Chatham, N.J.: Chatham House Publishers, 1980c), pp. 305-12.

315

24. Lexington Herald-Leader, "Whatever Happened to the Taxpayer's Revolution?" February 17, 1980, pp. D2, 3.

25. Lowery, David, and Sigelman, Lee. "Understanding the Tax Revolt: An Assessment of Eight Explanations" Unpublished manuscript, University of Kentucky, 1981.

26. Lucier, Richard L. "Gauging the Strength and Meaning of the 1978 Tax Revolt" in Managing Fiscal Stress, Charles H. Levine, ed. (Chatham, N.J.: Chatham House Publishers, 1980), pp. 123-36.

27. Mariotti, Steve. "An Economic Analysis of the Voting on Michigan's Tax and Expenditure Limitation Amendment," Public Choice 33 (Fall 1978): 15-26.

28. McCaffery, Jerry, and Bowman, John H. "Participatory Democracy and Budgeting: The Effects of Proposition 13," Public Administration Review 38 (November/December 1978): 530-38.

29. Mikesell, John L. "The Season of the Tax Revolt" in Fiscal Retrenchment and Urban Policy, John P. Blair and David Nachmias, eds. (Beverly Hills, Calif.: Sage Publications, 1979), pp. 107-130.

30. Mueller, E. "Public Attitudes Toward Fiscal Problems," Quarterly Journal of Economics 77 (May 1963): 210-35.

31. Musgrave, Richard A. "The Tax Revolt," Social Science Quarterly 59 (March 1979): 697-703.

32. Mushkin, Selma. Proposition 13 and Its Consequences for Public Management (Cambridge, Mass.: Abt Books, 1979).

33. Niskanen, William A. Bureaucracy and Representative Government (Chicago: Aldine and Atherton, 1971).

34. Peirce, Neal R. "Voters Give Second Thoughts to Jaws II," Public Administration Times, June 1, 1980, p. 2.

35. Rubinfeld, Daniel. "Voting in a Local School Election: A Micro Analysis," Review of Economics and Statistics (1977): 30-42.

36. Shapiro, Perry, Puryear, Daniel, and Ross, John. "Tax and Expenditure Limitation in Retrospect and Prospect," National Tax Journal 32 (June 1979): 1-10.

37. Sherwood, Frank. "Inflation Fuels Proposition 13," Public Administration Times, July 1, 1978, p. 1.

38. Tyner, Howard. "Tax Limitation Leaders Say Rebellion Continues," Lexington Herald-Leader, February 17, 1980, pp. D2, 3.

29. MUNICIPAL REVENUE BEHAVIOR
AFTER PROPOSITION 13*

Robert J. Cline and John Shannon

From 1977 to 1980 the pace and, in some cases, the direction of the long-run trends in city revenue sources were altered substantially...Particularly significant is the accelerating decline in the share of municipal revenues raised through property taxes and the sharp upswing in user fees and other nonproperty-tax revenues. The property taxes' relative decline can be partly attributed to the adoption of new state constraints on local expenditures and revenues during this period. Proposition 13 in California and Proposition 2 1/2 in Massachusetts are examples of limitations that actually rolled back property taxes and further limited the rate of increase in the local property tax base. Because the vast majority of the state restrictions relate only to the property tax, city officials are encouraged to expand the use of nonproperty tax revenues, including local sales taxes and benefit-based user charges and fees. The upsurge in the use of service charges reflects the most logical way for local policymakers to reconcile the need for more revenue with the realities of voter resistance to increased property tax levies.[1]

This article discusses the growth in state limitations on local governments and their impact on the revenue structure of municipalities. The changing composition of local revenues is documented by a survey conducted by the Advisory Commission on Intergovernmental Relations (ACIR) in collaboration with the Municipal Finance Officers Association (MFOA). The analysis of

* Reprinted from Intergovernmental Perspective, Summer 1982, pp. 22-28.

the survey results will focus on the increasing importance of user fees in the local revenue mix.

THE INFLUENCE OF STATE RESTRICTIONS ON LOCAL GOVERNMENTS

Although state restrictions on local taxing authority are not a new development, the pace of adopting state-imposed lids has recently increased substantially and has also changed decisively in character. The older traditional type of state restraint focused solely on the property tax. Indeed, all of the 31 state limits enacted before 1970 restricted the authority of local officials only with regard to the property tax and 29 of these 31 pertained solely to the property tax rate...

As a device for restricting the growth of local governments, property tax limits alone have proved insufficient. Restricting access to only one of the fiscal resources left local officials free to pursue several "escape hatches--in other words, local diversification.

States added 32 more restrictions in the eight years from 1970 to 1977 to the 31 adopted in the pre-1970 period. The states completed their arsenal of property tax curbs by adopting two new types of restrictions--limits on assessment increases and provisions for the full disclosure of property tax increases. The 1970s also witnessed the emergence of a new type of lid law--the TEL, that is, the tax or expenditure limit. While the TELs differ in detail, they share the characteristic of being more comprehensive in scope than restrictions applied only to the property tax. In general, the TELs limit the overall increase in local revenues or expenditures, with increases usually tied to a percentage change from a base year figure or to the growth in personal income. Adjustments are sometimes allowed for changes in the cost of providing public services--measured by population growth or changes in the consumer price

index, for example. Being more comprehensive in
scope, these TELs include local sales and income
taxes as well as nontax revenues, such as user
charges, in their more restrictive net.

Although TELs are the new and growing entry
on the restriction list, property tax limits still
dominate. Compared to the pre-1970 years, when all
31 state lid laws related solely to the property
tax, only 23 of the 32 limit laws enacted between
1970 and 1977 curbed the access of local officials
to the property tax. Since 1977 states have
enacted an additional 29 lid laws--almost equalling
the 32 adopted over the 1970-79 period and the
total of 31 enacted any time prior to 1970.
Twenty-five of the 29 lids adopted since 1977 apply
only to the property tax, while the four new TELs
are equally divided with two restricting local expenditures and two limiting revenue growth. The
rate of adoption of state limits, however, has now
slowed considerably with only two new limit laws
being imposed in the last year.

The vast majority of total state restrictions--
79 of the 92 currently in place--pertain solely to
the property tax. The adoption of property tax
limits reflects in large part continuing increases
in the share of total property taxes paid by homeowners. Although the property tax fell from 57.1%
of local own-source revenues in 1957 to 42.7% in
1977, higher relative rates of inflation in residential housing prices and increased business property tax exemptions resulted in an increase in the
share of property taxes paid by residential property as compared to the share paid by commercial
and industrial property. In Michigan, for example,
the share of residential property in total state
equalized value increased from 49.2% to 56.5% of
the total between 1972 and 1980. Similarly, in
California the homeowners' share of total net
assessed value increased from 33.7% in 1971-72 to
43% in 1978-79. Ironically, one important result
of Proposition 2 1/2 in Massachusetts appears to

be an increase in the relative burden of property taxes on homeowners as statewide property assessments are updated to reflect full market values in FY 1982.[2]

The Local Government "Escape Hatch"

Local governments can pursue a number of "escape hatches" in diversifying their revenue structures. The most direct approach is to increase revenue sources that are not constrained by state-imposed limits. In this case, the partial coverage of limit laws provides a "tilt" toward local sales and income taxes, special assessments and user charges and fees. Local governments can indirectly diversify their revenue structures by transferring certain activities, such as municipal water and sewer facilities to independent authorities exempted from limit laws. The independent authorities or special districts collect user fees, rather than property taxes, to cover the cost of their services.

The third option available to local policy-makers is "privatization" of a public service. This alternative involves transferring local government activities to private firms that charge consumers directly for the services provided. For example, municipal refuse collection could be turned over to a private firm operating under a government franchise. Summer school classes in California were provided on a user fee basis by private firms and volunteer groups when local school districts cancelled summer activities following the adoption of Proposition 13.

Another form of privatization is expanding use of the special fees and assessments collected from developers to finance capital facilities needed to service new residents and businesses. In California, local government increased development fees sharply following the mandated rollback in local property taxes. A survey of California cities six months after the passage of Proposition 13 found that 56% of the cities and 57% of the counties responding increased development fees.

321

In cities reporting increased service fees, the
average increase was 90%.[3] Overall, benefit-
related fees and charges grew from 22% of all
local revenues in FY 1976 to 24% in FY 1980.
Actual benefit-related charges increased by 55%
over this period for all local governments in
California. Information concerning the extent
of recent local diversification efforts across
the United States is presented in the next section.

THE ACIR-MFOA SURVEY

     If the property tax has undergone a long-
term decline and one that has quickened in pace
since 1977--what has taken its place as municipal
governments diversify their revenue structures?
The quick--and reasonably accurate--answer is
"everything" else. To track city nonproperty tax
actions, the Advisory Commission on Intergovernmental Relations, in collaboration with the Municipal Finance Officers Association, conducted a
national survey of 595 municipal finance officers.
Based on 438 replies, the following questions and
answers highlight developments in municipal revenue
diversification during 1980 and 1981.

     JUST HOW WIDESPREAD IS THE MOVEMENT TO DIVER-
SIFY MUNICIPAL REVENUE SYSTEMS THROUGH GREATER USE
OF NONPROPERTY TAX SOURCES IN GENERAL AND MORE IN-
TENSIVE USE OF SERVICE CHARGES IN PARTICULAR?
Raising the rates on existing user charges clearly
stands out as the most frequent nonproperty tax
action taken--72% of the respondents indicated that
this policy was followed by their communities during 1980-81... Local policy-makers seem to be reading the public mind quite accurately. A 1981 ACIR
public opinion poll documents the fact that taxpayers prefer user charge financing by overwhelm-
ing margins compared to other local tax increases,
if local taxes have to be increased.[4] When asked
specifically: "Suppose your local governments must
raise more revenue, which of these to you think
would be the best way to do it? 55% of the respondents in September 1981, selected user charges.

This percentage was more than 2.5 times that selecting local sales taxes, the second favorite choice.
Other revenue choices included local income taxes
and property taxes. Indeed, user charge financing
was the first choice in each of the individual
socio-economic demographic groups surveyed--and by
quite substantial margins in each case. Notably,
the support for user charges was highest in the
northeast where charges and fees are relatively
under-utilized.

Greater use of "benefit" taxation was also
reflected in responses to the questionnaire. Nearly 26% of the respondents reported action on the
special assessment front. As pointed out earlier,
local governments in California were quite active
in raising development-related fees and exactions
to replace lost property taxes. This shift may be
viewed as substituting a more narrowly defined
benefit tax for a broad-based general tax (the
property tax). However, special assessments fall
short of being a specific user fee because the
levy does not vary directly with use an individual
makes of the facilities.

IS THERE STRONG OPPOSITION TO GREATER USE OF
SERVICE CHARGES AND IF SO, WHY? Almost half of
the respondents indicated no strong community
opposition to greater use of service charges.
Among those who did indicate opposition, the regressivity of user charges was cited by 17% as an
"important" obstacle. Regressivity was deemed
"fairly important" by another 17%. Interestingly,
the fact that taxpayers cannot deduct local user
charges in calculating taxable federal income was
cited by only 7% as an important factor working
against more intensive use of municipal service
charges.

Although a number of respondents did oppose
expanding user charges for equity reasons, 60% of
the finance officers either were not opposed to
user charges or specified that possible hardships
on the poor were not an important reason for their

opposition to user fees. This strong support for
user fees may reflect a belief, at least at the
local level, that charging individuals for direct
benefits of government services (where identifiable) is more equitable than subsidizing their
consumption from general revenue sources.

DO CITIES DISPLAY A SIGNIFICANT DIFFERENCE IN
FISCAL BEHAVIOR WHEN CLASSIFIED BY THE PRESENCE OR
ABSENCE OF TAX AND EXPENDITURE LIDS? The quick
answer is no, although some differences exist in
the reasons cited for their actions. For example,
both tax limitation and nontax limitation cities
clearly favored greater use of service charges and
behaved about the same in "privatization" areas,
i.e., contracting out, and franchising...Cities with
TELs, however, were somewhat more active on the
special assessment front and more inclined to have
developers contribute toward the necessary public
services than were their non-TEL counterparts.
The greatest increase in developer fees occurred
in California.

When citing reasons for their behavior, only
California and Massachusetts cities put considerable
importance on the presence of tax lid legislation--
a not unexpected reaction given that their lids are
more restrictive than those imposed on communities
in most other states. Expenditure growth (due to
inflation), property tax pressures, and federal aid
cuts were all cited more often than limit laws as
reasons for taking nonproperty tax action.[5]

DOES SIZE OF PLACE MAKE A DIFFERENCE IN MUNICI-
PAL FISCAL BEHAVIOR? Yes. Large cities--with
populations over 250,000--clearly exhibited the
greatest willingness to make more intensive use of
nonproperty tax sources and to adopt privatization
policies.[6] The respondent large cities also cited
federal aid cuts and property tax pressures more
frequently than did responding small cities as
reasons for diversifying their revenue systems.

DOES GEOGRAPHY (REGIONAL LOCATION) CAUSE SIG-
NIFICANT VARIATIONS IN MUNICIPAL FISCAL BEHAVIOR?

324

Yes, there appear to be fairly significant regional variations in recent fiscal actions. The Rocky Mountain cities relied most heavily on user fee increases with 90% reporting increases.[7] The southwest and Great Plains cities followed in frequency of user charge increases. Sixty-seven and four-tenths percent of mideast cities reported increases in user fees, the lowest percentage among the regions. There is also a wide range in the use of special assessments--from a low of 15% among southwest cities to a high of 46% for the cities in the Great Plains region.

LIVING WITHIN FISCAL CONSTRAINTS: THE CALIFORNIA AND MASSACHUSETTS EXPERIENCES

The sharp increase in user fees and other non-property tax revenues is perhaps nowhere more evident than in California and Massachusetts, two states with the most restrictive taxing and spending lids....

An upward trend in the relative importance of user fees--when measured as a percentage of local own-source revenue accounted for by charges and fees--is readily apparent during the immediate post-Proposition 13 years. The sharp increases in the relative importance of fees during FY 1979 for most cities reflected a significant increase in user fees, as well as a substantial reduction in local property tax revenues. In San Francisco, for example, user fee revenues increased by more than 27% in FY 1979.

The renewed growth in property tax revenues and the distribution of part of the state surplus to local governments enabled large cities in California to avoid additional increases in their reliance on user fees during FY 1980. However, the state surplus is now exhausted and cities and counties in California face a 20% reduction in state aid in FY 1983. As a result, municipalities may be due for another upsurge in user fees.[8]

Although statewide data on changes in local
government finances in Massachusetts for the first
year following Proposition 2 1/2 are not yet available, Concord's experience provides an interesting
case study of the diversification strategies available to Massachusetts cities and towns.[9] To cope
with lost property tax revenues, Concord established
a policy guideline to "reduce tax support for areas
able to produce alternative revenues." Town officials identified the water and sewer departments,
recreation activities and ambulance services as
budget functions that should become self-supporting
immediately through the adoption of new user charges, as well as increases in existing fees.

The potential pitfalls of spiraling user fees
did not escape the attention of Concord's finance
director who noted:

> Injudicious use of fees and charges
> can undermine basic public support
> for the full range of local govern-
> ment activities while permitting
> the maintenance of services suscept-
> ible to pricing. It would be ironic
> if the move toward user charges re-
> sulted ultimately in the withering
> of services that remained to be
> financed from taxes.[10]

George Peterson of the Urban Institute also identified this potential problem in a recent analysis
of the fiscal effects of tax limitations.[11]
According to Peterson, local governments are "un-
bundling" municipal budgets by earmarking specific
revenue sources to finance more narrowly defined
public services and activities. Peterson notes
that the increased use of dedicated revenue sources
could potentially lead to a more fragmented budget
process and reduce budget flexibility in local
governments. This change may cause activities
financed by dedicated revenues or user fees to be
freed from expenditure and tax limits, while
general public services, including education,

326

public safety, general administration and income
redistribution programs, become more tightly
constrained.

CONCLUSION

It is becoming increasingly clear that the tax
revolt has had two distinct effects on the public
sector. The first was the blizzard of fiscal restrictions imposed on state and local governments
during the 1970s. Many students of public finance
will be quick to point out, however, that these
restrictions were more apparent than real. To put
it more directly, most of the legal restrictions
have significant loopholes giving state and local
policymakers considerable leeway if they choose to
exercise it.

The second--and far more important effect--
was the "go slow" message flashed to elected officials throughout the country. It signaled the need
for striking a more even balance between private
and public sector growth. Instead of growing at a
consistently faster rate than that of the private
sector, state-local spending should henceforth
either approximate or lag slightly behind the
growth in the taxpayers' income.

The tax revolt has also left its mark on the
revenue side of the fiscal equation. As underscored
by ACIR's public polls, the public now clearly
favors greater use of service charges if additional
revenue is needed to finance local governments.
Many voters may feel that user fee financing will
serve as an additional constraint on the growth of
specific public expenditures: services will only
be expanded if users are willing to pay for the
expansions. The mood of the country can be summed
up with a bit of doggerel--

Don't tax me and don't tax thee
But charge that user a darn good fee.

NOTES

1

User charges are defined by the Census Bureau as "amounts received from the public for performance of specific services benefiting the person charged and from sales of commodities and services, except those by liquor store systems and local utilities." Special assessments are mandatory payments from property owners who are assumed to benefit directly from public improvements. The other miscellaneous revenues category includes rents and royalties, proceeds from sale of property and interest earnings. The sharp increase in the relative share of this category primarily reflects the growth in the interest component. Interest earnings equaled 47% of miscellaneous revenues in 1980 compared to 35% in 1977.

2

A detailed analysis of the first-year effects of Proposition 2 1/2 in Massachusetts is found in Katherine L. Bradley and Helen F. Ladd, "Proposition 2 1/2: Initial Impacts, Part I and Part II," New England Economic Revenue, January/February and March/April 1982. The data on residential property tax shares are from Paul N. Courant, "The Property Tax," in Harvey E. Brazer, ed., Michigan's Fiscal and Economic Structure (University of Michigan Press, 1982) and William H. Oakland, "Proposition 13--Genesis and Consequences," National Tax Journal, Vol. XXXII, No. 2, Supplement, June 1979.

3

Reported in Dean J. Misczynski, "California's Nonplunge into Benefit Levydom," paper prepared for the Lincoln Institute of Land Policy and UCLA School of Law Conference, January, 1982.

4

See ACIR, Changing Public Attitudes on Governments
and Taxes, S-10 Washington, DC, 1981, p. 38.

5

For additional details concerning the differences
in responses by cities with and without TELs, see
John Shannon, "The Tax Revolt and Its Effects on
Municipal Revenue Behavior," paper prepared for
the Lincoln Institute of Land Policy and UCLA
School of Law Conference, January, 1982, table
A-3.

6

Ibid., table A-4.

7

Ibid., table A-5.

8

As reported in The New York Times, July 2, 1982.
In fact, preliminary results from a National
League of Cities survey of city fiscal conditions in the spring of 1982 indicate that
cities are raising existing fees to meet current
fiscal problems. Thirty-five out of 43 respondents (81%) reported increasing fees in FY 1982.

9

See Anthony T. Logalbo, "Responding to Tax
Limitation: Finding Alternative Revenues,"
Governmental Finance, March 1982.

10

Ibid., p. 19.

11

George E. Peterson, "The Allocative, Efficiency
and Equity Effects of a Shift to User Charges
and Benefit-Based Taxes," The Urban Institute,
January 1982.

30. Small Town Government: The Conflict of
        Administrative Styles*

Alvin D. Sokolow

More than 30 years ago Granville Hicks wrote Small
Town, an autobiographical account of an intellectual's
retreat to a small upstate New York community. Hicks
becomes a school trustee and fire commissioner, and in
the first chapter he describes his activities during a
typical week. A trip to the village store for a Sunday
paper results in a conversation about how the town's
Republican party erred in a recent political move. The
author exchanges comments about library and school
affairs with several persons leaving church, and in a
visit to a second store he discusses tax roll problems
with the storekeeper who is the school tax collector.
Dropping in at his neighbors for a social chat, the talk
turns to local politics. Later in the week, as school
trustee, he delivers a salary check to the school jani-
tor who, as a member of the board of assessments, men-
tions the valuation of the author's property.

The point is clear. Local government in such a
community is informal, personal and simple. It is accessible to its citizens because so many of them are
part of that institution and matters of government are
everyday topics of conversation. Furthermore, little or
no emphasis is given to distinguishing between politics,
policy and administration, as community leaders and citizens move freely from one role to another. These generalizations are part of the conventional wisdom about
life and politics in rural America that has come to us
from a number of autobiographical accounts, fictional
writings, and the works of sociologists and anthropolo-
gists.

It is no longer sufficient, however, to consider
them as quaint characteristics of a bypassed America.
Small communities are no longer isolated (if they ever
were) from the national mainstream. We are now in the
midst of a renewed interest in the fortunes of small
towns because of what startled demographers in the past
few years have been calling the "reverse" migration.

*Reprinted with permission from the National Civic
Review, October 1982, pp. 445-52.

For the first time in this century, nonmetropolitan areas of the country in the 1970s increased in population more rapidly than metropolitan areas, about twice as fast. More persons are moving from central cities and suburbs to small towns and the countryside than are migrating in the other direction, a turnabout from decades of net rural-to-urban migration. By no means is this new trend confined to a mere expansion of the suburbanization of the post-war years; the net migration rates since 1970 in fact have been highest in entirely rural counties located some distance from Standard Metropolitan Statistical Areas.

One implication of this population turnabout is that new issues about public administration and policy in small communities have to be addressed. Concerns about population loss, economic stagnation and aging populations have been replaced in part by a new attention to the capacity of small and rural communities to cope with growth and change. Increasingly, their local governments turn to new sources of administrative and policy expertise, whether in the direct employment of professional executives or in the use of assistance supplied by outside experts and consultants. This is not always a voluntary act on the part of local officials, but often because they face the demands of implementing the many state and federal mandates which originated in recent years as well as the local pressures of growth and change.

Whatever the reasons, these contacts are often accompanied by conflict and confusion. There are two worlds, with contrasting values and expectations. Informal operating styles, on the one hand, persist in most small communities. Traditional and particularistic values that emphasize friendship and primary group relations are dominant. On the other hand, the training and experience of professional public administrators generally emphasize more universalistic values, characterized by the norms of rationality and neutrality. What happens when the particularism of rural local government comes in contact with the universalism of professional and expert administrators? We turn to, first, an examination of several traditional characteristics of small town government.

331

SMALL AND MINIMAL BUREAUCRACIES

Informal behavior is due in large part to the small size and limited organization of rural local governments. While they may employ relatively large numbers of workers on a per capita basis, individually they are tiny bureaucracies. In 1977 the public payrolls in communities under 10,000 population averaged 15 employees (full-time equivalents) for municipalities, 16 for New England and mid-Atlantic towns and townships, one for mid-western townships, and 122 for counties. Most of these governments lack elaborate hierarchies of supervision and specialization, and the formal distance between the lowest employee and the top officeholder is minimal. Especially in small municipal and town governments, departmental organization is often absent and the few employees report directly to the elected council or board.

Small and simple organizations are also relatively visible and accessible. Citizens believe that their public officials will be close and responsive. Where elected officials and other public workers are friends, neighbors, relatives or otherwise well-known, it is expected that they will perform their duties in a friendly and personal manner. Informality, thus, is a natural companion of accessibility.

REGULATING FRIENDS AND NEIGHBORS

In such settings, the criteria for making public decisions are bound to be based on particularistic values. Sensitive to local circumstances and norms, local government officials may operate according to such subjective and personal standards as kinship, friendship and locality rather than the more objective and impersonal standards of general principle and written law. Robert Wood, in his 1968 book on suburbia, sees this as a means of bringing government into line with community mores: Legal and procedural requirements are overlooked and ignored. They are always to be adjusted to the "common sense, down-to-earth judgment" of the participants to take account of unique conditions and provincial peculiarities.

Being a "part" of the community--having close personal ties to constituents and maintaining first-hand knowledge of local conditions and attitudes--is an asset

332

for officials who make policy and administer public services. Information costs are minimal and often the compliance of individuals with government programs is facilitated. Furthermore, political risks and conflicts can be limited as officials' decisions are guided by their anticipation of how various groups and citizens would react to changed policies and programs.

Yet there are broad areas of policy and administration where close ties to citizens can be a decided handicap. Some local government programs involve the regulation of private activity, and here the styles of informality and personal government often work against fairness and the rule of law. Where administrators deal with citizens on a first-name and neighborly basis it is difficult to apply laws and regulations consistently across the board. The clearest examples are in small-town police work, as Otto Hoiberg's description of the job of the law enforcement officer suggests:

> The difficulty of his task is closely related to the number and the closeness of the personal bonds which tie him to the people he serves. It is more difficult to issue a ticket for an illegal U-turn on Main Street to one of his kinfolk, to an elder of his church, to a fellow Legionnaire . . .than to a person with whom he has no personal relationship whatever. In the average small community the local peace officer is more or less personally acquainted with most of the persons who come under his jurisdiction, and the typical situation which calls for official action causes him some degree of emotional concern.

Another area of regulation of increasing importance to small-town government is the implementation side of land use planning--the enforcement of laws that deal with land development, zoning and building. Such regulations are inherently unpopular in rural communities because of the strong belief that private ownership of real estate should convey virtually absolute control of its uses. To many small-community residents, land use ordinances are the most blatant examples of governmental interference in personal liberty. Farmers, for example, have always disliked rural zoning, despite its justification as a means of protecting land values and preserving agriculture from urban development.

As in police work, it is difficult for government officials and employees involved in the implementation of land use controls to push around their friends and neighbors. Decisions about applications to develop land or construct buildings, or requests for variances, are more often than not made on a case-by-case basis. The criteria involve the applicant's status and reputation in the community. Knowing the economic and social circumstances of local residents, officials frequently soften the law to accommodate "hardship" cases--the wish of a widow to conduct a small business in her home, for example, or the plan of a farmer to place a mobile home on his land to serve as a residence for an aged parent. Judgments based on such personal and emotional standards are frustrating for professional planners and land use attorneys, concerned as they are with consistency rather than individual accommodation.

VOLUNTARISM

Still another dimension of the accessibility of small-town government to citizens is the tendency of many people outside of government to volunteer their time and energy to public programs. The best known example is the volunteer fire department, the dominant arrangement throughout rural America for public fire suppression. Typically, tax funds allocated by a local government support equipment and operational costs (perhaps the chief's salary and a per-fire stipend for others), while the manpower is donated by members of the volunteer organization. In effect, a social club takes on a public responsibility.

Many other public services are provided, in whole or part, by volunteers in rural communities. Recent examples in a Michigan township included the organization of work parties to destroy roadside weeds, farmers arranging for the oiling of gravel roads, a women's society helping to maintain the public cemetery, and a church-operated softball program on township land providing summer recreation for youngsters. In other small communities, volunteers staff public libraries, work as police or sheriff's reserves, and drive ambulances as emergency medical technicians.

It cannot be denied that such contributions of time and energy are an important public resource for small communities. The costs of local government are subse-

334

quently reduced. Voluntarism strengthens local democracy by encouraging people to have a direct hand in
making government programs work, and it reinforces
strong and spirited community identification.

But this delegation to private citizens of activities for which governments are legally responsible often
also results in community conflicts and problems. It
may constitute a threat to professionals and other paid
employees in local government, suggesting that their
skills and contributions can be replaced by less costly
ways of running small governments. For their part,
volunteers may see employees as less interested in the
best welfare of the community than in their paychecks.
A basic issue for elected officials is the accountability of voluntary activities--who controls the administration of the public service, for whose benefit, and
for what purpose? The selfless generosity of volunteers
in giving so freely of their time and energy makes it
difficult for the responsible authorities to direct or
otherwise control their work; volunteers cannot be
disciplined, reduced in rank or fired. In fact volunteers are usually very protective of the programs in
which they participate, resisting the efforts of elected
officeholders to change their activities and shift funds
to other purposes.

THE DISTRUST OF EXPERTISE

Finally, in this inventory of the characteristics
of informal government in rural communities, we have the
basic distrust of expertise--a sentiment shared by elected officials and citizens alike. One reason is the
perception that an informal approach to administration
is incompatible with one based on the application of
abstract principles to specific tasks. The reliance on
technical or expert skills implies a burdening of the
governmental process; simplicity is reduced by the proliferation of facts, paperwork and formal methodologies.
Expertise sometimes is seen as the opposite of common
sense.

Experts represent foreign values, another source of
distrust, because they have been trained elsewhere and
the professional norms and techniques they carry are
usually urban in origin. Often they are responsible for
implementing at the local level unpopular state and
federal mandates in such programs as planning, environ-

335

mental protection and welfare. Furthermore, there is a
matter of the "status inequality" between the experts
and others in local government--a gap that includes age
differences (experts are often younger than the governing board members who employ them), a distinction between cosmopolitan and local views of the world, and
the sense of superiority that specialists on a subject
convey to generalists.

Nevertheless, the employment of policy and administrative professionals by rural local governments has
mushroomed in recent years. Small cities and rural
counties now employ far larger numbers of chief execu-
tives--whether called managers, executives, administrators, coordinators, etc.--than they did a decade ago.
Specialized professionals such as planners, recreation
administrators and trained police chiefs have also increased in number. More impressive, perhaps, is the
amount and variety of expertise and technical assistance
tapped by rural governments from outside sources such as
private consultants, regional planning agencies and
development districts, state government, cooperative
extension services, and universities and colleges. Nonmetropolitan California municipalities of less than
10,000 population, for example, usually obtain all of
their legal, engineering and planning services from
part-time consultants.

Why this new proliferation of expertise? One might
say that it has been forced on small governments, a result of their need to deal with the complexities of
intergovernmental relations, rather than resulting from
the need to deal with strictly local problems and conditions. The desire to improve grantsmanship abilities
was perhaps the single most common reason for employing
professional managers in small municipalities in the
1970s. Likewise, the belief that only communities with
comprehensive plans would be eligible for federal grants
stimulated the initial employment of professional planners, a pattern later reinforced by the emergence of
state planning and environmental mandates for local
governments. As for civil engineers, the great employment boom in rural local government came primarily in
the design and construction of costly wastewater treatment systems which were mandated by the federal and
state clean water standards of the 1970s.

Greater familiarity with expertise in these various forms does not necessarily eliminate the feeling of distrust. One reason is that part-time elected officials are often uncertain of their ability to effectively control and evaluate the work of specialists; thus, they are wary of consultants hired for special and highly technical tasks. It may be a different story for in-house professionals employed in more general capacities, such as chief executives or administrative coordinators, since they are more directly controlled by the elected governing boards that employ them. Often the job of the appointed executive is seen as one that does not involve a great deal of technical skill. Any successful businessman or other competent person can administer the general governmental programs of a city or county, many governing board members and other small-town residents believe. Consequently, appointed executives are often recruited from sources other than professional public administration, such as business and the military.

Small-town executives usually are not the strong and independent administrators that their compatriots in larger communities are assumed to be. They are generalists, responsible for the diverse management needs of small local governments. Multiple responsibilities prevent them from devoting much time and effort to executive leadership. City managers in municipalities under 10,000 population may act as directors of finance, purchasing agents, city engineers, street superintendents, building inspectors and civil defense directors. And they perform these combined jobs without administrative staff, sometimes without secretarial assistance.

CONCLUSION: PROFESSIONAL ADMINISTRATORS AND THE RURAL COMMUNITY

There is the error of overgeneralization in thus expanding a simple observation about informal and personal government into an extended discussion of administrative styles in rural communities. Granville Hicks' upstate New York town of 30 years ago may not represent well the characteristics of most small localities today. Much has happened in American society to reduce the traditional homogeneity, stability, isolation and conformity of small communities. The sources of change include the cultural pervasiveness of television and other national media, federal programs and funds, as well as the new population influx from urban areas. Neverthe-

337

less, one senses that certain institutions, especially local governments, are much slower to change than communities as a whole. Informal ways of governing are still treasured aspects of life in small towns and countryside areas simply because they seem to foster citizen accessibility and familiarity.

As rapid growth presents small communities with new problems of service delivery and regulation, however, the traditional styles of administration come under attack. Informality in government is seen by some as encouraging inefficiency, amateurism, inequality and resistance to change. In the rush to improve governmental competence in small communities, the emphasis is on replacing informal styles of administration with more bureaucratic and presumably rational and neutral methods. The usual prescriptions include employing professional administrators, obtaining technical assistance from outside agencies, and improving such procedure as budgeting, personnel management and purchasing.

Quite often the shift in administrative styles generates community conflict. Contrasting and basic sets of values are at issue, the particularism that stresses a "friends and neighbors" approach to government as against the universalistic norms of neutrality and distance. We see the clash of values expressed in such changes as the effort to professionalize a local police department and the employment of the first professional manager by a small municipality.

It may be that the central political question for small communities undergoing change today involves the appropriate balance between administrative competence and traditional informality. How do you build the first without diminishing the second? By no means is the question irresolvable for individual communities, considering the characteristics of the current migration from urban to rural areas. Many of the newcomers in small towns want to accept not challenge the traditional patterns of their new communities. In fact, the perceived openness of government is probably a part of the package of community amenities that attracts them to the rural areas.

More problematic is the position of professional administrators who come to work in rural communities, and those who work with such communities as representa-

338

tives of federal, state and regional programs. If insensitive to local traditions and circumstances, they may contribute to rather than helping to resolve the problems of administrative transition in such communities. It is up to the professionals to help bridge the gap between the contrasting values. The elected decisionmakers have already done their part by agreeing to employ the professionals in the first place and thus compromising some of the public traditions of their communities.

What can we suggest to the professional administrator newly arrived in such a community about how to be effective? Anything that can be done to dispel the perception of an outside expert prepared to apply superior wisdom, and who intends to use the experience to land a more challenging and better-paid position in a larger jurisdiction, will be advantageous. Obviously, the importance given locally to informal aspects of government should be recognized and the administrator should operate accordingly. An open and receptive style is preferable to retreating behind a desk, budget and professional status. For there is a distinction between those dimensions of informality that hinder effective and fair administration and those that promote citizen participation and closeness to government. As much as the elected official, the professional administrator in small-town government needs this citizen interest and support. Effectiveness in helping the community to cope with change and make the transition in administrative styles depends on it.

31. Lay Local Government
Charter-Writing Commissions*

David K. Hamilton

In recent years, local governments have been
given more freedom to alter their basic structure
through the adoption of a home rule charter or the
selection of an optional form of government.
Approximately three-fourths of the states now allow
local governments some discretion in framing their own
charters [11, p. 6]. This allowance has produced a
substantial increase in local government charter-
writing activity. For example, of the 84 home rule
counties that adopted new charters through 1980, 56
had been written since 1965 and 39 since 1970 [14,
p. 72].

The charter-writing process is one of the most
important parts of the local government change effort.
A National Academy of Public Administration publication comments on the charter-writing phase: "The
selection and composition of the study commission is
critical to its eventual success or failure. This is
true not only because of what the individual members
are able to contribute, but also because the
commission's membership will affect its credibility
with the larger community" [14, p. 19].

Despite the great importance of this phase for
the total change effort, relatively little research
has been conducted on charter-writing commissions.
Studies tend to concentrate on the efforts of opponents
or proponents to convince the voters to support or
oppose the charter and/or on analyses of charter
itself [2, 3, 14, 19, 20]. In recent years some
research has been done on local government study commissions [6, 11]; however, there is a need for much
more. Attention should be given to the commission
composition. What are the possible different

*Reprinted from State and Local Government, Vol. XIV,
No. 3, September 1982, pp. 124-27 by permission of
the Institute of Government, University of Georgia.

substantive orientations of commission members on structural changes? What is the impact of personal motivations of members on structural change preferences? The intent of this inquiry is to provide some insights on these questions, thus adding another dimension to the literature on local government change efforts.

First, the traditional, appointed study commission with its predictable goals and structural change orientation is reviewed. It is argued that this type of commission probably cannot be obtained when commissions are elected. Models are developed to categorize and explain change preferences of members of elected commissions. A typology of members' personal goals is offered to aid in analyzing their change preferences and behavior on the commission. The models are applied to describe orientations of members on major structural issues. Finally, a case study that used the framework is briefly described.

BLUE-RIBBON CHARTER COMMISSIONS

To the extent that charter writing is covered in the literature, it is usually procedural and prescriptive in nature. Reform-oriented agencies such as the Governmental Research Association [18], the National Municipal League [15, 16] and the International City Management Association [17]; university-based groups, such as the Bureau of Public Administration at the University of Maine [7], and state executive departments, such as the Pennsylvania Department of Community Affairs [10], publish guides for charter-writing commissions. These guides outline proper procedure, discuss substantive charter issues, and often include model charter provisions.

The assumption in these publications seems to be that charter-writing commissions will be appointed as blue-ribbon commissions, groups of concerned citizens selflessly giving their time and talents to improve their municipalities. One guide for charter-writing commissions explicitly states that only those who have been active in civic leadership positions or who are knowledgeable about state and local government through education or experience should be commission members [5, p. 8].

The blue-ribbon commission invariably considers

341

economy and efficiency in government as its major
priority. Its recommendations usually follow the
"good" government literature. However, due to the
makeup of the commission, the optimum of current
thinking on economy and efficiency in local government
may not be reflected in the charter recommendations.
There are generally a few members (e.g., labor leaders
and politicians) who do not have economy and efficiency
as their first priority. The reform-oriented members
who dominate the commission are generally pragmatic
and willing to compromise on proposals as long as the
resulting charter promises improvement in government
economy and efficiency.

FRAMEWORK FOR STUDY OF ELECTED
CHARTER COMMISSIONS

According to Adrian [1, p. 138], most local
government charter-writing committees are elected by
the voters. Members of elected commissions may have
structural preferences and personal motivations
different from those of members of appointed commissions. Indeed, those members advocating structural
reforms espoused in the good government/reform
literature may not be in the majority on an elected
commission.

Cornwell, Goodman, and Swanson [4] have developed
and tested a framework relating the values and
motivations of members of state constitutional conventions with their preferred constitutional changes.
The framework was useful in their study of the
functioning and decision-making of state constitutional
conventions. Some of their findings are used as a
point of departure in developing a framework for
analyzing local government study commissions. This
material was used because definite similarities exist
between state constitutional conventions and elected
local government study commissions. For example,
there are no pre-established patterns of internal
structure and behavior. People with various attitudes,
interests, and personal goals are brought together for
intensive, goal-directed periods of time. The
knowledge of members on the subject matter varies
widely. Personality conflicts and operational issues
may escalate to the point of becoming the major focus
of the group. Also, the entire substantive product is
put before the voters for approval, a factor

342

overshadowing the group's deliberations.

There are, however, substantial differences
between state constitutional conventions and local
government study commissions. Constitutional conventions are composed of much larger groups that generally
require different organizational procedures and may
elicit individual behavior different from what a small
charter-writing commission would elicit. Constitutional
conventions generally take place in a shorter, more
intensive time period than do the local government
commissions. Also, the concerns surrounding a basic
law for the state differ from those for a local government.

Cornwell, et al., propose three models to describe
orientations of members of state constitutional conventions. These were a guide in developing models
applicable to local government charter commissions.
The models applicable for local government charter
commissions are the status quo model, the reform model,
and the populist model. Adherents of the status quo
model see the commission as a political body, a subsystem within the existing, larger political system.
Major changes that will substantially alter structure
or existing power relationships are not sought. Cues
are generally taken from the political leaders. Commission members are considered as part of the political
process. Therefore, they should be concerned with
maintaining and enhancing existing political goals.

The reform model is an idealized view of what a
charter should contain. Adherents of this model
closely follow the models and tenets put forth in the
reform/good government literature. Efficiency and
professionalism are major aims. The process of writing
the charter should be above ordinary politics. With a
duty to draft a "higher law" document, members should
behave as impartial law givers, rising above normal
loyalties, interests, and conflicts of everyday
politics. The issues should be carefully and
abstractly weighed, the end goal being the creation
of an ideal document subtly attuned to the needs of
the community.

The populist model is a variation of the reform
model. Adherents of this model also seek changes in
the existing government. They seek to make government

343

more accessible and accountable to the "common" people.
The commission should not be influenced by politicians
or by the business community. It should remain
independent. By remaining aloof from community economic
and political interests, the commission can better
provide for more democratic government. Provisions
are sought to encourage citizen participation and
eliminate centers of political power.

Members seek to achieve certain personal goals
through commission membership. These goals, or
"hidden agendas," affect members' preferences on
structural changes. The following is a typology of
potential commission members' goals and the change
model members would likely favor [9, pp. 52-53].

1. Standpatters. These people are generally
   office holders or government employees.
   They seek to preserve their present
   positions and protect the political power
   structure generally and specifically in-
   sofar as it affects them. They favor the
   status quo model.

2. Dabblers. These are individuals who are
   active in neighborhood groups and special-
   interest associations. They seek increased
   neighborhood esteem and recognition and/or
   represent special interests. Dabblers are
   generally not concerned with overall
   government reform per se, but they do have
   special concerns and interests. They are
   usually well-educated, upper- or middle-
   class community members, able to devote
   considerable time to furthering their
   interests. They lean toward the populist
   model.

3. Reformers. These people are generally
   knowledgeable in the theory of government
   and are familiar with the literature on
   local government reform. They are
   interested in broad government reform,
   not just special concerns. They adhere
   to the reform model.

4. Statesmen. Knowledgeable of government
   processes, these people either hold or

344

have held elected offices in government for many years. Their service has been on a nonpartisan basis, or they are perceived as having risen above partisan politics. They may harbor some political ambitions but these are secondary. With their knowledge and stature, statesmen mediate conflicts between members and are often looked to as group leaders. They may prefer any model, but would appear more readily to favor the reform model.

5. Aspirants. These are generally young professionals seeking to advance themselves politically. They may have an existing political power base such as a minor elective office or the support of a few influential party members. The aspirants view the commission as a stepping-stone for future political success. Their structural preferences will be dictated by their perceptions about what would be best for their political careers. Aspirants probably lean toward the status quo model but will often favor some change to enhance their public image.

The commission membership mix is substantially affected by the selection method. An appointed commission will generally be a blue-ribbon commission dominated by reform model adherents with membership heavily drawn from those in the business, civic, and academic sectors of the community. Partisan elections will increase the possibility of electing adherents of the status quo model. Party slating of candidates and the use of party resources in being elected will ensure the influence of political leaders. Nonpartisan elections, usually have minimal qualification requirements for a position on the ballot. Therefore, many candidates will stand for election. The populist model will probably predominate since the possibility of electing people with particular concerns and interests will be maximized [4, pp. 42-44].

APPLICATION OF THE FRAMEWORK

The following section considers change preferences

345

on basic structural change, the legislative body, method of election, and election or appointment of administrative row officers (treasurer, sheriff, etc.).

Status quo model adherents would favor the status quo in all areas. The only changes they support would be those that enhance the power of the party or that would be acceptable to the entrenched politicians.

Reformers advocate change and follow the reform/good government literature on structural questions. Such literature has traditionally advocated a city-manager or county-manager form [15]; however, in urban areas with heterogeneous populations and partisan political activity, reformers often accept an elected executive with a separation of powers and a corresponding system of checks and balances. Reform model adherents would advocate an at-large system of election or possibly a combination of at-large and district election. Elections should be non-partisan. A small, full-time legislative body of five to ten members is preferable [10, pp. 71-72]. On the question of election or appointment of row officers, adherents would follow the tenets of the reform literature and would advocate that the only elected positions should be policymaking ones and, ultimately, that all administrative officers should be responsible to one chief administrative officer. Therefore, all elected administrative row offices should become appointive.

Populist model supporters also seek change from the current system. They would probably advocate the establishment of a separation-of-powers system with adequate checks and balances to avoid the centralization of power. However, they may react against a strong mayor system by favoring a council-manager plan to eliminate any possibility of a mayor accruing too much power. Populist model adherents desire to provide citizen access, better representation, and diminished political party control for the legislative body. They would favor an election system that would disrupt the existing political control. They would normally advocate nonpartisan district elections as the ideal to encourage more participation by the "common" people in the political process. They would also favor having a large number of council members.

Concerning row offices, populist model adherents

on the one hand seek increased citizen access that may
be possible through an elected office. On the other
hand, they also favor reducing political control by the
dominant political party. The decision on row officers,
therefore, is not clear. It would depend upon the
individual's perceptions of the degree of citizen
access under the current system. Populists would
probably favor a change in the status quo in an attempt
to destroy old power bases and open up new avenues of
citizen access.

In the reform-status quo cleavage, populists and
reformers would appear to be allied against status quo
model adherents. Members of both models may agree on
the need for change and the general direction of
change. However, they may not agree on the degree of
moderation of that change. Reformers would be more
willing to compromise and accept lesser changes as
long as the compromise guaranteed some improvement.
Populists are less willing to compromise. They would
continue to insist on much greater change, possibly
bordering on the extreme, than would the reformers.
Figure 1 is an indication of the change-status quo
orientations of the models.

Figure 1: Continuum of the Degree of Change
Preferences of the Three Models

no change	moderate change	extreme change
status quo model	reform model	populist model

THE EFFECT OF GROUP DYNAMICS

Specific recommendations favored by adherents of
each model may be inserted in the charter. These
recommendations will result not only from the initial
preferences of members but also from group dynamics.
Moreover, for various reasons, members classified in
the same model may have differing structural
preferences on a specific issue.

Such was the case with the Allegheny County,
Pennsylvania, Charter Writing Commission [8]. This

347

commission existed from 1972 to 1974. The seven-member elected commission had three populists, three status quo model supporters, and one reformer. The general orientation of the group was toward change: however, the reformer did not agree with the populists on all issues because he felt that some of the populists' stands were too extreme.

Through group dynamics, some members were convinced to support stands other than those they normally would have adopted. The resulting charter had recommendations advocated by reform and status quo model supporters, although recommendations supported by populist model supporters predominated. For example, the reformer pushed the separation-of-powers concept with a separately elected executive. He did not have any trouble convincing two of the three populists who wanted to disrupt the political system. The third populist had to be convinced that the separation-of-powers system was better than the council-manager system he preferred. The reformer's eloquence also persuaded one of the three status quo model adherents to vote for the separation-of-powers. The other two status quo model adherents continued to favor the existing system. Status quo model adherents favored only a modest increase in the three-member legislative body (easier to retain political party control), while populists favored a large body to maximize citizen access. In this instance the reformer sided with the political model adherents.

The populist model adherents won on district elections because they were joined by a status quo model adherent, an aspirant, who felt his chances of election would be enhanced by district election. He was a Republican in a heavily Democratic county. The reformer and the other two status quo model adherents favored the existing at-large system or a partial district, partial at-large compromise. Populists also won on other measures to increase citizen access and participation by underrepresented sectors of the community. This included mandating female and black membership on all appointed boards and commissions. They were also successful in their desire for charter specificity to reduce possible political maneuvering by future officeholders.

CONCLUSION

The framework described in this paper is useful in studying the charter-writing phase of the charter revision effort. The framework was useful in the case study of the Allegheny County Home Rule Study Commission. It provided a frame of reference and an organizing focus for analyzing decision-making on various charter recommendations. It should be useful in the study of charter commissions in the following ways.

1. It is useful in organizing and presenting data.
2. The models should be invaluable in analyzing the differences in structural change preferences among members.
3. The typology should have utility in the description and analysis of the personal motivations of members and the relationship between personal motivations and structural change preferences.
4. Group processes and the behavior of individual members in the group context can be effectively analyzed using the framework.

REFERENCES

1. Adrian, Charles R., and Press, Charles. Governing Urban America, 5th ed. (New York: McGraw-Hill, 1977).
2. Advisory Commission on Intergovernmental Relations, Sub-state Regionalism and the Federal System, Regional Governance: Promise and Performance, Vol. II (Washington, D.C.: U.S. Government Printing Office, 1973).
3. Bowden, John H., and Hamilton, Howard D. "Some Notes on Metropolitics in Ohio." Political Behavior and Public Issues in Ohio, edited by John J. Gargan and James G. Cole (Kent, Ohio: Kent State University Press, 1972).
4. Cornwell, Elmer E., Goodman, Jay S., and Swanson, William R. State Constitutional Conventions: The Politics of the Revision Process in Seven States (New York: Praeger Publishers, 1975).
5. Cullen, Richard. "Preparing A County Charter." Guide to County Organization and Management

(Washington, D.C.: National Association of
Counties, 1968).
6. Gamm, Larry. Community Dynamics of Local Govern-
ment Changes (State College, Pa.: Pennsylvania
Policy Analysis Service, Pennsylvania State
University, 1976).
7. Haag, J.J. Introduction to the Charter Drafting
Process (Bangor, Maine: Bureau of Public Adminis-
tration, University of Maine, 1970).
8. Hamilton, David K. "Areawide Government Reform:
A Case Study Emphasizing the Charter Writing
Process." Ph.D. dissertation, University of
Pittsburgh, 1978.
9. _____. "Exploratory Research on the Behavior of
Members of Elected Local Government Charter Commis-
sions." Journal of Urban Affairs 3 (Fall 1981):
51-61.
10. Karlesky, Joseph. Home Rule and Optional Plans, A
Guide for Pennsylvanians (Harrisburg: Pennsylvania
Department of Community Affairs, 1972).
11. Marando, Vincent L., and Florestano, Patricia S.
"State Commissions on Local Government: A
Mechanism for Reform." State and Local Government
Review 9 (May 1977): 49-53.
12. Morgan, David R. Managing Urban America (North
Scituate, Mass.: Duxbury Press, 1979).
13. Murphy, Thomas P. Metropolitics and the Urban
County (Washington, D.C.: Washington National
Press, 1970).
14. National Academy of Public Administration.
Metropolitan Governance: A Handbook for Local
Government Study Commissions (Washington, D.C.:
U.S. Department of Housing and Urban Development,
Office of Policy Development and Urban Research,
September 1980).
15. National Municipal League. A Guide for Charter
Commissions (New York: National Municipal League,
1974).
16. _____. Model County Charter (New York: National
Municipal League, 1956).
17. Platsky, Robert A. Local Government Structure and
Organization, A Handbook for Local Officials
(Washington, D.C.: International City Management
Association and National Association of Counties,
1978).
18. Reed, T.H. Revising A City Charter (New York:
Governmental Research Association, 1947).
19. Temple, David G. Merger Politics: Local Govern-

ment Consolidation in Tidewater, Virginia (Charlottesville, Va.: University Press of Virginia, 1972).

20. Williams, J.D. The Defeat of Home Rule in Salt Lake City (New Brunswick, N.J.: Eagleton Institute Cases in Practical Politics, Rutgers University, 1960).

32. A "FAIR" VOTING SYSTEM FOR LOCAL GOVERNMENTS*

Joseph F. Zimmerman

Unrepresentative local governing bodies have been a long-standing problem in the United States, with blacks and minority language groups being affected most adversely by at-large plurality elections in many large cities. In a democratic system of government based on majority rule, there is an unavoidable clash between the views of the majority and the minorities on numerous issues. What is needed is an electoral system that provides for majority rule and direct minority representation in a city where there is ethnic, racial or other bloc voting.

The issue of the best election system for local governing bodies was a prime concern of the original municipal reform movement in the early years of this century. The reformers were convinced that the ward system of election promoted and perpetuated "invisible" city councils controlled by corrupt political machines, and resulted in councils that did not represent the citizenry at large. The movement sought to replace a large, bicameral city council with a small, "visible," unicameral council, ward elections with at-large elections, and partisan elections with nonpartisan elections. The reformers generally were successful.

In the 1960s, the municipal reform model was re-assessed by observers convinced that the quality of municipal government had been improved but concerned with the new system was relatively insensitive to the special needs and desires of blacks and Spanish speaking citizens because the at-large council tended to overrepresent a white middle class majority and aggravate feelings of political impotence in minority communities.

---

*Reprinted with permission from the National Civic Review, October 1979, pp. 481-87 and 507.

Enactment by Congress of the Voting Rights Act in
1965 added impetus to the movement to change local
electoral systems. Acting by authority of this act as
amended, the United States Department of Justice and
the federal courts have been insisting that cities
wishing to make any change in their electoral systems,
no matter how minor, must adopt the single-member
district system, which, of course, is the old ward
system under a new label.

CANONS OF FAIR REPRESENTATION

Based on the assumption that there are no impedi-
ments to citizens registering and voting for a local
governing body, it is possible to develop canons of a
good electoral system that will produce "fair" representation for all citizens. These canons, or criteria,
can measure the quality of representation that will be
produced by the various methods of selecting the
members of a city council. The criteria are inter-
related rather than discrete.

Effectiveness of Ballots Cast. The effectiveness
canon refers to the potency of each ballot cast by a
registered voter and indicates that a proper electoral
system does not cancel or dilute invidiously the
effectiveness of ballots cast by any citizen or
identifiable group. In particular, in the eyes of a
minority group, the election of a city council must be
more than a type of periodic consultation ritual that
is meaningless to the group because their ballots are
rendered ineffective by the design of the electoral
system. If a minority group perceives that the
electoral system makes it politically powerless,
participation in the political process will be low and
the public interest will suffer accordingly.

Maximization of Participation. A good electoral
system encourages the enrollment of eligible voters
because they can visualize that their exercise of the
franchise will be effective. Logically, voter turnout
by a group will be in direct relation to the possible
influence that the group can exercise. Low voter
registration and turnout on election day may result
as much from feelings of alienation--a sense of
powerlessness--as from apathy.

Responsiveness of Elected Officials. Representa-

tion of all competing interests is an important feature
of an electoral system that is functioning properly.
In a large city, there is a natural divergence between
citywide and neighborhood interests. A good electoral
system is structured to produce council members who
simultaneously are attuned to citywide needs and have
a special sensitivity to the needs of ethnic, neighborhood, racial and other groups whose interests are more
circumscribed. A truly representative council will
treat all citizens fairly in the process of accommoda-
ting competing interests. An electoral system that
guarantees direct representation on a city council for
members of a sizable minority group will facilitate the
necessary political accommodation and help to ensure
responsiveness by the council to the needs of the group.

Maximization of Access to Decision Makers. A
proper system of voting will result in the selection of
council members who are willing to listen to, and seek
out, the views of all groups in polity. Consultation
with constituents must be genuine and not pro forma or
else alienation will be promoted. The best system
ensures that all council members are accessible to all
concerned citizens.

Equity in Representation. Fairness in representation is the hallmark of a democratic political system.
If members of a group are convinced that they can be
represented most effectively only by a member of the
group, the selection system should be one that will
guarantee that a sizable minority group will be able
to elect a member to the council. Direct representation for such a group should not be a product of
happenstance.

Legitimization of the Council. An important
function of an electoral system is to legitimize the
city council in the eyes of citizens, thereby facilitating the implementation of its policy decisions.
The effectiveness of a city's policies depends in many
instances on the active cooperation and support of the
citizenry. A widespread view that decisions are
designed deliberately to favor one group over another
will seriously weaken the perceived legitimacy of the
policy makers.

THE FEDERAL VOTING RIGHTS ACT

Through the Voting Rights Act in 1965, Congress

regulated elections for the first time since 1871. The act was extended for five years in 1970, and was broadened and extended for seven years in 1975.

On determination that the act applies to a state or political subdivision, the covered unit becomes subject to the pre-clearance requirement, forbidding the enactment or administration of any change in the election system unless the Attorney General of the United States or the district court for the District of Columbia, in response to an action initiated by the covered unit, issues a declaratory judgment that the change would not abridge the right to vote of citizens protected by the act.

Two important decisions of the United States Supreme Court have extended substantially the coverage of the act. In 1968, the court ruled that the act must be given "the broadest possible scope" to reach "any State enactment which altered the election law of a covered State in even a minor way" (Allen v. State Board of Elections, 393 U.S. 544 at 566-67, 1968). Three years later, the court held that annexation comes under the purview of the act (Perkins v. Matthews, 400 U.S. 379, 1971). The court's insistence on the single-member district system as the price of annexation by a covered city with at-large elections has complicated central city annexation of unincorporated territory to prevent white residents of the territory from incorporating and setting up a separate municipality or a separate school system (City of Petersburg, Virginia v. United States et al, 410 U.S. 962, 1973; City of Richmond v. United States, 422 U.S. 358, 1975).

The court upheld a racial gerrymander in favor of blacks in United Jewish Organizations of Williamsburg, Incorporated v. Carey (430 U.S. 144, 1977), reversing its 1960 decision in Gomillion v. Lightfoot (354 U.S. 339, 1960) that invalidated racial gerrymandering. Gomillion, in effect, has been discarded if the clearance requirement of the Voting Rights Act is involved. Chief Justice Warren M. Burger, in the Williamsburg case, was most accurate in writing that "the assumption that 'whites' and 'non-whites' in the County form homogeneous entities for voting purposes is entirely without foundation."

AN EVALUATION

The single-member district system, replaced in many large cities by voters accepting the recommendation of municipal reformers, is being resurrected by decisions of the Department of Justice and the federal courts. This fact necessitates that the system be evaluated in terms of the canons of a "fair" electoral system. If the single-member district system is found to be wanting, citizens, Congress and the courts should give serious consideration to alternatives.

A ballot cast by a member of a sizable minority group in a single-member district system may or may not be effective in helping to elect a candidate representing the group. A group that is geographically dispersed in a city where bloc voting is prevalent will be unable to elect a candidate. Furthermore, in the Williamsburg case, the Department of Justice decided that only a deliberate, or affirmative, racial gerrymander producing a district with a black population of 65 percent would guarantee the election of a black. It is apparent that with the single-member district system the map makers can determine the nature of representation on the council to a greater degree than can the electorate whose choices will be limited by the shape of the district lines. One must not overlook the possibility that a deliberate gerrymander could be employed to reduce the voting strength of a minority, particularly one not protected by the act; and its voting strength in the absence of frequent reapportionment also might be sapped by a "silent" gerrymander, i.e., population shifts.

An at-large system may enable a minority group to exercise more influence in the decision-making process of the city council since it allows the group to mobilize its electoral strength as a "swing" vote rather than by attempting to elect one of its own members. A "balance-of-power" role may afford a minority group more leverage with the city council than holding a small number of council seats.

The single-member system will facilitate maximum participation in the electoral process if the voters in each district perceive that the effectiveness of their votes is guaranteed. The system, however, does not offer such a guarantee. This will discourage

356

participation at the polls. In addition, the media focus on city-wide issues and provide less coverage of the activities of a district councilmember. As a result, the public is less aware of the important role than the councilmember plays in governing the city and is less motivated to participate in the electoral process.

The ward system strengthens the position of council members whose goal is to gain benefits for their respective areas, even at the expense of the common good of the city. This system means, of course, that council members will tend to be responsive to the requests of many of their constituents. This may prove to be divisive, however, if councilmembers are hostile to the needs of minorities within their districts. The smaller the districts in terms of population, the more probable is the election of "extremists" who will discriminate against their opponents within the districts. One must also not forget past experience showing that the single-member district system may pit one district against others in a struggle for the distribution of resources, or may produce a compromise by which resources are distributed equally regardless of citywide or district needs.

Should members of a minority group become convinced that they will have greater access to a decision maker if they pool their voting strength in a single district, they will be encouraged to remain in segregated neighborhoods or to move to districts where others of their race or ethnic group live. In other words, the system may promote the perpetuation of separate societies. A second access problem with the district system is the fact that a voter has no other direct representative on the council to turn to for assistance should the district member be insensitive. The problem would be most severe for a voter who supported the losing candidate in the district. A related problem is that discernible ethnic and racial enclaves do not exist in all municipalities and a dispersed minority will be unable to elect an effective district representative who would provide effective access for the group to the council.

The greatest failure of the single-member district system is its inabiliity to ensure equity in representation. The system fails to guarantee that minorities

357

will be represented in proportion to their voting
strength even when there is no deliberate gerrymander
designed to dilute their votes, or that the majority
of council members will be sympathetic to the special
needs and problems of minorities. Of particular
concern is the tendency of the single-member district
system in a city covering a considerable geographical
area to produce a large and unwieldy council with real
power being exercised by committees less representative
of the citizenry at-large than the council. Also, the
single-member system does not provide as much legitimacy
for the council as an at-large system because each voter
has the opportunity to help elect only one member
instead of all or a majority of the council members.

The single-member district system, then, has a
number of undesirable features and consequences. There
is an alternative to the single-member and plurality
at-large systems that ranks high in terms of criteria
for a good electoral system.

The single transferable vote system of Proportional
Representation (P.R.), developed by Thomas Hare in 1857,
ensures that various parties and groups are represented,
with mathematical exactness, in proportion to their
voting strength.

Voters in a P.R. election indicate their preferences by placing a number after each candidate's name.
A "1" is placed after the name of the first choice
candidate, a "2" after the second, et cetera. A
candidate must receive a number of votes equal to the
quota to be elected. The quota is determined by
dividing the total number of valid ballots by the
number of councilmembers to be elected plus one, plus
one ballot. If 100,000 valid ballots are cast to elect
a nine-member city council, the quota would be

$$\frac{100,000}{\text{Number of Councilmen} + 1} + 1 = 10,001.$$

After the quota is determined, the ballots are
sorted by first choices. A candidate is declared
elected if he or she receives a total of number "1"
ballots equal to or exceeding the quota. If any
candidates receive more than the quota, their surplus
ballots are transferred to the remaining candidates

358

according to the second choices indicated.

The candidate who receives the smallest number of "1" votes is declared defeated and those ballots are distributed to the remaining candidates according to the second choices marked on them. A ballot is distributed to the third choice in the event the second choice candidate already has been elected. A new count is conducted and candidates with a total of number "1" and number "2" ballots equal to or exceeding the quota are declared elected. Their surplus ballots, if any, are transferred to the remaining candidates. The process is continued until the full council is elected.

P.R. measures up well against the effectiveness canon, as most ballots help to elect a candidate either by first choice or by transfer. In contrast, the ballots of voters in a single-member district system cast for the losing candidate may be viewed as wasted. P.R., in other words, ensures that each voter, with relatively few exceptions, may have an equal effect on the final outcome of the election.

Maximum participation will be promoted by P.R. since it facilitates the selection of the most responsive and talented candidate, regardless of her or his place of residence. Consequently, voters will be encouraged to turn out at the polls. In addition, P.R. eliminates the need for a primary and thus guarantees that the council members will be selected in an election with a relatively large turnout of eligible voters.

Responsiveness of council members will be increased, as their election will be dependent in large measure on their ability to develop a program with broad citizen support instead of a one-issue platform appealing to the majority or plurality of voters in a single district. Since a vote has an equal weight regardless of the polling place at which the vote is cast, candidates will be seeking support throughout the city, and that support will be dependent on their responsiveness to the needs of citizens. Access to decision-makers is facilitated, since a vote cast for a council member in any district of the city carries an equal weight.

Clearly, the most important canon is equity, and
P.R. measures up exceptionally well in terms of this
criterion since majority rule with guaranteed minority
representation is its chief advantage. It will be
impossible for a faction with a small majority of the
votes to elect all members of the council. Assuming
that a minority group votes as a bloc, the group will
be represented fully yet cannot benefit from a split
among opposition groups and elect a majority of the
members of the council, as is possible with limited
voting and cumulative voting. P.R. also helps to
ensure equity by eliminating gerrymandering, deliberate
or silent, and the need for periodic reapportionment of
the council.

P.R. reduces the possibility of election frauds.
The selection of members of the council by single-
member districts and plurality voting tempts unscrup-
ulous individuals to try in various ways to influence
the counting of ballots in districts where the election
races are close. Since P.R. is an at-large system and
the ballots are counted in a central location, the
possibility of tampering is minimized. P.R. also helps
to legitimize the city council by ensuring the election
of highly qualified candidates who develop a program
with broad citywide support.

CONCLUSIONS

A good local electoral system makes representative
government a reality by ensuring that sizable minority
groups as well as the majority have direct representation on a city council. While the goals of the United
States Department of Justice and federal courts in
Voting Rights Act cases are proper, one must object to
their attempts to impose a racial and ethnic quota
system on cities attempting to adjust to changing
conditions.

Democratic government should function best when
the electors cast ballots only for the best qualified
men and women seeking public office without regard to
the ethnic, racial, religious or other background
characteristics. Nevertheless, full recognition must
be accorded to the pervasiveness of bloc voting.

A city council selected in an at-large plurality
election may be unrepresentative because of partial or

total disfranchisement of large minority groups. The single-member district system, however, is not the most desirable alternative to eliminate malrepresentation. While the single-member district system improves the chances of blacks electing candidates in a city such as Houston where they tend to be concentrated geographically within the sections of the city, the system does not help Mexican-Americans who are spread throughout the city. Only P.R. would provide direct representation for both, assuming that they give their ballot preference to their own group.

Under P.R., particular and general interests can be represented simultaneously, as council members belonging to an ethnic, racial or other group must build a citywide coalition of electoral support in most instances to win a seat on the council. The principal advantage of P.R. is the fact the system elevates rather than submerges minority voting strength and relies on design rather than chance to produce direct and "fair" representation.

33. Evolving Decentralization
in New York City*

Joseph F. Zimmerman

The 1898 consolidation of all local governments
within a five-county area to form New York City has not
proved to be a panacea for service delivery problems.
A need arose for a new mechanism--administrative
decentralization--to coordinate effectively the delivery
of services on a sub-city basis. By 1970, administrative decentralization by regular city departments had
resulted in the creation of 23 health districts, 75
police precincts, 58 sanitation districts, 31 school
districts, 44 social service centers, and a large
number of recreation areas. The proliferation of
districts not enclosed within identical boundaries
slowed interagency coordination and baffled residents
attempting to register complaints or obtain information.

THE 1975 CITY CHARTER AMENDMENTS

During a five-year period, the State Charter
Revision Commission for New York City carefully studied
the existing system of administrative decentralization
and proposed ten amendments to the city charter. Six
received the sanction of the electorate in 1975. One
of the new charter sections provides for the development of service districts with identical boundaries.
Exceptions are community school districts and fire
department districts. The charter also links these
coterminous service districts to reconstituted
community boards. Section 2704 of the city charter,
effective January 1, 1980, stipulates the following
services must be provided within community districts:
police patrol services, street cleaning and refuse
collection services, local parks and recreation areas,
and social services.

---

*Reprinted from State and Local Government Review, Vol.
XIV, No. 1, January 1982, pp. 16-19 by permission of
the Institute of Government, University of Georgia.

The following services must be provided either on
a community district or multi-community district basis,
depending upon whether each district is large enough to
achieve economy and efficiency in providing the
particular service: housing code enforcement, neighborhood preservation and related housing rehabilitation
services, street maintenance and repair, sewer
maintenance and repair, and health services other than
municipal hospitals.

The Police Department requested an amendment to
the charter to allow operation outside the prescribed
boundaries while new precinct houses are being con-
structed in the Bronx, Queens, and Manhattan. On
November 28, 1979, Mayor Edward I. Koch announced his
support for an amendment allowing the department to
operate as requested until the results of the 1980
federal census of population are available [9, p.B-5].

Section 2704 (d) of the charter stipulates that
"the head of each designated agency shall assign to
each such district at least one official with
managerial responsibilities involving the exercise of
independent judgment in the scheduling, allocation and
assignment of personnel and equipment...." Each
agency, in addition, is required to prepare an annual
list of priorities, projected activities, and programs
within each community district; to report its direct
operating expenses within each district to the community
board; and to provide each board with current information on agency operations and programs.

COMMUNITY BOARDS AND SERVICE CABINETS

Although proposals for the creation of community
boards date from 1947, no one took action on these
proposals until 1951 when Manhattan Borough President
Robert F. Wagner, Jr., created 12 community planning
councils with 15 to 20 appointed members. Renamed
community planning boards, their original role was to
serve as advisory mechanisms to improve citizen input
into the city's decision-making process. Section 84
of the 1963 city charter provided for the creation of
community planning boards by each of the five borough
presidents. Sixty-two board members were appointed.
The charter was amended in 1969--New York City Local
Law 39--to change the name of the boards to community
boards and to enlarge their membership to a maximum of

50. The amendment also stipulated that all city departments and agencies required to hold public hearings must refer matters to the concerned community board.

Under provisions of a 1975 city charter amendment, each of the 59 boards has as many as 50 unpaid members appointed by the borough president for overlapping two-year terms. Half the members are appointed from nomination lists submitted by members of the city council representing the borough. The councilmen are nonvoting members of the board, which is responsible for

a. preparation of plans for the growth, improvement, and development of the community district.
b. submission of capital and revenue expense budget priorities.
c. participation in the planning of individual capital projects funded in the capital budget and review of scopes and designs for projects.
d. initial review of all applications of public and private agencies and developers for use of land in the community district.
e. assistance to agencies in the preparation of service statements for the community district.
f. dissemination of information about city services and programs and the processing of complaints and inquiries of district residents [7, p. 13].

Section 2800 (f) of the city charter authorizes each board to appoint a district manager to serve at its pleasure and to monitor the delivery of services by city departments. In cooperation with city agencies providing services, including the fire department, the manager is directed by Section 2705 of the charter to establish a district service cabinet for coordinating the delivery of services. Section 191 (b) (5) of the charter requires a representative from the Department of City Planning to serve on the cabinet, which holds monthly meetings.

Since the community school districts were

364

established by Chapter 330 of the New York Laws of 1969, the city charter could not require these districts to have boundaries coterminous with those of the community boards. Nor could the charter require that the school districts be represented on the district service cabinets. A certain amount of inter-locking of the community school boards and community boards has occurred because a number of individuals elected to the school boards have been appointed to serve on the community boards by their borough presidents. In addition, several district service cabinets have invited a community school board to designate a member to serve on the cabinet. The chairperson of the community board is an ex officio member and the district manager is the cabinet chairperson.

To strengthen relationships between the city government and neighborhoods, Mayor Edward I. Koch issued on February 8, 1978, executive order Number 6 creating a Community Board Assistance Unit (CBAU). The CBAU provides professional assistance to the boards and district managers and coordinates imple-mentation of the revised city charter. The executive order also established a community liaison unit to maintain contact with community groups--including civic, block, neighborhood, and tenant associations-- to ensure that the complaints and problems of these groups receive attention from high-level city officials. The two units have adjoining offices and work closely together.

In July 1978, the Nova Institute and the CBAU launched a pilot program designed to improve communi-cations between the members of the boards and the dis-trict service chiefs. A survey of participants revealed the following:

> [T]he principal problem with the...project
> was that it asked the district service
> chief to make decisions that went beyond
> his responsibility. Since the decisions
> he was asked to make were basic managerial
> decisions on the scheduling and allocation
> of manpower and resources assigned to his
> service district, this comment points out
> how important it is for city government to
> implement the command decentralization
> requirements under the revised Charter [6,p.6].

The report also noted "the need for better measures of district-level agency performance" which, together with the failure to delegate sufficient authority to the district chiefs, "limit the present effectiveness of the district plan and report as a managerial tool for district operations" [6, p. 7].

To help board members understand the city's budget-making process, the CBAU issued a Guide to Community Board Participation in the Budget Process for Fiscal 1980. The Guide stresses that the $13.5 billion "executive budget. . .comes in three volumes, none of which can be recommended as light reading," and reports that none of the data in the 1,000-page computer-printed supporting schedule "applies to service districts that even remotely correspond to community districts" [10, pp. 5-6]. In July 1978, the unit published agency service statements on a borough basis containing data on equipment and staff for local service districts of city agencies. However, the information is not based on districts having identical boundaries.

In 1979, seven city agencies--Environmental Protection (Division of Water Resources), Fire, Housing Preservation and Development, Parks and Recreation, Police, Sanitation, and Transportation (Bureau of Highway Operations)--consulted community boards as part of the budget preparation process. The Guide cautions board members that they "have to recognize that only a small fraction of the overall expensse budget is likely to be subject to influence by community boards in any single fiscal year" because a large portion of the budget is "un-controllable" and "even the 'controllable' portion... includes many activities that are largely outside the jurisdiction of community boards such as elementary, secondary, and higher education" [10, p. 42].

EVALUATION

Very little evidence is available to judge the effectiveness of the new system of colinear adminis-trative district boundaries and the reorganized community boards. The former were not implemented fully until January 1, 1980, though the latter have been operating since 1976.

City Controller Harrison J. Goldin prepared a detailed report in 1975 projecting the annual cost of
service districts within the same boundaries at $193.7
million [8, p. 22]. The State Charter Revision
Commission, however, estimated that the one-time costs
of transition to coterminality would be $3 to $4
million, and that annual costs of coterminous service
delivery would range from slightly under $2 million to
$3 million [7, p. 4]. City Sanitation Commissioner
Anthony Vaccarello in December 1977 predicted that
matching the sanitation district boundaries with the
community board districts would cost the city an
additional $30 million "with no consideration to the
ease of picking up garbage" [1, p. 39].

In 1979, the CBAU released a report on the cost
of and the progress made in implementing coterminality.
The report revealed the State Charter Commission's cost
estimates generally were on target, with the exception
of the police department. That department had to
build and staff two new precinct headquarters because
there were no precinct facilities in Bronx Community
District Number 11 and Queens Community District
Number 3 [4, p. 13].

Because each board is allocated only $60,000 per
year, doubts may be raised about its ability to achieve
the goals established for the boards by the charter
drafters. Several boards have supplemented their city
grant with federal and foundation grants. Nevertheless, a study by the Nova Institute concluded that the
boards should be granted some "direct decision-making
capability over specific funds" if the boards are to
be able to influence service delivery [11, p. 28].

Many political leaders have recognized the increased importance of the community boards since the
city charter was amended in 1975. This increasing
awareness can be seen in the political battles to
elect chairpersons of the boards in many districts,
notably the disputes between Manhattan Borough
President Andrew J. Stein and borough city councilmen.
These disputes focused on the appointment of community
board members after the expiration of the term of
office of all board members on December 31, 1978.
Borough President Stein did not appoint to community
boards several nominees of city council members. On
January 31, 1979, city councilman Theodore Silverman

367

succeeded in having the chairperson of the Crown
Heights Community Board in Brooklyn replaced [14, p. B-
6 and 2, p. B-3]. One reason for the battles over
board nominees is that the boards can serve as training
grounds for future elected officials.

The City's Board of Estimate--the mayor, city
controller, president of the city council, and five
borough presidents--acquired power under the 1975 city
charter amendments to review decisions of the Board of
Standards and Appeals. This board may grant variances
and special permits under the zoning law. The Board
of Estimate reviewed 41 decisions of the Board of
Standards and Appeals in 1977 and 1978 and reversed
20 of them. Nineteen of the reversals involved cases
initiated by community boards [13, p. A-30].

The City Planning Commission, required to consult
community boards on most land-use questions, reported
that in 98 percent of the cases the commission concurred with the recommendations of the community boards
[3, p. B-1].

The community boards participated for the first
time in the city's budget-making process in connection
with the preparation of the fiscal 1980 city budget.
Boards were requested to recommend capital projects
and to rank city services by priority. Police patrol,
fire protection, and local parks maintenance ranked
high, but central support services, such as sewer
treatment, as well as city zoos, skating rinks, and
golf courses ranked low.

The boards submitted over 2,000 proposals for
community development capital items, and 57 percent
of them were approved. The high approval rate is
explainable because the boards were coached carefully
about likely city priorities and were discouraged from
submitting a wish list with items such as new schools.
Most capital projects involved repaving streets,
installing new sewers, and rehabilitating parks. Many
projects had been recommended in the past and
deterioration dictated corrective action. Relative
to the expense budget, approximately 40 percent of the
boards' requests were approved. One positive result
of the boards' participation in the process is that
many city operations have become more targeted because
the boards know their districts and what needs

improvement.

CONCLUSIONS

The political centralization theory dominated New York City from the 1890s until the 1960s and guided the structuring of city government. Nevertheless, concern about citizen input into the decision-making process of a monolithic city government surfaced after World War II and found expression in community boards. These mechanisms for citizen input into the decision-making process received important new advisory powers when voters approved the 1975 amendments to the city charter. Charter provisions for a full-time manager clearly enlarged the potential effectiveness of the part-time lay boards in monitoring the delivery of services by city agencies. A second charter provision for service districts with identical boundaries and for a neighborhood cabinet of service delivery officials greatly enlarged the opportunity for the citizen boards to participate in the governmental process. The commonality of administrative district boundaries in particular holds promise for improving the coordination of service delivery by district administrative agencies and for increasing the accountability of service delivery agencies to the citizens.

The neighborhood cabinet serves as a barometer of the quality of services as perceived by citizens. It also affords district agency heads the opportunity to explain to citizens the reasons for service delivery problems, such as the breakdown of equipment or the shortage of manpower, and for initiated corrective action.

The future effectiveness of community boards will depend heavily upon the development of a cooperative spirit by the boards and the district agency administrators. Should boards engage in only critical rhetoric and fail to support the administrators, the boards will be of no value as advisory mechanisms, and the district cabinets will fail to serve as accountability mechanisms.

The ability of community boards, coterminous districts, and district cabinets to achieve goals established by the drafters of the charter amendments will depend on the willingness of commissioners in

city hall to delegate sufficient authority to district
administrators. The administrators must be able to
adjust to a new situation in which they make decisions
previously made by their city hall superiors.

Centripetal and centrifugal forces will continue
struggling for dominance. Some political and administrative leaders will favor the centralization of
decision-making in city hall to ensure that citywide
needs are addressed in a priority order. Other
political leaders and administrative officials will
support a greater role for neighborhoods in the city's
decision-making process. Political leaders with
neighborhood constituencies and district heads of
administrative agencies desiring additional discretionary authority may discover it in their respective
interest to work together to weaken city hall's
decision-making authority. The community boards
already have formed a citywide coalition meeting
regularly to discuss common problems and to develop
a united front on issues whenever possible.

The community boards and the city administrative
officials clearly are engaged in learning new roles.
The results of the new approach to citizen input into
the city's decision-making process undoubtedly will
vary from district to district and will depend upon
the competence of the boards and district adminis-
trators--and upon their degree of dedication to making
the new system work. Boards representing higher
income areas are apt to have more success than those
representing poor neighborhoods in channeling additional city resources into their neighborhoods. The
higher income boards have more members with political
clout, including direct access to the mayor's office.

REFERENCES

1. Bird, David. "Making Community Boards Work Is
    Now Full-time Job." The New York Times,
    December 28, 1977, p. 39.
2. Carroll, Maurice. "Black Supplants Rabbi as
    Crown Heights Board Chief." The New York Times,
    February 1, 1979, p. B-3.
3. _____. "Neighborhoods Gain New Power in
    Political Shift." The New York Times, February
    19, 1979, p. B-1.
4. Coterminality for New York City: A Report on

    Planning in Progress (New York: New York City
    Community Board Assistance Unit, March 15,
    1979).

5. Coterminality for New York City: Final Report
    (New York: New York City Community Board
    Assistance Unit, July 15, 1979).

6. The District Plan and Report (New York: The Nova
    Institute, January 1979).

7. Final Report of the State Charter Revision Com-
    mission for New York City (New York: The
    Commission, August 21, 1975).

8. Fowler, Glenn, "Cost of Charter Revisions Put at
    330 Million a Year." The New York Times,
    October 27, 1975, p. 22.

9. _____. "Koch Agrees to Delay City Charter Mandate
    on Lines of Precincts." The New York Times,
    November 28, 1979, p. B-5.

10. Guide to Community Board Participation in the
    Budget Process for Fiscal 1980 (New York: New
    York City Community Board Assistance Unit,
    1978).

11. Khiss, Peter. "Koch Urged to Speed Local Parti-
    cipation on Budget." The New York Times,
    December 19, 1977, p. 28.

12. McNeil, Donald G. "Until the Old Ballfields are
    Fixed, Canarsie Wants No More Parks." The New
    York Times, May 13, 1978, pp. 1 and 11.

13. Oser, Alan S. "Zoning Appeals Raise Issue of
    Jurisdiction of 2 Boards." The New York Times,
    December 22, 1978, p. A-30.

14. "Stein Disputing Council Choices for Local
    Panels." The New York Times, January 9, 1979,
    p. B-6.

15. Tracking Community Services in New York City (New
    York: The Nova Institute, June 1978).

16. Uniform Land Use Review Procedure (New York: New
    York City Planning Commission, June 1, 1976).

17. You and Your Community Board (New York: League
    of Women Voters of the City of New York, 1978).

34.   COPING WITH METROPOLITAN PROBLEMS/
      THE BOUNDARY REVIEW COMMISSION*

Joseph F. Zimmerman

METROPOLITAN PROBLEMS have been attributed partially to the jurisdictional morass resulting from
the failure of some State Legislatures to facilitate
the annexation of unincorporated land by central
cities and to restrict the incorporation of new
units of local government in metropolitan areas.
However, not all States have been inactive. Nine
States - Alaska, California, Michigan, Minnesota,
Nevada, New Mexico, Oregon, Texas, and Washington -
have created boundary review commissions. To cite
only one illustration, the 1959 Minnesota Legislature (Chapter 414) reacted to the problem of increasing local governmental fragmentation by establishing
the Minnesota Muncipal Commission with authority to
approve, disapprove, or modify proposals for the incorporation of municipalities in metropolitan areas,
annexation of unincorporated territory, consolidation of municipalities, and detachment of territory
from a municipality.

This article will examine the powers and
operations of boundary review commissions in the
nine States.

In terms of control, commissions in five of the
States - Alaska, New Mexico, Oregon, Texas, and
Washington - are state controlled, commissions in
California and Nevada are locally controlled, and
commissions in Michigan and Minnesota are under
joint state-local control.

POWERS OF BOUNDARY COMMISSIONS

The determinations of the commissions in
California, Oregon, and Texas are final. Although

* Reprinted with permission from State Government,
   Vol. XLVIII, No. 4, Autumn 1975, pp. 257-60.

a commission in Nevada has the power of review -
to approve, modify, or disapprove an annexation
proposal - it must disapprove a proposal if protests are made by a majority of the real property
owners in the proposed annexation area. Certain
annexation proposals in Michigan, Minnesota, New
Mexico, and Washington are subject to a popular
referendum.

ALASKA

     The 1959 Alaska constitution (Article X,
Section 12) directed the Legislature to establish
a local boundary commission with authority to propose boundary changes to the Legislature during
the first 10 days of a regular legislative session.
A proposed change becomes "effective forty-five
days after presentation or at the end of the
session, whichever is earlier, unless disapproved
by a resolution concurred in by a majority of the
members of each house." The five-member Alaska
Local Boundary Commission, appointed by the
Governor for overlapping five-year terms, has
functioned since 1959 and also possesses the power
to establish procedures whereby boundaries may be
changed by local action.

MINNESOTA

     Three members of the Minnesota Municipal
Commission, one of whom must be "learned in
law," are appointed by the Governor for six-year
terms, and two county commissioners serve as ex
officio members whenever the commission considers
a proposal for incorporation of a village, consolidation of a municipality with one or more towns,
or annexation of unincorporated territory to a
municipality located in the county commissioners'
county.

     The 1973 Minnesota Legislature amended the
enabling law (Chapter 621) to provide that in
cases where the proceeding for annexation was not

initiated by a majority of the property owners in
the proposed annexation area, a commission order
for annexation must fix a date 20 to 90 days in the
future for a referendum by voters in the proposed
annexation area; the order becomes effective only
if approved by an affirmative majority vote.

CALIFORNIA

Rapid population growth in California during
a period when incorporation statutes were highly
permissive resulted in a complex local government
system. "Special interest" incorporations, designed to provide tax benefits for residents of unincorporated areas, and "defensive" incorporations,
designed to prevent annexation by a contiguous
city, occurred with relative frequency. Special
districts benefiting developers and other special
interest groups were formed with the same degree of
ease as new cities.

Although the Governor's Commission on Metropolitan Area Problems in 1960 had called for the
liberalization of annexation laws and the establishment of a gubernatorially appointed State
Metropolitan Areas Commission to control boundary
changes and new incorporations,[1] strong political
opposition led to a 1965 compromise law (Chapter
587) providing for the establishment of boundary
commissions on the county level. A five-member
Local Agency Formation Commission (LAFCO) was
formed in each county with the exception of the
City and County of San Francisco. The county board
of supervisors appoints two of its members to the
LAFCO, a city selection committee appoints two
city officials, and a fifth member representing
the general public is appointed by the other four
members. Members serve for four years. A commission is authorized to review and approve, reject,
or modify all proposals for the incorporation or
disincorporation of a city, annexation of territory
to a city, detachment of territory from a city, and
creation of special districts. The District Reorganization Act of 1965 (Chapter 2043) strengthened

LAFCOs by increasing their powers over the reorganization of special districts, including the abolition
of districts.

NEW MEXICO

The three-member gubernatorially appointed New
Mexico Municipal Boundary Commission (Chapter 300
of 1965) may approve or reject annexation petitions
anywhere in the State with the exception of the
Albuquerque metropolitan area, where such petitions
are under the jurisdiction of the five-member gubernatorially appointed Metropolitan Boundary Commission (Chapter 248 of 1967). A referendum must be
held on the approval of an annexation petition by
the latter commission if the petition is signed by
15 percent of the real property owners in the affected area and "filed with the clerk of the municipality within thirty days of filing of the final
order of the Commission." Less than six annexations
have occurred under provisions of the 1965 law and
no annexation petition has been processed by the
Metropolitan Boundary Commission.

WASHINGTON

Eleven-member boundary review boards were
created by the 1967 Washington Legislature (Chapter 189) in Class AA (population of 500,000 or more)
and Class A (population of 210,000-500,000) counties,
and other counties were authorized to establish
five-member boards. Each board is appointed by the
Governor and is authorized to approve, modify, or
reject petitions for (1) annexation of territory,
(2) incorporation, consolidation, or dissolution of
municipalities and nonschool special districts, (3)
"assumption by a city or town of all or part of the
assets, facilities, or indebtedness of a special
district which lies partially within such city or
town," and (4) extraterritorial extension of sewer
or water service by a city, town, or special
district. Negative decisions of the board are
final. If the board approves a petition, "it shall
be presented under the appropriate statute for

375

approval by a public body and, if required, a vote
of the people."

MICHIGAN

The incorporation of cities in Michigan was
supervised by the Secretary of State and to a
limited extent by county boards of supervisors until
1968, when the Legislature created the State Boundary (Public Act Number 191). The Governor appoints
three commission members for three-year terms with
the advice and consent of the Senate, and the pre-
siding probate judge in each county is directed to
appoint two members--one from a city and one from
a township -- to serve on the commission whenever
it considers an incorporation or consolidation petition from that county. Located in the State Department of the Treasury, the commission is authorized
to review petitions for the annexation of territory,
incorporation of new cities and villages, and consolidation of two or more cities, villages, or
townships as a new city.

After reviewing an incorporation or consolidation petition, the commission may approve or
reject the petition. During its review, the commission may revise the boundaries of the area proposed for incorporation or consolidation. Rejection
of a petition by the commission is final. Approval
of an incorporation petition with or without a
boundary revision is final 45 days after the date
of the order unless a petition for a referendum
signed by 5 percent of the registered voters residing in the proposed incorporation or consolidation
area is filed with the commission. If a referendum
is held, the decision on incorporation is made by a
majority vote of the electors in the proposed incorporation area. If a consolidation referendum is
held, the decision is made by a separate majority
vote in each affected municipality.

NEVADA

Whereas the 1967 Nevada Legislature granted relatively broad annexation powers to cities located in counties with a population exceeding 200,000, a City Annexation Commission (CAC) was established in each county in the 100,000 to 200,000 population range (Nevada Revised Statutes, §§ 268.570). Each CAC is composed of the chairman and one other member of the board of county commissioners and one member of the governing body of each city. Members serve for a two-year term and have the power to review and approve, modify, or disapprove annexation proposals. Annexations must be disapproved if protests are made in writing or at a public hearing by a majority of the real property owners in the proposed annexation area or by "owners of real property whose combined value is greater than fifty percent of the total value of real property in the territory proposed to be annexed, as determined by assessment for taxation." A protest, however, may be overridden if the proposed annexation territory is completely surrounded by the city, does not exceed 40 acres, and is subdivided for residential, commercial, or industrial purposes, or provision of public services is necessary to protect public health, safety, convenience, or welfare.

OREGON

The 1969 Oregon Legislature created (Chapter 494) a local government boundary commission in each of the State's three metropolitan areas, effective July 1, 1969, to guide the establishment and growth of cities and special districts, prevent illogical extensions of local government boundaries, and assure the provision of adequate public services and the financial integrity of each local government. A commission may be established in other areas by resolution of the county board of each county within the jurisdiction of each proposed commission. A commission has 11 members if its jurisdiction includes a population exceeding 500,000 and seven members in all other areas. All members of each commission are appointed by the Governor with

377

Senate approval for four-year terms.

In contrast to California's LAFCO's, no appointed or elected local official may serve on an Oregon local government boundary commission. A five-member advisory committee composed of local elected officials, however, must be appointed by each boundary commission. A commission has the power to review and approve, modify, or reject all proposed changes in the boundaries of cities and nonschool special districts within its jurisdiction without a referendum. The extraterritorial extension of sewer or water services by a city or special district requires commission approval, as does the creation of private sewer and water firms. In addition, a single-purpose special district desiring to provide an additional service must obtain the commission's approval prior to assuming responsibility for a new service.

Each commission is funded by the State and the base budget has not been increased since 1970. As a consequence, the commissions are only able to react to requests and are unable to conduct in-depth studies of problems in their areas.

TEXAS

Although Texas lacks a general law regulating all proposed boundary changes, the 1971 Legislature enacted a law (Chapter 84) granting the Texas Water Rights Commission authority to approve or reject petitions for the creation of a municipal utility district responsible for control and distribution of water, reclamation and irrigation of arid or semiarid land, drainage of overflowed land, development of water and hydroelectric power, navigation on inland and coastal waters, and protection and restoration of the purity of water. Land within the corporate limits or extraterritorial jurisdiction of a city may not be included in a district unless the city council enacts a resolution or ordinance granting the city's consent for the inclusion of its land within the district.

378

CONCLUSION

Although the activities of boundary control
commissions have not been subjected to an in-depth
analysis, available evidence suggests that the
commissions generally have been successful in
carrying out their assigned duties. Writing in
1968, Ronald C. Cease concluded:

> All operating boundary review boards
> have been successful; that is, they have
> significantly reduced the proliferation
> of local governments. The Canadian re-
> view boards are the most successful;
> they have broader powers than the boards
> in the United States and they do not
> appear to have financial and staffing
> problems.[2]

The Advisory Commission on Intergovernmental
Relations reported in 1973 that the Local Government Boundary Commission in the Portland, Oregon,
area reduced the number of special districts over
a two-year period from 303 to 198, chiefly by
providing for the absorption of highway lighting
districts into a county service district.[3]

The Minnesota Municipal Commission has been
successful in preventing the incorporation of
small, economically unviable municipalities.
During the nine years preceding the establishment
of the commission, 62 municipalities with an
average size of only 7.6 square miles were incorporated; one had only 43 residents. This may be
compared with five municipalities with an average
size of 31.13 square miles incorporated in the
nine years subsequent to the creation of the
commission.[4]

In 1974, the California Task Force on Local
Government Reform reported that LAFCOs had performed satisfactorily "in resolving annexation
disputes and in providing advisory information to

379

citizen groups interested in changing their governmental arrangements."[5] The task force, however, accused LAFCOs of thwarting "local level decentralization" and of favoring "larger agencies over smaller ones, annexation over incorporation, general purpose agencies over special purpose agencies, and county controlled districts over independent ones."[6] The reader should be alerted to the fact that the task force favored the existing decentralized system of local government and in effect accused the LAFCOs of doing exactly what they were supposed to do.

It must be pointed out that a boundary control commission's potential is limited in most cases to the prevention of further fragmentation, as the commission usually lacks authority to correct problems resulting from past sins of commission or omission. It is recommended that each Legislature provide for the creation of boundary review commissions which, in addition to the usual duties of such commissions, would have the authority to order the dissolution of existing special districts subject to bondholders' approval.

NOTES

1. Meeting Metropolitan Problems (Sacramento, California: The Governor's Commission on Metropolitan Area Problems, December 1960), pp. 16-17 and 20.

2. Ronald C. Cease, A Report on State and Provincial Boundary Review Boards (Portland, Oregon: Portland State College, August 1968), p. 32.

3. Advisory Commission on Intergovernmental Relations, Substate Regionalism and the Federal System, vol. 1: Regional Decision Making: New Strategies for Substate Districts (Washington, D.C.: U.S. Government Printing Office, 1973), p. 26.

4. 1974 Annual Report (St. Paul, Minn.: Minnesota Municipal Commission, n.d.) p. 13.

5. Local Government Reform (Sacramento, Calif.: California Task Force on Local Government Reform, 1974), p. 42.

6. Ibid.

35. The Federal Voting Rights Act:
Its Impact on Annexation*

Joseph F. Zimmerman

Annexation, the most common method of adjusting
local boundaries, may have several advantages. Service
levels in the annexed area may be raised, governmental
responsibility may be consolidated, economies of scale
in service provision may be achieved, orderly growth
may be promoted in the annexed area, benefits of the
city's services may be better correlated with its
taxing jurisdiction as spillovers are reduced, the tax
base of the city may be expanded significantly, and
the governmental structure in the area will be
simplified and new incorporations frustrated.

It is important to point out that the power to
annex land can be abused. In some states, cities have
annexed only areas that add significantly to their tax
base, such as strips of land along major highways and
shopping centers. A second major criticism of
annexation is the charge that it has been used
deliberately to dilute the growing political strength
of blacks in central cities.

Annexation was at a low level during the Depression and World War II. Since 1945, however, a large
number of municipalities has annexed territory. To a
large extent annexation follows a regional pattern.
According to the Municipal Year Book for 1972, the
amount of territory annexed by cities in the period
1950-1970 was below average in the northeast and east
north central regions; average in the west north
central, south central and pacific regions; and above
average in the southeast, Oklahoma-Texas and mountain
regions. During this same period, the land area of
290 larger cities increased from 7,610 to 15,588
square miles, yet little territory was added to the
larger cities in the northeast in contrast to the south
where 94 out of 101 cities annexed land.

---

*Reprinted with permission from the National Civic
Review, June, 1977, pp. 278-83.

Table I contains data on annexations by incorporated munucipalities with more than 2,500 population
in the period 1970-1973. Although 23,698 annexations
were reported, the average annexation involved only
61.36 persons and 0.147 square miles. The process is
used seldom in New England and often in Illinois,
California, Texas and Ohio.

TABLE I
MUNICIPAL ANNEXATION
UNITED STATES
1970-1973

Year	Number	Area (nearest square mile)	Population (thousands)
1970	4,602	663	256
1971	5,803	925	359
1972	6,767	965	539
1973	6,526	930	300

Source: United States Bureau of the Census, Boundary
and Annexation Survey 1970-1973 (Washington,
D.C.: United States Government Printing
Office, 1975), p. 1

While annexation is a local process, there is also
a federal dimension. Congress first gained the power
to regulate state and local elections under specified
conditions on March 30, 1870, when the fifteenth
amendment to the United States constitution was
declared to be in force. A law was enacted that year
making private and/or public obstruction of the right
to vote a federal misdemeanor punishable by imprison-
ment for no less than one month and no longer than one
year [16 Stat. 140 (1870)]. Amendments to the law
adopted in 1871 authorized federal oversight of the
election of United States Representatives in every
city and town over 20,000 population "whenever . . .
there shall be two citizens thereof who . . . shall
make known, in writing, to the judge of the Circuit
Court of the United States for the Circuit wherein
such city or town shall be, their desire to have said
registration, or said election, or both, guarded and
scrutinized . . ." [16 Stat. 433 (1871)]. The most
important sections of these two acts were repealed in
1894 and states became relatively free of direct

federal supervision of elections. The United States
Supreme Court remained as the principal protector of
the voting rights of blacks and struck down grandfather
clauses in 1915, procedural obstacles in 1939, the
white primary in 1944, discriminatory application of
voting tests in 1949 and racial gerrymandering in 1960.

Reacting to continuing charges of racial discrimination in voting, Congress in 1965 again decided to
use its fifteenth amendment powers and enacted the
voting rights act [79 Stat. 437, 42 U.S.C. 1973 (1964
Supp.)]. The act was extended for five years in 1970
and for seven years in 1975.

The act applies automatically to any state or
political subdivision if the Attorney General of the
United States determines that as of November 1, 1964,
a test or device has been employed to abridge the
right of citizens to vote because of race or color,
and the director of the United States Bureau of the
Census determines that less than 50 percent of the
persons of voting age were registered to vote on
November 1, 1964, or that less than 50 percent of the
persons of voting age exercised the franchise in the
1964 presidential election. The 1975 amendments
change the dates to November 1, 1972, and the 1972
presidential election. When a determination is made
that the act applies to a state or political subdivision, the United States District Court is directed
to authorize the appointment by the United States
Civil Service Commission of federal examiners to enforce the constitutional voting guarantees.

The 1975 amendments broaden the coverage of the
act to include language minorities defined as "persons
who are American Indian, Asian American, Alaskan
Natives, or of Spanish heritage," and cited the
fourteenth amendment as well as the fifteenth as the
authority for the act [89 Stat. 402, 42 U.S.C. 1973a,
1973d, 1973l (1975 Supp.)].

The constitutionality of the act was challenged
on the grounds that Congress encroached on powers
reserved to the states and that the act violated the
principle of the equality of the states. Rejecting
these arguments, the United States Supreme Court
decided in 1966 "that the sections of the Act . . .
are an appropriate means for carrying out Congress'

384

constitutional responsibilities and are consonant with all other provisions of the Constitution" (<u>South Carolina v. Katzenbach</u>, 383 U.S. 308). In 1968 the court held that it was the intent of Congress that the act be given "the broadest possible scope" to reach "any State enactment which altered the election law of a covered State in even a minor way" (<u>Allen v. State Board of Elections</u>, 393 U.S. 566-67).

The act was designed specifically to end voting discrimination in several southern states, but the United States District Court for the District of Columbia held in 1974 that the act as amended in 1970 applied also to New York congressional and state legislative districts in Manhattan, Brooklyn and the Bronx. The decision necessitated a special session of the state legislature to redraw district lines in the three boroughs.

Objections to some of the new district lines were made by representatives of Brooklyn's Hasidic Jews who argued that the new state Assembly districts divided the community and made it the victim of a racial gerrymander. On July 1, 1974, the United States Attorney General approved the new districts and dismissed the objections of Hasidic Jews and Irish, Italian and Polish groups on the ground the act was designed to prevent voting discrimination on the basis of race or color, not on the basis of ethnic origin or religious beliefs.

The Attorney General's ruling was appealed by the Hasidic community, but the appeal was rejected in 1974 by the United States District Court for the Eastern District of New York and the United States Circuit Court of Appeals for the Second Circuit on the ground "there is no federal constitutional right either to contiguity or compactness of voting districts" (<u>United Jewish Organizations of Williamsburgh v. Wilson</u>, 377 F. Supp. 11641).

On March 1, 1977, the United States Supreme Court by a seven-to-one vote upheld the lower court ruling that the 1974 redistricting was constitutional. Chief Justice Warren E. Burger, however, labelled the majority decision "racial gerrymandering" and said that "racial quotas . . . are evil and dangerous because there is no semblance of justification for them."

The act also served as the basis for the finding
in October 1976 by Federal Judge Virgil Pittman of the
Southern District of Alabama that the three-member
Mobile city commission, elected at large, "precludes a
black voter from effective participation in the
election system" and the judge's order that the
commission be replaced in 1977 by a mayor elected at
large and a nine-member city council elected from
single-member districts.

The voting rights added a federal dimension to
annexation proceedings in several states, particularly
in the south. The United States Supreme Court held in
1971 that annexation comes within the purview of the
act (Perkins v. Matthews, 400 U.S. 379). The case involved Canton, Mississippi. The special three-judge
District Court for the District of Columbia in 1969
dissolved a temporary injunction issued by a single
federal judge against the holding of city elections
and dismissed the complaint on the ground that "the
black voters still had a majority of not less than 600
after the expansions were effected" (Perkins v.
Matthews, 301 F. Supp. 567). A total of 82 black
voters and 331 white voters had been added to the city
by annexation in 1965, 1966 and 1968, no white voters
were added to the city by a 1965 annexation. The
United States Supreme Court overturned the decision of
the district court.

In Richmond a 1970 annexation increased the city's
population and real property tax base by 19 percent and
23 percent, respectively. A group of black voters
objected on the grounds that the annexation was
designed to dilute black voting strength, thereby
violating their rights under the fourteenth and
fifteenth amendments to the constitution and section
5 of the voting rights act. Fifty-two percent of the
city's pre-annexation population was black and this
percentage was lowered to 42 by the annexation.

The United States District Court for the Eastern
District of Virginia in 1971 ruled in favor of the
plaintiffs and wrote that "the evidence before the
Court shows a concern not only of the officials of the
City and County, but of State officials as well, that
the City of Richmond not become a city of the old, the

386

poor, and the Black. Once again the Court points out that the concern of not all who so expressed themselves was primarily racially motivated" (Holt v. City of Richmond, 344 F. Supp. 233). The court added, however, that "the Fifteenth Amendment forbids a deprivation of one's vote by reason of race--this Court interprets that to mean dilution as well." Declaring that de-annexation would be impracticable because the city had appropriated millions of dollars for improvements in the annexed area, the court ordered that the city be divided into two districts for purposes of new council-manic elections. Seven councilmen would be elected from the district comprising most of the pre-annexation city and two councilmen would be elected from the annexed area and a small part of the pre-annexation city.

The district court's decision was reversed in 1972 by the Circuit Court of Appeals which ruled that "for perfectly valid reasons Richmond's elected representa-tives had sought annexation since 1966" (Holt v. Richmond, 459 F. 2d 1093 and 1099). The United States Supreme Court in 1972 denied certiorari, thereby up-holding the decision of the circuit court (Holt v. Richmond, 408 U.S. 931).

In a related case, the United States Supreme Court in 1973 affirmed a decision of the United States District Court for the District of Columbia denying Petersburg, Virginia, the right to annex 14 square miles of land because the boundary extension would increase the percentage of the white population from 45 to 54 in a city which elects its councilmen at large, thereby discriminating against black voters (City of Petersburg, Virginia v. United States et al., 410 U.S. 962).

The annexation ordinance was adopted unanimously by the five-member at-large city council. Two members, including the one who introduced the ordinance, were black. The three-member district court found that the purpose of the annexation was to expand the city's growth and tax base and there was no evidence that the annexation had a racial motive. The Court, however, stated that the city has "a long history of racial segregation and discrimination," and "that almost total bloc voting by race has been the well established pattern in Petersburg." The court also found that the city council generally had been unresponsive to the black community's needs and desires.

Conceding "that an at-large system of electing city councilmen has many advantages over the ward system," the court ruled that the annexation could be approved only if the city substituted ward elections for the at-large election of the city council which had been expanded from five to seven members by action of the Virginia legislature in 1972.

In 1972 Richmond sought federal district court approval for the 1970 annexation, refused twice by the United States Attorney General. The Richmond city council was elected at large in 1970 with voters from the annexed area participating; only one black councilman was elected. According to the District Court for the District of Columbia, "it is conceded here that Richmond conducted these elections illegally in violation of Section 5. It did not, prior to diluting by annexation the votes of the citizens residing within the old boundaries, obtain the approval of the Attorney General or a declaratory judgment from this Court that this dilution did not have the purpose and would not have the effect of abridging the right to vote on account of race or color. Richmond has held no councilmanic elections since 1970; the illegally elected City Council continues to serve to this time" (City of Richmond, Virginia v. United States, 376 F. Supp. 1344).

The court concluded that Richmond's change from at-large to single-member district elections subsequent to the annexation was "discriminatory in purpose and effect and thus violative of Section 5's substantive standards as well as the Section's procedural command that prior approval be obtained from the Attorney General or this Court." Richmond relied on the Supreme Court's decision in the Petersburg case and argued "that the annexation was made lawful by the adoption of its single-member district plan."

The Supreme Court reversed the lower court decision in 1975. Delivering the majority opinion, Justice Byron R. White pointed out that blacks would not be underrepresented on the city council if its members were elected by wards and, consequently, the annexation does not "deny or abridge the right to

388

vote. To hold otherwise would be either to forbid all
such annexations or to require, as the price for
approval of the annexation, that the black community
be assigned the same proportion of council seats as
before, hence perhaps permanently overrepresenting them
and underrepresenting other elements in the community,
including the nonblack citizens in the annexed area"
(City of Richmond v. United States, 422 U.S. 371).

The Supreme Court remanded the case to the district
court for further proceedings to determine "whether
there are now objectively verifiable, legitimate reasons
for the annexation." The district court on August 10,
1976, issued a declaratory judgment that Richmond had
"complied with the Voting Rights Act of 1965 with
respect to the annexation of 1970 in the context of
the ward plan for councilmanic elections." And on
November 12, 1976, federal District Court Judge Robert
Merhige, Jr., set March 1, 1977, as the date for the
new council election. The new council contains five
black and four white members.

The proposed annexation by an older central city
of territory in which a large number of whites resides
may bring two goals into sharp conflict: (1) the need
to increase the present and potential tax base of the
city to enable it to finance services, including those
needed by the disadvantaged, and (2) the desire to
maintain the voting strength of blacks in the central
city. The Supreme Court wisely decided to allow
annexation even though it reduces the political power
of the black community in the city.

The Supreme Court recognized that conventional
at-large elections do not adequately and accurately
represent all citizens in a city with a large disadvantaged population as, generally, only candidates
who command wide support throughout the city will be
elected. As a consequence, conventional at-large
elections frequently overrepresent the middle class
and often result in no direct representation for
minorities, who thus are isolated from the center of
decision making. Furthermore, basic policy decisions
may be made by a city council and a school board
unaware of and insensitive to the problems of poor
neighborhoods and minority groups.

In rejecting the proposal that blacks in an

389

enlarged city be guaranteed their pre-annexation representation, the Supreme Court considered only the single-member district electoral system as an alternative to the conventional at-large system. While using single-member districts increases the possibility that each group will be able to elect a representative, the system does not guarantee such representation and has a tendency to pit districts against each other in a battle for the distribution of resources, or may result in an agreement to distribute resources equally among the districts regardless of the needs of particular districts and the whole city. Furthermore, a single-member system in a city with racially segregated housing patterns may result in the election of councilmen in several districts hostile to the needs of the black community and may encourage people to move to districts where others of their race live.

Other alternatives include combined at-large and district elections, at-large elections with residence requirements, limited voting, cumulative voting and proportional representation.

As of July 30, 1976, municipalities in 10 states were required by the voting rights act to submit 3,011 annexations to the United States Attorney General. One hundred forty six of these, only 4.5 percent, were found to violate the voting rights of groups protected by the act. In addition, relatively few citizens are involved in the typical annexation, and the vote of the black or language minority electorate in the annexing city is not significantly diluted.

36.   Recommendations for Unified Government
in Dade County*

Irving G. McNayr

This is a report designed to bring into focus the
most fundamental local issue facing us today: the role
of the cities and the county in providing governmental
services to our citizens. This problem has doubtless
given you much thought. It has also been uppermost in
the minds of other local public officials and civic
leaders as well as the general public. We are asked
almost daily, "When will we have a single occupational
license?" "When will we have a unified police force
and fire department?" "When will Metro provide the
badly needed municipal services in the unincorporated
area?" "Which services is the county responsible for
and which are the cities responsible for?" "Why must I
take out a building permit in each city as well as the
county once I have passed the county-wide contractors'
examination?" These problems all resolve into the
fundamental question of the future role of the cities
and the county in local government . . .

MUNICIPAL BOUNDARIES

Municipal borderlines were established at a time
when towns were isolated places, many of them small in
size. They have now lost their meaning and new settlements have filled in the area between and around them.
Further complicating the pattern was the rapid incorporation and annexation of the Florida "boom" period,
and the ensuing contraction of the cities after
collapse of the boom, when the cities' financial
conditions left them unable to service their expansive
areas.

The sizeable contractions of the municipalities
rarely left logical and orderly boundary lines in their
wake. Individual property owners frequently "sued out"
of their respective cities, leaving jagged, often

---

*Reprinted from A Report to the Chairman and Members of
the Board of County Commissioners (September 25, 1962).

391

weird, boundaries--a legacy of the past that plagues governmental efficiency today. South Miami is now literally a "city in pieces," with parts of the city geographically separated from the city proper, forming islands within the cities of Hialeah, El Portal, and North Miami Beach. The entire unincorporated area weaves in, around, about, and through the cities in an illogical and irregular path.

This haphazard pattern of jurisdictional boundaries has important effects on the government of the area. The problems of providing local services are accentuated by this fragmentation; it makes it difficult and costly for the cities to service themselves and even more difficult for Metro to service the unincorporated areas. Police patrol, fire response areas, garbage collection routes, and sewerage systems are crisscrossed, overlapping and ineffectual. The existing boundaries prevent the efficient and economical deployment of public works forces and equipment. The many small, irregularly joined governmental units make it difficult to bring the area's full resources to bear on the task of providing better services, particularly those which require large scale capital investments and central facilities such as water, sewers, garbage disposal, and so forth. Only about one third of Dade's residences are now connected to sewerage lines. The area's water supply system is a complexity of contractual arrangements, primarily with the city of Miami, with many residents still relying on their own individual wells. Several cities are presently contemplating large investments for the construction of waste composting plants and incinerators in an effort to meet their immediate problem. However, there is a strong possibility that such efforts may compound rather than solve area problems.

Numerous examples can be cited where Metro patrols one side of a street and municipal police the other side. Similarly, county waste trucks service one side of the street while city waste collectors are picking up garbage on the other side. On some streets in the South Miami maze, it was actually necessary for the city to supply the county with the house numbers of the homes they service and of those which we service.

At the present time, the only public functions which can avoid the waste and inefficiency which is imposed by these boundary patterns are those which have been removed from the jurisdiction of the municipal governments. If reasonable efficiency and economy in government is to be achieved, the existing jurisdictional boundaries must be eliminated. They presently provide only a deterrent to efficient and logical service and fail to recognize that this is one metropolitan community regardless of political boundaries. City streets are traveled by the residents of other cities, by residents of the unincorporated areas and by tourists. Nor are the thoroughfares in the unincorporated areas magically cut off from travel by municipal residents. A thief residing in one municipality may find the practice of his "trade" more lucrative in another, thereby placing the cost of his apprehension on the second municipality. South Miami residents shop in Coral Gables and vice versa. Residents from the entire metropolitan area visit the race track in Hialeah, the Orange Bowl in Miami, Crandon Park in the unincorporated area . . . .

Another impediment to progress is the multiplicity of governing jurisdictions. The frictions and areas of dispute are not limited to city-county relationships but are found among the cities themselves. Competition arises between them for attracting trade, industry and tourism without regard to the overall needs of the community. This diversity of interest has often prevented necessary action on a community-wide level. Frequently, cities have failed to cooperate in matters where we should offer a common and united front in asserting ourselves with state and federal agencies.

It is necessary also to explode several myths which are advanced by those who would attempt to retain fragmentized government. We often hear that unified government will cause "loss of community identity," or that the communities will be "swallowed up" by the larger government. Coconut Grove, Ojus, and Perrine were once cities which dissolved themselves but which retain their identity and character. Carol City, Cutler Ridge, Westwood Lake, and Key Biscayne, on the other hand, are all examples of communities which have never been incorporated yet whose residents display strong community identification and civic interest.

393

The statement, "Our standards will be lowered," is still another myth. There is simply no basis for this argument. Has anyone ever seen a large city where all neighborhoods had the same characteristics, standards, and amenities? One can look right here in the city of Miami where both low rent districts and luxury neighborhoods exist. Has Coconut Grove deteriorated by virtue of its consolidation with Miami? Does the luxury community of Bay Point have the same standards as the blighted areas of Miami? The same conditions exist in Miami Beach--all classes of neighborhoods, from the areas in transition to the luxury islands. This argument simply will not stand up in the light of logic and experience.

To those who say, "Our officials will no longer be responsive to us," it is believed that the reverse is true. In a single city there will be single responsibility and single accountability. No longer can there be "buck passing" and confusion over jurisdiction and responsibility. There will be one set of elected representatives and one set of appointed officials, without overlap and duplication. Community service centers will answer complaints and inquiries. Police substations will service neighborhoods. Libraries and fire stations will not be moved but will be expanded into logical service areas. Garbage routes can be districted logically for more efficient service and waste trucks can deposit their loads at the nearest disposal center rather than driving miles further as presently. The nearest fire station will respond to an alarm without regard to the present illogical political boundaries. No longer will policemen be confused over jurisdictions when accidents occur on municipal boundaries . . . .

FISCAL PROBLEMS

Over 400,000 persons now reside in the unincorporated area of Dade County. Most of these people reside in areas which have all the characteristics of cities-- high population density, sizeable commercial and industrial centers, traffic congestion, and the entire spectrum of urban requirements. Yet, there is a vast difference between the levels of services offered to the residents of cities and those offered residents of

394

the unincorporated areas. Some of the shortcomings in
the unincorporated area are: police and fire protection, inadequate street maintenance, sidewalks, sewerage and water supply, no auto inspection stations and
libraries, virtually no street lighting and fire
hydrants.

The residents of these areas can look only to
Metro to provide the public services they need. Thus,
Metro is required to act as a city government in the
unincorporated areas while simultaneously serving as a
metropolitan-wide authority. Yet our fiscal powers, as
a county, are still geared to a government designed to
have primary responsibility for rural areas. In the
1940s and 1950s, a number of previously municipal
functions were transferred to the county government--
health, hospitals, airports, and so on. Under Metro,
still more functions were turned over and many others
contemplated. Unfortunately, while the Metro charter
gave the county the power to carry on a central metropolitan government, it was unable to grant the new
government any taxing powers other than those it
previously possessed as a county. This resulted in the
paradoxical situation where governmental responsibilities were shifted from municipal governments, with
wider taxing powers, to the county with much narrower
taxing powers.

The differences between the revenue-raising
authorities of Metro as a county and its potential
revenue as a city are rooted in the rights granted by
the state to its counties and to its cities. The
state, recognizing the additional requirements placed
upon governments operating in urban (as compared to
rural) environments, granted greater fund raising
powers to the cities. The counties, on the other hand,
were viewed essentially as agents for the performance
of state functions and for governing rural areas. Its
chief functions, traditionally, were judicial administration, tax assessment and collection, election
administration, construction and maintenance of rural
roads, and rural law enforcement. As such its
financial needs were relatively small, and with less
responsibility, it was reasoned that the counties
needed less broad revenue raising powers.

The cities' greater revenue-raising abilities stem essentially from their powers to levy excise taxes and franchise taxes, and to regain from the state the taxes collected from the sale of cigarettes within the municipalities. Cities may impose excise taxes on utility bills. Residents of areas outside city limits are not so taxed. The state-imposed cigarette tax is a source of considerable strength to cities as 95 percent of the taxes so collected are returned to the city. The taxes on cigarettes sold in the unincorporated areas are retained in their entirety by the state, and the county receives nothing. During 1960-1961, the City of Miami alone received more than $5 million from these two sources--more than one fifth of all its general revenues . . . .

Municipalities also have greater freedom in deriving franchise taxes from utilities. Although the county has been successful in levying a similar tax on the Florida Power and Light Company for its operation in the unincorporated areas, it does not levy a franchise tax on other utility enterprises.

To illustrate the effect of such differences in taxing powers between the cities and Metro, compare the general revenue sources of Metro, the City of Miami, and the City of Hialeah. Over 90 percent of Metro's tax revenues are obtained from ad valorem taxes, as compared to 65 percent for Miami and 37 percent for Hialeah.

This vividly illustrates the financial strait jacket in which Metro is bound and brings us to a situation that further compounds the problem. Under state law, ad valorem taxes levied by the counties must by levied uniformly county-wide. In addition, the municipalities levy separate property taxes within their respective boundaries. Thus, the resident of a municipality pays property taxes to two governments, Metro and the city in which he lives, while the resident of an unincorporated section is taxed only by Metro. Since some of Metro's receipts must be used to provide strictly local services in the unincorporated areas, the residents of the municipalities are placed in the position of having to finance services from which, on the surface at least, they receive no benefits. About 70 percent of Metro's tax base is within the municipalities; thus any increase in the level of local services in the unincorporated areas must increase the subsidy the city residents are now paying to those areas. Naturally, Metro has been loathe to pursue such a course. The inevitable result has been that Metro has not provided an adequate level of local service in the unincorporated areas. Inasmuch as the unincorporated areas are growing at about four times the rate of the municipalities, the demands for local services in those sections will continue to increase, placing ever-mounting pressures on the county government.

The logical and obvious solution to these financial problems is the total incorporation of Dade County as a city, retaining also our identity as a county. As a single city, we would qualify for over $6 million in revenues not presently available to us as a county. This amount is greater than our entire present expenditures for the local services which are restricted to the unincorporated area. This additional revenue alone, available to this area as a single city, would enable us to more than double our present services to the unincorporated area.

At the same time avoidance of duplication of jobs, the ability to deploy personnel and equipment where needed without regard for municipal boundaries, the establishment of one central purchasing facility, and all the other devices for providing needed services to the whole community if under one government should greatly reduce the costs of government throughout the area.

MUNICIPAL OPPOSITION

There is still another factor concerning present city-county relationships which should be frankly faced and openly discussed. It is the political opposition that municipal officials have placed in the path of almost every area-wide endeavor attempted. They have obstructed, or attempted to obstruct, Metro's progress every step of the way, and continue to do so. The League of Municipalities has openly used taxpayers' funds to finance anti-Metro movements. In supporting the autonomy amendment which was subsequently defeated

397

at the polls, the cities freely used municipal personnel, equipment and tax monies . . . .

This opposition has been so intense that at one
point it seems that the City of Miami went so far as to
release traffic violators rather than permit their
trial in Metro Court. The concept of Metro Court was
fought all the way to the United States Supreme Court
in a two-year court battle. When that failed, the
recently proposed charter amendment attempted to do at
the polls what the courts refused to do. County-wide
traffic engineering was attacked in the courts. Work
on the Dodge Island Seaport was delayed for years by
the opposition of officials of Miami Beach. The City
of Miami attempted to stop the transit take-over by
court action and by every other means. The cities have
refused a county-wide automobile inspection system and
the City of Miami Beach even refuses to use a uniform
inspection sticker. City councils have openly favored
charter amendments restricting Metro even though their
residents have consistently voted pro-Metro. They have
fought uniform hours for the sale of liquor, a uniform
building code, a uniform traffic code, and virtually
every effort made to implement the charter. These are
the public and open areas of opposition. We daily
encounter others in every area of contact.

This lack of cooperation is often laid at Metro's
doorstep by city officials. But the actual record
indicates that lack of cooperation tends to stem
primarily from municipal officials . . . .

In every transfer of a function to the county, we
have had to pay taxpayers' money for equipment and
facilities already paid for by taxpayers who would
still get the same benefit from it. As we increase our
taxes, in assuming these new functions, the cities do
not lower their taxes . . . .

There has been a standing offer to the cities to
use our purchasing division, one of the best in the
country and which has attracted nationwide attention
through the methods it has used in bringing prices
down. Not a single city has fully accepted this
readily available economy.

398

Municipal cooperation to date in developing area-wide services has occurred only rarely, and every bit of progress by Metro has been made despite, rather than in concert with, municipal officials. If we are ever to move ahead, it must be with a unity of purpose. City officials have openly and defiantly demonstrated that they do not intend to cooperate in the development of metropolitan area government.

CONCLUSION AND RECOMMENDATION

These then are the three major obstacles to progress in this area:

1. The illogical and haphazard municipal boundaries which impede the provision of services by the cities as well as the county.

2. The financial strait jacket of both the county and the cities: the county losing millions of dollars annually due to the state restriction on its revenues as a county; and the cities due to their size, unable to finance many major improvements.

3. The political opposition created by city officials who have fought every Metro attempt to make progress.

The 27 cities and the unincorporated area of metropolitan Miami should unify into one city. It is one city in every sense of the word, except for the purposeless political boundaries now existing. As the City and County of Miami, the area would retain its identity as a county for our relationships with the state and in meeting legal requirements. As a city, the government would release itself from the financial condition which serves the rural counties adequately, but which ties the hands of an urban government serving over a million residents. Double taxation of the city residents would be eliminated . . . .

Advantages of one city-county government are vast and almost endless. The following list is not intended to be all inclusive but rather to illustrate some of the many benefits and savings to be derived through this unification:

399

FINANCIAL

One tax assessment; one tax bill; one purchasing
system which through competitive bidding on volume
buying will afford countless savings; one consolidated
insurance program at huge savings; one budget for
balanced programming and elimination of intergovernmental charges.

POLICE AND FIRE

One central police and fire communications system
providing one emergency telephone number for immediate
response regardless of political boundaries; one police
and fire academy to provide minimum and uniform training; one standard uniform, insignia and vehicle; one
police and fire chief; one crime laboratory providing
complete county-wide modern crim investigation; one
central jail and stockade system eliminating the costly
expense of individual municipal jails; one police
records bureau providing complete files on all known
criminals regardless of political boundaries; one auto
inspection system; one vice squad; one homicide division to handle all capital crimes; one juvenile bureau
with properly trained personnel; one firefighting
system with uniform equipment.

The lack of coordination of police services, perhaps, is the key factor in this area finding itself
year after year listed by the FBI in its Uniform Crime
Reports as among those areas in the nation with the
highest incidence of crime in most categories.

PUBLIC WORKS

One capital improvements program properly coordi-
nated and implemented on the basis of need rather than
political boundaries and pressures; one water and sewer
agency using the City of Miami system as a nucleus to
serve the entire county; uniform maintenance and
construction of all roads; one agency to coordinate
road and expressway planning, engineering and construction, fuller utilization of heavy equipment, government
facilities and forces; logical routing of waste and
trash collection routes regardless of existing political boundaries; implementation of the master waste
disposal plan.

GENERAL

One voice, cognizant of the areas' needs, to deal with state and federal officials for funds and programs; one governing body with the responsibility and authority to handle the Miami River problem; an area-wide library system; one county-wide industrial development and general publicity program; one standard weights and measures system; one occupational license, taxicab permit, bicycle license, liquor store license, charity drive and soliciting license; one uniform liquor law pertaining to hours of operation; uniform building and zoning inspection control; uniform personnel rules, pay plan and retirement provisions for all local government employees.

In summary, the issue of one city for Dade County has long been avoided in the face of popular support and logic. It has been and will be no doubt strongly opposed by the local municipal office holders. The problems facing this area have been generally stated as well as recommendations for their solution. Much study remains to be done in detail and with deliberation. This is the most important local issue which will face us in this decade at least. Many more facts need to be gathered, aired and discussed.

Accordingly, it is respectfully urged that the Board of County Commissioners of Dade County appoint a board of its choosing, composed of outstanding citizens representative of the various areas and elements of the community, to undertake this study, hold public hearings, and present its findings to the Board of County Commissioners and citizens of Dade County for the orderly implementation of this proposal.